Mary and Human Liberation

THE STORY AND THE TEXT

Tissa Balasuriya OMI

EDITED BY

Helen Stanton

INTRODUCED BY

Edmund Hill OP

TRINITY PRESS INTERNATIONAL
HARRISBURG, PENNSYLVANIA

Compilation © Mowbray, a Cassell imprint, 1997

Mary and Human Liberation first published in *Logos*, volume 29, nos 1 and 2 (March/July 1990) by the Centre for Society and Religion, Colombo; expanded edition 1994; 3rd reprint, including 'A Marian Way of the Cross', January 1997

Trinity Press International, P.O. Box 1321, Harrisburg, PA 17105
Trinity Press International is a division of the Morehouse Group

Library of Congress Cataloging-in-Publication Data
Balasuriya, Tissa.
    Mary and human liberation: the story and the text/by Tissa
Balasuriya.
        p.   cm.
    Includes bibliographical references.
    ISBN 1-56338-225-3 (pbk. : alk. paper)
    1. Mary, Blessed Virgin, Saint – Theology – Controversial
literature.   2. Mary, Blessed Virgin, Saint – Cult – Controversial
literature.   3. Liberation theology.   4. Catholic Church – Doctrines –
Controversial literature.   5. Balasuriya, Tissa.
    6. Excommunication – Catholic Church – Case studies.   I. Title.
BT614.B35   1997
232.91–dc21   97–23821
                                                                          CIP

The publishers would like to thank the following for permission to use their work:
The Catholic Bishops' Conference of Sri Lanka; *Catholic Messenger* (Sri Lanka); Ecumenical Association of Third World Theologians; Oblates of Mary Immaculate, Rome; Oblates of Mary Immaculate, Sri Lanka; Sacred Congregation for the Doctrine of the Faith, Rome.
Particular thanks are due to Frs Daniel Corijn and Marcello Zago OMI for permission to reproduce their letters in full, and to
Francis Pimentel-Pinto for his invaluable help in assembling the documents.

Typeset by York House Typographic Ltd, London
Printed and bound in Great Britain by
Redwood Books, Trowbridge, Wiltshire

97 98 99 00 01 02 10 9 8 7 6 5 4 3 2 1

Contents

Letter to the reader

Dear Reader

Mary and Human Liberation first appeared as a modest double issue of *Logos*, the quarterly review of the Centre for Society and Religion in Colombo, Sri Lanka. It was published in 1990, and its 600 copies would, like the other numbers of this review, have found their place in libraries and archives, if it had not been for the attention the book received from the officials of the Magisterium of the Roman Catholic Church. It is presented here in a form that is close to the original, and in response to the huge public interest that it has generated throughout the world. This interest has been generated as much by the controversy that has surrounded the book as by the work itself, and we have therefore taken the decision to include in this volume the full text of the main documents that tell the story of the progress of this controversy, and also of my own excommunication. I am delighted that Dr Radhika Coomaraswamy, United Nations Rapporteur on Violence Against Women, has agreed to write a Foreword.

In my view, the main issues raised by the material contained in this book are as follows.

Theological issues

(1) The relationship between the sources of revelation and their subsequent interpretation by different generations of Christians throughout history.
(2) The relationship between defined dogma and its interpretation in different cultural contexts.
(3) The role, authority and limits of the Church's teaching power, spotlighting in particular the Magisterium, and also the Congregation for the Doctrine of the Faith (CDF), its membership, its accountability and its contribution to sacred tradition.
(4) Gender justice.

Procedural issues

(1) The methods used in dealing with theological writings, and the due relationship between judgement and trial, punishment and proof, penalty and right of appeal.
(2) The need for judicial processes for the most serious of Church penalties.
(3) How is the exercise of supreme judicial authority by the Pope to be reconciled with the right of appeal to the Supreme Court of the Holy See?
(4) How are such procedural questions to be reconciled with the Vatican II approach of openness, participation and subsidiarity?

Relationship issues

(1) How have the relationships between the local Church and the central authorities in Rome functioned in this case?
(2) What is the relationship between the different dicasteries of the Holy See – for instance the CDF and the Commission for Justice and Peace, and the Secretariats for Other Religions and for Ecumenism?

Spirituality issues

(1) Different theologies have generated different models of Mary and Jesus. How legitimate are these?
(2) What is the relationship between truth, power and faith? What is the value of lifelong witness as a criterion of fidelity to the Catholic Church?
(3) How far are the demands of social justice within and among countries relevant for spirituality and the mission of the Church today?

World Church issues

(1) The role of the mass media in this issue, and the significance for the catholicity of the Church of the international interest it has aroused.
(2) The shift in balance in the Catholic Church in these years. It is becoming very much a Church of the South (Asia, Africa, Latin America), but power is still concentrated in the North, particularly in the organs of the Roman Curia.

The issues set out above, while they have some relevance to the case of *Mary and Human Liberation*, are central challenges of our time for

Christians and others everywhere. I welcome this book, because it contributes to the debate.

Personally, while going through the pain of excommunication with all the loving kindness and equanimity (*metta, karuna, muditha* and *uppekkha*) I can muster, may I bear its cross in the spirit of Colossians 1.24. May I do this for the cause of theology in Asia, for the rights of women in society and Church, and for human rights in the Catholic Church globally.

May I also take this opportunity to thank the thousands of people from all continents who have communicated with me since this issue came to the fore, and have affirmed my being INCOMMUNIONED spiritually in the Church, the mystical body of Christ. I hope I can say, with St Paul, 'Bonum certamen certavi, cursum consumavi, fidem servavi' (I have fought the good fight, I have completed my course, I have preserved the faith).

TISSA BALASURIYA OMI
15 April 1997
Centre for Society and Religion
Colombo
Sri Lanka

Foreword

For those of us involved in the struggle for women's rights within society, religion and its representation of women has been a major site for debate and discussion. In fact of all the areas in which there has been discourse on women's rights, religion and women remains the most controversial. Women seeking vindication of their rights within religious discourse have been vilified and attacked by the more patriarchal discourses within religious tradition. Men who have supported them have also faced enormous opposition. Father Tissa Balasuriya is one such man, who in attempting to foster a vision of mature, independent womanhood has had to face the reaction of more orthodox forces within his own religion.

As a non-Christian, I am unfamiliar with the debates within Christianity of what is termed 'The Marian Way of the Cross'. Yet as a citizen of the world, I am aware of the powerful symbolism of Mary and have felt the strength of her power as reflected in Michelangelo's *Pietà* and in other works of art which are part of our world heritage. To one outside the Christian faith, Mary represents the values of compassion, love and struggle. To our Christian friends she was obviously a powerful role model who gave them strength and vision during times of crisis. To elicit notions of women's liberation from Mary's life is therefore a natural path for men and women working for women's liberation within the Christian faith.

In all the world's religions a great debate is taking place. The women's liberation movement of recent years has led to a questioning of traditional interpretations of women's roles. While some women have chosen to move away from religion, the vast majority have retained their religious faith and have chosen instead to find liberation and salvation from alternative interpretations that do not uphold patriarchal assumptions. This debate about the representation of women within religions is taking place everywhere, among Muslims, Hindus,

viii

Buddhists and Christians. Everyone is agreed that the spirit of all the world's religions is towards equality, but man-made laws and practices interpreting religion have led to ideological manifestations which inhibit women's equality. Women and men within religions are attempting to question these interpretations and are striving to put forward alternative readings which would allow for a more empowered portrayal of the female form and feminine destiny. Father Tissa Balasuriya is an important part of this movement towards alternatives. His vision of Mary is an integral part of his vision of social justice and human rights. To him religion is an essential part of the struggle for this justice and religious symbolism is a powerful ideological tool helping society strive towards this goal.

The liberated modern woman is the vision of the Enlightenment personality. It is the notion of independent women, endowed with rights, guided by reason, striving for change and social justice in their societies. The Mary who emerges from the pages of *Mary and Human Liberation* is one such personality. She is a 'strong woman with great powers of endurance' and 'her words can be an inspiration for radical action for changes of consciousness in people and in the structures of societies'. Woman is therefore chosen with 'God ... dependent on a woman for the carrying out of the divine plan of redemption' (pp. 57–8). As Father Tissa writes, 'What the Gospels present, however, is the story of a mature, adult woman facing some of the most difficult problems of womanhood and motherhood, and thereby sharing their common trials'. He argues that 'It is necessary to rediscover these facets of the story in order that the life of Mary may have more meaning for ordinary women who undergo such trials' (p. 59). Father Tissa's Mary is an empowered, committed woman who is an integral part of the Christian message of salvation.

Father Tissa is not alone in putting forward this vision of women in Christian theologies. Many feminists working from within the religious tradition have articulated similar positions and reflective hypotheses. They have argued that we must move away from a male interpretation of Mary towards a feminist articulation. Similar approaches are available in other religions, with Muslim women appropriating Ayesha, the Prophet's wife, Hindu women reanalysing the Goddess in Hinduism and Buddhist women turning to the examples of Buddhist nuns. They are turning to these religious representations to give them strength and sustenance to deal with their daily lives in the modern world. Father Tissa's contribution to this debate is exemplary in that these interpretations are usually put forward by female theologians, but he is a male priest brought up in an earlier time when these ideas were not so prevalent.

   Father Tissa's extraordinary sensitivity to the life experience of women and his empathetic portrayal of Mary are a testament to the deep spirituality which conditions his life and work. That spirituality, which breaks man-made boundaries to capture the essential goodness of other people, is a precious gift which should be protected and nurtured in these difficult times. This 'context-smashing' humanism which has the capacity to reach across races, cultures, civilizations and gender is suppressed in our societies by tradition, ritual and social and political structures. Those who attempt to liberate this humanism are often at the receiving end of a great deal of hostility. And yet they need to be strengthened and celebrated as brave individuals who protect the spiritual core of religious faith. In the final analysis, perhaps, we can take strength in the future, since time, like God, must be on their side.

RADHIKA COOMARASWAMY
United Nations Rapporteur on Violence Against Women,
including its causes and consequences

Introductory essay: The Balasuriya file

On 2 January 1997 the Vatican Congregation for the Doctrine of Faith (CDF) issued, in Italian, a 'Notification on the Work of *Mary and Human Liberation* of Fr Tissa Balasuriya OMI', a document of some four pages listing what are considered to be the errors of the book and incompatible with the faith. Its last paragraph but one states: 'In publishing this present *Notification* the Congregation considers itself likewise obliged to declare that Fr Tissa Balasuriya has deviated from the integrity of the truth of the Catholic faith, and therefore cannot be regarded as a Catholic theologian, and has furthermore incurred excommunication *latae sententiae* (can. 1364, para. 1).' The final paragraph states that the Pope has approved this Notification, which was agreed upon in the ordinary session of the Congregation, and has authorized its publication. It is signed by Joseph, Cardinal Ratzinger, Prefect, and Archbishop Tarcisio Bertone, Secretary of the Congregation. Canon 1364, 1 reads, in the translation of the Canon Law Society of America (CLSA), 'with due regard for can. 194, para. 1, n. 2, an apostate from the faith, a heretic or a schismatic incurs automatic (*latae sententiae*) excommunication'. Canon 194 specifically provides for loss of ecclesiastical office as an administrative consequence of abandoning the Catholic communion.

This announcement immediately created something of a furore in – what shall we say? – well-informed Catholic circles and indeed wider Christian circles too. *Latae sententiae* excommunication means effectively that the subject of it is to be considered as having excommunicated himself or herself by persisting in his or her errors, and that there is therefore no need for a formal trial and, if convicted and refusing to recant, excommunication by an actual judgement, *ferendae sententiae*. The leading article in the 11 January issue of the British journal *The Tablet* states that he has been denied his freedom and rights (their loss being a consequence of excommunication): 'Where is the due process of law? Without that process there is tyranny.' Fr Charles E. Curran, himself banned by the Vatican from teaching moral theology, wrote to the US *National Catholic Reporter* as follows:

> Only my identity as a Catholic theologian was attacked by the Vatican, but if action against you destroys the most fundamental identity of your life as a baptized Catholic, a theologian, and a priest, I was hurt by the action against me, but you must be devastated by what has happened to you.

One more quotation, from the mass of letters to *The Tablet* which the excommunication provoked, will show how its 'fall-out' extended beyond the limits of the Catholic Church. The Revd Roy Robinson, of the United Reformed Church, wrote from Norwich:

> As for Fr Balasuriya's excommunication, can the Pope really be serious in inviting us, the representatives of the churches of the Reformation, to discuss with him the role of the papacy, when he gives such examples of the abuse of papal authority.
>
> (Letters, *The Tablet*, 25 January 1997, p. 110)

The main issue, in fact, in the whole affair is not the rightness or the wrongness of Fr Balasuriya's theology, but the appropriateness or otherwise of the reaction to it by the ecclesiastical authorities, both in Sri Lanka (for that is where the pot is boiling over) and in Rome. Readers of this documentation will have before them the material on which to make up their minds on both points, and we shall have to consider them both, I hope objectively, in this introductory essay. But first we must introduce Fr Balasuriya more fully with a brief sketch of his life and his work, and then go on to a factual account of the way in which the whole affair has unfolded, from the publication of his book in 1990 to his excommunication in January 1997 – and beyond.

Balasuriya's life and work[1]

Sirimevan Tissa Balasuriya was born on 29 August 1924 in the small village of Kahatagasdigiliya in the central province of Ceylon, as it was then known, where his father was an apothecary in government service. The family was Catholic; one of his sisters, who died in 1991, joined the Congregation of the Holy Family. Tissa was sent to school at Maris Stella College in a village of Catholic fisherfolk by the sea, called Negombo. He was two years at St Patrick's College, Jaffna (1939–40) and at St Joseph's College, Colombo (1941–2).

He attended the University of Ceylon from 1942 to 1945, graduating in Economics and Political Science. In 1945 he joined the Congregation of Oblates of Mary Immaculate (OMI), making his religious profession in 1946. He was sent to Rome to do his philosophical and theological studies at the Gregorian University; he obtained his licentiate in both subjects, and was ordained in Rome in 1952. Back in Sri Lanka he was assigned to teach in Aquinas University College, a Catholic institution which prepared students for external university degrees. In 1962 he came to Europe again for further studies: to Oxford for a year, where he gained a diploma in Agricultural Economics; then to Paris for studies in theology, catechetics and sociology, at the Institut Catholique.

Back once more in his native land in 1964, he was appointed Rector of Aquinas College, a post he remained in until 1971. He was also at times during these years national chaplain to the Ceylon Catholic Students Federation, and Asian chaplain for Pax Romana Catholic Students movement 1969–79. In 1971 he resigned from Aquinas College to found his Centre for Society and Religion, of which he became the director. He resigned his directorship in 1994, but still takes part in the work of the Centre. In 1976 he became a founder member of the Ecumenical Association of Third World Theologians (EATWOT), launched in Dar es Salaam, Tanzania, and for ten years was the Asian co-ordinator of this organization.

He has been editor of *Voices of Third World Theology*, 1985–92; of *Social Justice and Sadaranaya* since 1987; and of *Logos*, which is, or has become, the house journal of his Centre for Society and Religion, since 1971. Besides his book *Mary and Human Liberation*, which triggered off the recent *brouhaha*, he has written *Jesus Christ and Human Liberation*, *The Eucharist and Human Liberation*, *Planetary Theology*, *Right Relationships* and other works on economics and sociology.

Unfolding the affair[2]

1990: *Mary and Human Liberation* published as a double issue of *Logos*.

1992, December 1: an *ad hoc* body, called for convenience from now on the Ad Hoc Theological Commission (AHTC), was convened to review the book. Present were Vianney Fernando, Bishop of Kandy, Malcolm Ranjith, Assistant Bishop of Colombo, Fr Dalston Forbes OMI and Fr Emmanuel Fernando, Rector of the national seminary.

1993, January 7: at the request of Nicolas Marcus Fernando, Archbishop of Colombo, Fr Balasuriya attended a meeting at the office of the Catholic Bishops' Conference of Sri Lanka (CBCSL). There Bishop Ranjith distributed what he claimed to be the observations of the AHTC on the book, in which it was said, *inter alia*, that they all felt that Balasuriya 'seems to deny the divinity of Jesus Christ', and that 'he denies *in toto* the following classical theological presentation of the nature of Jesus':

All mankind is under original sin;

Redemption is to be freed from the power of original sin;
This can be done only by a divine-human Saviour;
Jesus Christ is that Saviour.
Through his death and resurrection he saves us ontologically from original sin;
Therefore Jesus Christ is the divine-human Saviour and God's Son.

Fr Balasuriya's presentation, says Bishop Ranjith's statement, is based on the following propositions:

There is no original sin;
no redemption is necessary;
no Saviour is necessary;
Jesus Christ is not the Saviour; he is not God.

According to Fr Forbes (who was present at this meeting) this surely rather idiosyncratic presentation of 'classical theology' was a travesty of the Ad Hoc Theological Commission's discussion a month earlier, and also of Balasuriya's views, and he very naturally dissociates himself from it entirely. But it was to form the basic charges of the CBCSL against Balasuriya.

At this meeting there was no discussion with Balasuriya; he was simply requested to present his answer in writing as soon as he could.

- 1994, January 7: exactly a year later he sent the bishops his reply in great detail, pointing out, among other things, '6 falsifications, 5 distortions, and 3 manipulations of my text'.
- 1994, April 20: Fr Balasuriya was summoned to CBCSL meeting in Kandy and informed that the bishops would soon make a public statement. There was no discussion of the issues involved.
- 1994, June 5: the bishops published their statement on the book in the *Catholic Messenger*, mentioning 'four glaring errors', and warning Catholics against reading it. Balasuriya's reply to the charges was not published, in spite of his requests that it should be.
- 1994, July 22: the Congregation for the Doctrine of the Faith (CDF) in Rome sent Balasuriya their Observations, having now taken the matter out of the hands of the CBCSL. The Observations had no authenticating signature, and were sent in Italian; Balasuriya had to ask for an English translation.
- 1995, March 14: he sent his reply.
- 1995, December 18: Fr Balasuriya received a letter from the CDF saying his reply was 'unsatisfactory', and enclosed for him to sign before witnesses, 'a Profession of Faith' formulated by 'this dicastery', the rather pompous Greek word meaning a court of justice, which the curial congregations in Rome, especially the CDF, now

like to call themselves. It was a profession of faith specially drawn up for Balasuriya for this occasion, and so he declined to sign it.

- 1996, May: accordingly he received a fax from the CDF, bidding him to sign by 15th of the month, or be excommunicated. So on May 14 he signed Paul VI's *Credo of the People of God* with the added rider that he did so 'in the context of theological development and Church practice since Vatican II, and the freedom and responsibility of Christians and theological researchers under Canon Law'.
- 1996, December 7: The Nuncio in Sri Lanka read out to Balasuriya the Notification of Excommunication, and told him it would be published and take effect if he did not sign the CDF's Profession of Faith forthwith. He was then informed that the Profession of Faith of Paul VI signed by him was not sufficient as the added rider invalidated it.
- 1997, January 2: the Notification was published.
- 1997, January 21: the Oblates of Sri Lanka issued their statement in support of Balasuriya, and highly critical of the procedures both of the Catholic bishops in Sri Lanka and of the CDF in Rome. They conclude their statement as follows:

We therefore insistently urge that the CDF should repeal the penalty of excommunication. Other means should be devised to deal with these alleged theological errors of this book, and to place them before the international theological community of the church.

- 1997, January 24: Cardinal Ratzinger gave his justification of the CDF's proceedings in a press conference.

Further developments will be mentioned in the final section of this introductory essay.

Assessment of the book *Mary and Human Liberation*

The Observations of the CDF on the book begin with the somewhat lukewarm compliment: 'Good intentions can certainly be found in this work', and among them it mentions 'the desire to offer a view of the figure of the Blessed Virgin that illuminates the values of mature and responsible womanhood'. The other good intentions are concerned with interfaith relations and inculturation. But we will concentrate on the first one, because one comes away from the book with the strong impression that Balasuriya's primary motivation in writing it was his wholehearted sympathy with, and indeed commitment to, the feminist movement in general and feminist theology in particular. And the nameless members of the CDF who composed that tepid eulogy at the beginning of their observations – damning with faint praise before getting down to the business of damning in earnest – could have been a little more generous in granting that at least on this point he did largely achieve what he desired.

Chapter 4, 'Mary: a mature adult woman', seems to have been the nucleus of the book. Its contents were the subject of talks given in Ireland in 1988. On the basis of an imaginative – and entirely proper – interpretation of the New Testament evidence, mainly in Luke's Gospel, and certainly not excluding the infancy narratives, he presents Our Lady as 'an ordinary woman of her time who went through the process of living in very difficult circumstances'. He emphasizes her 'strength of character' 'as a poor, courageous woman'. She 'foreshadows the trials and struggles of women of our time too'. 'Mary as a mature and ageing woman accepted the changed relationship [with her son]. She co-operated in Jesus' liberative action. She shows a way in which older women, including widows, can participate in personal and societal liberation.'

In all this he is not eliminating but supplementing the traditional image of Mary – so disproportionately, perhaps, that of the Madonna and Child – in a way that is surely positive and valuable. He has a magnificent comment on the Magnificat, which has God casting the mighty down from their seats and exalting the humble and meek, filling the hungry with good things and sending the rich empty away: 'The pity ... is that the Christian tradition has succeeded in domesticating Mary so much that she is known as the comforter of the disturbed, rather than as a disturber of the comfortable.'

Unfortunately, Balasuriya is not content with thus simply supplementing traditional Marian devotions and theology. He has adopted the style of argument, much favoured by newspaper controversialists, which speaks in terms of 'either this or that'; 'not this, but that'.

So his arguments tend to run on the following lines. We should *not*, he says, espouse the old classical Catholic theology (a favourite turn of expression – as if there were only one old classical Catholic theology!), which is patriarchal, male-dominated, governed by Western, Greco-Roman cultural presuppositions (one such 'presupposition', incidentally, being the interpretation of the doctrine of original sin). On the contrary, we should turn to the new feminist, liberation, inculturation, dialogue theologies. But are the two mutually exclusive? If only his argument had tended more towards a 'both ... and', 'not only ... but also' emphasis, things might have turned out very differently.

He does not deny the defined Marian dogmas, from Mary's virgin motherhood and her being the *Theotokos*, the God-bearer, to her Immaculate Conception and Assumption. He does, however, undervalue them as being the products of Hellenistic, Western, patriarchal values and concerns, which have taken Our Lady out of the arena of the everyday life of most women in the world. One small instance of this kind of oversimplistic contrast: he writes 'While most spiritual writers have interpreted Mary's *fiat* as a sign of her submission to God's will in respectful docility, some feminist theologians have stressed that God was dependent on a woman for the carrying out of the divine plan of redemption.' Yet the second reading of the breviary's Office of Readings for 20 December is from the sermon by that archetypal feminist St Bernard, in which the preacher addresses the Virgin thus: 'You have heard that you shall conceive and bear a Son ... The angel is waiting for your answer; it is time for him to return to God who sent him. We too are waiting, O Lady, for the word of pity ... Answer, O Virgin, answer your Lord. Speak the word, receive the Word ... Why delay? Why tremble? Believe, speak, receive. Let your humility put on boldness, and your modesty be clothed with trust ... ' And so on till the climax: 'And Mary said ... '

It is the same in the other areas of theology and doctrine that he deals with. His method leads him to call in question the long prevalent interpretation of original sin as a 'presupposition', based partly on a literal interpretation of Genesis; and ineluctably therefore to question the doctrine of consequent interpretation of the doctrine of redemption by Jesus Christ, the saviour of the whole human race. He is so keen, and laudably so, to respect the other religions with which he is in dialogue, and their founders, that he seeks to reinterpret one of the first principles of inter-faith as one of ecumenical dialogue, and that is that participants must not compromise their own basic religious tenets; and one basic tenet of Christianity (not just of Catholicism) is that Jesus Christ 'is the saviour of the world' (John 4.42), and that 'there is salvation in no one else, for there is no other name under heaven given among mortals by which we must be saved' (Acts 4.12).

To be sure, these texts do not oblige us to believe, in any crude literal sense, that only fully professed Roman Catholics can be saved. Nor would any of the theologians of the CDF, its Prefect included, consider that it does; after all, when the CDF was still the Holy Office, back in 1949, it excommunicated a certain Fr Feeney for persistently maintaining just that. But the basis of all the Christian missionary enterprise is that Jesus Christ, the incarnate divine Word of God, is of a unique relevance to every single human being and their ultimate eternal salvation. For those who are saved, whether they profess other religions or none at all, their salvation is dependent on their living according to the light given to them by their consciences. It is therefore through the grace won for them by Christ's redemptive death and resurrection that their salvation is achieved.

So it is not surprising that the Sri Lankan bishops were alarmed by Balasuriya's book – and indeed they would have been failing in their duty of episcopal oversight if they had not taken notice of it. What is rather surprising is that they took so long to do so, something like two years after its publication. But this now brings us to the last point we must consider in this introductory essay.

Assessment of the reaction of the ecclesiastical authorities

There are two things to be looked at here; first, the justice or otherwise of the procedures applied in dealing with Tissa Balasuriya and his book – and it is this that has claimed all the attention and publicity surrounding the case; and secondly the pastoral appropriateness of the actions taken.

(1) The questionable justice of all the procedures. They have all been applied, to be sure, in accordance with some canons of the Code of Canon Law, though Balasuriya maintains that other canons have been flouted, which is why he thought he could appeal. Some further contributors to the debate on the affair have said that it is unreasonable to fault these canons on the grounds that they do not tally with the accepted procedures or principles of Anglo-Saxon Common Law. But the main objection has been that they do not tally with the requirements of natural justice. This can be immediately illustrated when we come at last to the end of the story.

Balasuriya appealed to the curial dicastery, the Signatura, against the procedures applied to him, precisely on the grounds that they contravened various canons. These were canons 50 and 221, on the rights of those against whom disciplinary action is taken or contemplated; also the document of the 1971 Synod of Bishops, *Justice in the World*, sec. III. After some initial hesitation they agreed to hear his appeal, and asked him to choose counsel to plead his case from a list of names they supplied him with. He did so; but before they received the name of his nominee the papal Secretary of State informed the Signatura, on the Pope's instructions, that they had no competence to try the case. His Holiness had personally approved the procedures, and the final excommunication in *forma specifica*, and there is no appeal from such papal decisions, without another direct mandate from the Pope. In other words, the right of appeal is forestalled by the highest court of appeal judging (or rather prejudging) the case in first instance.

However, Balasuriya sent an appeal to the Pope, through the Signatura, for a mandate (under can. 1405, 2) to allow his appeal to go ahead.

He also offered, responding to a suggestion of Cardinal Ratzinger's, to sign the *Credo* of Paul VI without the rider he had attached to it; but asking that if he did so the excommunication would be lifted and that any alleged errors in his book should be referred to an independent board of theologians acceptable to both sides.

He says that this response is now with the Oblates' Procurator General to the Holy See.[3]

And then the excommunication itself, *latae sententiae*, saving the CDF from the trouble of formally having to try him, and then, if finding him guilty and on his declining to recant, excommunicating him *ferendae sententiae*. The only analogy in secular law that I can think of is the ancient penalty of outlawry. I suppose Robin Hood and his merry men were declared outlaws before they were ever arrested and brought to trial. But here is the comment of the Canon Law Society of America (CLSA) on can. 1364, 2, which the 'Notification' invoked, in its edition of the Code:

> This law does not define apostasy, heresy or schism (they are defined in can. 751), but simply specifies that they warrant latae sententiae excommunication ... This represents a relatively late change during the consultative process (in preparation of the new code), during most of which a ferendae sententiae penalty has been envisioned for these offences. In maintaining that a latae sententiae penalty be incurred in these instances, Church authorities need to be sensitive to the complex issues raised by these offences. It is difficult to determine precisely when an individual or group is guilty of heresy according to law. This is especially true given increased theological pluralism and ecumenical contacts, and confessional boundaries that are not as sharply defined as formerly.

Of course the excommunication of 2 January did not come out of the blue. Balasuriya had plenty of warning beforehand, as we have seen. But he for his part maintains that throughout these years, from 1992 onwards, he was never given the opportunity to discuss the objections officially raised against his book. There was never any debate, any argument giving the pros and cons. It is true that he was invited to reply, first to the comments of the Sri Lankan bishops, and then to the Observations of the CDF. This he did at very considerable length; but the local bishops, he says, just ignored his reply, while the CDF responded with the single word 'unsatisfactory', and then required him to sign the Profession of Faith which they composed especially for his benefit.

Cardinal Ratzinger, in his justification of his 'dicastery's' action already referred to, said 'to avoid an interminable discussion which would not be useful to anyone, the CDF opted for a more positive way forward by inviting him to sign a profession of faith. One does no wrong to any Catholic by inviting him to profess his faith'; and the Cardinal went on to say that the Profession of Faith presented to Balasuriya was formulated only from solemn pronouncements of the Magisterium.

This, not uncharacteristically of the curial style, is less than candid, not to say disingenuous. Since when has 'Rome', which likes to say it thinks in centuries, been in such a hurry that it wants to avoid interminable discussions? Not useful to anyone? Possibly of use in getting at the truth. One does no wrong to a Catholic by asking for a profession of his or her faith; but this particular Catholic was being asked to subscribe to a particular, one might almost say somewhat slanted, statement of faith (which included the inordinability of women) as seen by the CDF. It is trenchantly analysed and criticized by an Indian Jesuit theologian, Samuel Rayan. He makes the point that this Profession of Faith mixes indiscriminately 'bits from ecumenical councils ancient and modern, from doctrinal definitions and explanatory observations, from papal letters, from pastoral creeds and from what is referred to as the CDF Professio fidei'. Is all this 'only solemn pronouncements of the Magisterium'? The Cardinal says that inviting Balasuriya to subscribe was a more positive way than interminable discussion. Fr Rayan says: 'It is difficult to see in this creed and in the accompanying letter some pastoral concern, some fraternal love, some sensitive search for the truth. They dictate rather than dialogue ... The voice therefore of documents like this creed is the voice of the Inquisition of shameful memory rather than the voice of the Good Shepherd.' And he concludes his criticism by saying: 'The CDF would do well to publish a scholarly faith-criticism of Balasuriya's book, and to have that criticism met by believers and scholars everywhere.'

Which brings us to our second point, on which we can be very brief.

(2) The pastoral appropriateness of the actions taken. Here I am thinking of pastoral concern not for Balasuriya himself, but for the faithful, above all in Sri Lanka. As we have noted, there are certainly grounds for objecting to the book *Mary and Human Liberation*. But by taking what seems to have been purely disciplinary action, alleging serious errors and even heresies in the book, first of all the Sri Lankan bishops left Balasuriya and his book in possession of the field in that country, at least among the educated who could read English; and then the CDF made sure that he and his book would be in possession of the field in the rest of the English-speaking world. What was called for was precisely the discussion, the argument that he was requesting all along; a reply to him in terms of the popular theology he was writing in.

Finally, and in the long run this is even more serious, the way the

Holy See, indeed, the Pope himself, and the CDF have acted in this case has done more than almost anything in the present pontificate to bring discredit to the Holy See and to undermine its authority. Respect for authority can never be taken for granted; it has to be earned – and regrettably can be forfeited. And that is what is happening now over this case. In a letter to *The Tablet*, 1 February 1997, Professor James O'Connell hopes that this case may prompt the Church to 'face up to reform' in several areas. 'The Church', he writes, 'might rethink its witness of integrity in relation to the great social and personal issues . . . and it might surely revise its organisational structures, not just the Curia, but the working of the dioceses, the recruitment and formation of clerics . . . ' Not just the Curia, no. But first and foremost, the Curia; and most urgently the Church, the Holy See, needs to revise, reform, rethink the whole working of the Curia and all its dicasteries, especially those of the Congregation for the Doctrine of the Faith.

EDMUND HILL OP
Cambridge, England
April 1997

Notes

1 I am indebted for my information to Bernadeen Silva and Basil Fernando.
2 For much of this information I am indebted to Fr Dalston Forbes OMI and to Robert Cruz of Colombo.
3 Fax to Steve Alston of CAFOD, and friends, received by SA 3 March 1997.

Mary and Human Liberation

Dedication

to my mother

VICTORIA BALASURIYA
(1901–1985),

the Congregation of the
Oblates of Mary Immaculate,
also my Mother since 1945,

and all the women
who have enriched my life

Preface

Mary is very important in Catholic spirituality. Teaching concerning her and devotion to Mary are among the most difficult issues within ecumenical dialogue. Many Protestants think that Catholics give her an almost divine place in the plan of salvation. Attitudes towards Mary are also important in the current theological dialogue around feminism and Third World theologies. Mary has been interpreted to favour male domination and conformism to prevailing social inequalities. We have, therefore, to ask ourselves how contemporary Mariology developed in the Catholic tradition.

Marian theology raises critical issues of hermeneutics, as does almost any branch of theology. Mariology has been linked to a theology of domination that has held sway over Western Europe, and has been transposed, with the missionary expansion of the Church, to most of the Catholic world. How and why did this theology arise? The search for a more meaningful Marian theology and spirituality has led to a questioning of many of the assumptions, or presuppositions, of traditional Christian theology.

The translation of certain significant texts of the Bible is important for Mariology also, for example in relation to the virginity of Mary, and whether she had other children in addition to Jesus. Marian theology is influenced by the way the scriptural texts concerning Mary have been selectively utilized and emphasized, so that, for example, the socially radical significance of the Magnificat, attributed to her, was bypassed for many centuries.

Traditional theology has often been dependent on a literal interpretation of the first few chapters of Genesis. A non-literal interpretation of these texts was officially accepted by the Church only in this century, through the Biblical Commission. Prior to that, even though there were theologians who spoke of the allegorical nature of these narratives, the main focus of the Church's teaching was to present them as actual historical events. This literal interpretation was a foundation of the doctrine of original sin, communicated through procreation to all humanity. This explanation of original sin was, in turn, the basis for the doctrine of the Immaculate Conception, one of the principal privileges attributed to Mary.

As feminist theologians point out, the male authorship of the books of the Bible may explain the androcentric emphasis of the scriptures in their presentation of the Jesus story. Each of the evangelists has his own constituency and priorities in writing a Gospel. Connected to this also is the silence of the scriptures concerning many aspects of Mary's life which might have been recorded if a woman had written a Gospel. We might then have known more about Mary, her personality, identity and sense of personal mission in those troubled times.

Marian theology is connected to and depends on the general core and construct of the rest of theology. Christian theology is about God, the universe, human life, redemption and our destiny after this life. Teaching on these has evolved historically through the interpretation given to the scriptures, and the message of Jesus, by the Church authorities. The theological controversies and the Councils of the Church have been the occasions for the development and definition of some of the central doctrines of Christianity. Mariology has been intimately linked to these decisions about the identity, nature, personality, mission and role of Jesus Christ. Mary's own personality, privileges and role in the divine plan are significantly linked to the Church's teaching concerning her son Jesus.

The definitions of the Councils of Nicaea, Ephesus and Chalcedon in the fourth and fifth centuries were crucial in the evolution of Christian theology, particularly Christology. These definitions concern matters that are beyond human comprehension, and belong, in human terms, to the area of inscrutable mystery. The question then arises of how the Councils reached their conclusions concerning these issues: What is the role of ecclesiastical authority in determining the truth concerning these mysteries? What is the role of the civil and political powers that were also involved in resolving these theological controversies? How far are the traditional interpretations of Mariology dependent on this conciliar process, which involved a compromise between the Church and the imperial powers of the day?

In this connection the concept of original sin and its consequences is crucial for subsequent Christology and Mariology. A re-thinking of human nature in relation to sin and redemption would imply a change in the understanding of the life and role of Mary. The nature of human redemption is a critical background issue for Mariology.

Since these theological doctrines and definitions are about matters which are beyond the competence of human understanding, we can question whether they are truths communicated to us by God, or whether the human imagination itself has contributed towards their elaboration. What, then, is the role of imagination in the evolution of theologies? How far can the accepted myths of a society contribute towards this process?

Ideology, too, may have had a significant role in the elaboration of Marian theology. Male domination may have contributed to theological perceptions concerning Mary, and these may, in turn, have helped consolidate the privileged position of men in both religious and social spheres. Is it possible that the self-interest of the decision-makers and power-holders had a role to play in the development of Marian theology?

Throughout the Catholic world, popular religion has enhanced Marian devotions. There is a warm and eager recourse to Mary as mother, protectress and intercessor. She softens the image of God as the just judge. The apparitions of Our Lady have contributed to popular religion as well as to the confirmation of theological doctrines. The shrines, places of pilgrimage, prayers, hymns, litanies, novenas and preaching of the Church nourish people's devotion to Mary.

It is in this overall context that I try to reflect on the meaning of Mary, especially for our times, and in the circumstances of an unjust world. I propose some criteria for the critique and evaluation of theological propositions and presuppositions. I try to evoke the life and message of Mary from a reading of the Gospel story itself. I have also given some space for my imagination. My aim is not, however, to engage in speculation on humanly incomprehensible issues, but rather to understand what sort of a life Mary and her companions might have lived in tumultuous times of social injustice, burdensome religion, foreign occupation, and a people's rebellion against these.

I reflect on the Gospel evidence, scanty though it be, about the life of Mary. I see her as a mature adult woman who was concerned about the conditions of her people. She supported the struggle of her son and the group that gathered around him in a search for integral human liberation. In this book my reflection on Mary is very much related to the life and mission of Jesus. It is from the perspective of an understanding of Jesus that is different from that of traditional Christology, however. My presentation may be subject to the criticism that Mary is not considered independently, in her own right, but in relation to Jesus. While there is some truth in this, my perception of Mary is quite different from her portrayal in traditional theology. I see her as a woman of real life, involved in the day-to-day struggles of ordinary people at individual and community levels. Her experience would thus be close to that of today's women, and men also.

In Chapter 7 the message of Jesus is expressed as a call to conversion from a state of sin to one of virtue. Some of the words used to describe this process, such as 'from pride to humility and service', need some clarification. As the feminist movement stresses, in a certain sense, women need more often to affirm than to efface themselves. A sense of self-worth and a legitimate pride in oneself are good and necessary. Women's sense of service is often exploited by others, especially by men. My words concerning conversion should, therefore, be understood in such a way as to be ennobling for all, and not an encouragement to an undue self-abnegation of women, leading to their alienation.

The perception of Mary presented in this book, I think, can be meaningful for people everywhere, and not merely for those of us in poor countries. As the world is one of injustice, Mary's message of justice and liberation is relevant for the poor and the rich, for the victims of injustice as well as those who are oppressors. Marian spirituality can be an inspiration for the profound conversion that is required in our world of hunger in the midst of plenty, of war and threats of war, of the exploitation of people and of nature, and of the large-scale death and destruction caused by human selfishness and unconcern for others. I urge a rethinking of Mary so that devotion to her may be a means not of human alienation, but of overall human betterment for women and men everywhere.

I am conscious of treading on ground that is delicate, and capable of arousing strong reactions among some Catholics. *My intention is not to dilute Marian devotion but to help make it more meaningful and truly fulfilling for everyone.* It can motivate us towards new ministries required for our times: commitment to justice, inter-faith dialogue, action for peace, the liberation of women, caring for nature. All these can deepen practices such as novenas, family prayers and group reflections. Marian shrines, with a renewed theology, can be centres of renewal for the Christian community and all pilgrims. This new perception of Mary can also foster understanding among the Christian Churches. I hope the dialogue that may be generated by this work will shed further light on the issues involved.

The main ideas of the last two chapters were first published in *Logos* on 'Woman in Asia' in August 1974. I received many favourable comments on it from various parts of the world. These two chapters were also the subject of lectures at Milltown School of Theology in Dublin, Ireland, in May 1988. Chapter 6, 'Presuppositions in theology', was developed for the Russell Chandran Lectures at Union Theological College, Bangalore, India. Chapter 7, 'The presuppositions of original sin', and the rest of the book were included in lectures to the Daughters of Charity and at Turramurra Theological Faculty in Sydney, Australia, the Asian Young Christian Workers in Hong Kong, the Oblate Retreat Centre in Crewe, England, the Mission Institute of the Maryknoll Sisters at Ossining, New York, and at our own Centre in Colombo.

The thinking of this book can be complemented by my other theological writings: especially *Jesus Christ and Human Liberation, The Eucharist and Human Liberation, Planetary Theology* and *The Liberation of the Affluent.*

I am grateful to the numerous persons who have given me the benefit of their counsel, and to the hundreds who have participated in lectures, seminars and retreats based on the material of this book. Their responses convince me that it is worthwhile offering these ideas to a wider audience.

Dogma and the development of theology

Christian dogmas defined in past centuries are generally expressed in the language, philosophies and metaphors of those times. They are interpreted and lived according to the needs and understandings of different ages and peoples. They relate to God and the fundamentals of human life.

God is infinite and not fully comprehensible by our finite human minds. Our human language can never totally exhaust the Divine. Hence, all that we say of God is understood metaphorically and analogically. We can speak of the Divine only in human terms, of the Absolute only in relative language, of the Eternal only in temporal expressions. As St Thomas Aquinas and other mystics say, what we can say of God is in negative terms only, of what is not, rather than what God is.

Hence, while dogmas try to capture the reality of God in a human formula, they are never complete or adequate. God cannot be enclosed in any of our human categories. Mystics appreciate silence before the Infinite. God is to be sought without ever being found fully in human life. The development of theology takes place through different interpretations of human categories concerning God, expressed in a given culture and philosophy.

The Church endeavours to maintain the same faith by keeping the same words for dogmas and giving them varying meanings, or changing the priorities among doctrines. Pope John XXIII recalled this in his opening speech to the Second Vatican Council on 11 October 1962:

> *The substance* of the ancient doctrine of the deposit of faith is one thing, and *the way in which it is presented* is another.

Thus, God is presented through different images according to different cultural understandings, for example, as an old man, a lawgiver, a judge, or a creative spirit. When I write

> What is the nature of the divinity of Jesus? It is one thing to say Jesus is divine, another to claim to be able to understand, and even theologically define, the way and extent to which Jesus is divine,

I am not denying the divinity of Jesus. On the contrary, I am affirming it and trying to discuss some aspects of my understanding of it. In general, the mainstream theology of the official Church in the West tries to express the ultimate reality in specific terms, categories, definitions and dogmas. The Eastern mind, like the mystical-prophetical theology of the West, is more analogical, descriptive and does not view the divine as so easily captured in human formulas. God is an experience, an intuition, an inspiration, more than a definable substance. God is Spirit, God is love, God is truth – but cannot be contained in and exhausted by our human formulations.

Likewise, Mary has been imaged differently throughout the ages. To try to present another image of Mary, more relevant to our peoples, is not to deny her dogmas or her dignity, but rather to appreciate her better and more meaningfully today.

The task of theological explorers is to endeavour to present the content of the faith in a way that is intelligible and meaningful for the people of our time, place and culture. This has been, and is, an accepted ongoing process in the Church. It has contributed towards the development and elucidation of doctrine. It is from this perspective that what I have written concerning the dogmas of the faith can be evaluated. This requires an attentive and meditative reading of what I have written.

Preparation for Millennium 2000

Pope John Paul II has invited all Catholics to prepare for the Great Jubilee of 2000 in commemoration of the birth of Jesus. Regarding this occasion he has written an Apostolic Letter *Tertio Millennio Adveniente*, 'The Drawing Near of the Third Millennium'. He invites Catholics to repent of our past faults in relationships within the Church and with others:

> Another painful chapter of history to which the sons and daughters of the Church must return with a spirit of repentance is that of the acquiescence given especially in certain centuries, *to intolerance and even the use of violence in the service of truth.*
>
> It is true that an accurate historical judgment cannot prescind from careful study of the cultural conditioning of the times, as a result of which many people may have held in good faith that an authentic witness to the

truth could include suppressing the opinions of others or at least paying no attention to them. Many factors frequently converged to create assumptions which justified intolerance and fostered an emotional climate from which only great spirits, truly free and filled with God, were in some way able to break free. Yet the consideration of mitigating factors does not exonerate the Church from the obligation to express profound regret for the weakness of so many of her sons and daughters who sullied her face, preventing her from fully mirroring the image of the crucified Lord, the supreme witness of patient love and of humble meekness. From these painful moments of the past a lesson can be drawn for the future, leading all Christians to adhere fully to the sublime principle stated by the Council: 'The truth cannot impose itself except by virtue of its own truth, as it wins over the mind with both gentleness and power' (Vatican II Declaration of Religious Freedom, I).

(Pope John Paul II, *Tertio Millennio Adveniente* (Rome, 1994), no. 35)

This is one of the rare statements of a Pope that tries to deal with the problem of the mistakes of the Church over a long historical period, and in many lands. The Pope calls for an examination of conscience, and repentance, for these shortcomings. The Church needs to seek and correct the deeper theological motivations for such violence by the disciples of the loving and lovable Jesus and of his mother Mary.

This book may help somewhat in this painful task of asking ourselves where we Christians (in Asia and the rest of the world) went wrong during centuries of violence and disregard for the rights of others, including women. A more than merely superficial expression of repentance is required for a genuine openness to others in frank, respectful dialogue and united action for the common good of humanity and the care of nature. The Pope has indicated a way forward, it is up to us to develop the necessary theological background to meet this challenge.

The Second Vatican Council's criticism of the past has shown that there have been many shortcomings in attempting to interpret revelation. This means that theology is always exploratory and never final. This is true also of my work, which shares in the normal fallibility of the Church.

Therefore, as I suggest in this book, my work is also open to criticism and correction in a climate and context of genuine search for the truth.

TISSA BALASURIYA OMI

1

Mary in Catholic devotion

The importance of Mary in Catholic devotion

Mary the mother of Jesus has a very special place in Catholic devotion. In chapter 8 of the Dogmatic Constitution on the Church, *Lumen Gentium*, the Second Vatican Council explains the 'nature and basis of the cult of the Blessed Virgin':

> Mary has by grace been exalted above all angels and men [*sic*] to a place second only to her Son, as the most holy mother of God who was involved in the mysteries of Christ; she is rightly honoured by a special cult in the Church. From the earliest times the Blessed Virgin is honoured under the title of Mother of God, whose protection the faithful take refuge together in prayer in all their perils and needs [*Sub tuum praesidium*].
>
> Accordingly, following the Council of Ephesus, there was a remarkable growth in the cult of the People of God towards Mary, in veneration and love, in invocation and imitation, according to her own prophetic words: 'all generations shall call me blessed, because he that is mighty hath done great things to me' (Luke 1.48).
>
> (Vatican II: Constitution on the Church, 1965, 66)

In the Constitution on the Sacred Liturgy (1963) the Vatican Council records the place of Mary in the liturgy:

> In celebrating this annual cycle of Christ's mysteries, holy Church honours with a special love the Blessed Mary, Mother of God, who is joined by an inseparable bond to the saving work of her Son. In her the Church holds up and admires the most excellent fruit of the redemption, and joyfully contemplates, as in a faultless image, that which she herself desires and hopes wholly to be. (Art. 103)

These two texts of the most recent and most important Council of the Catholic Church offer an understanding of Marian devotion in the Catholic Church during the centuries up to the 1960s.

Mary is venerated and loved as Mother of God, invoked in peril, and when in need of protection and refuge, and she is to be imitated as the most perfect human being after Jesus.

I shall endeavour to reveal how the traditional devotion of the Church has influenced Christian theology.

In keeping with the central place of Mary in the life of Jesus and the Church, Christians, particularly in the Catholic and Orthodox Churches, have developed their piety and spirituality in a close and deep relationship with Mary. Perhaps no other person has so many churches and shrines dedicated to them in the whole world. People have built large and beautiful cathedrals in her honour. The world's most popular pilgrimages focus on Marian shrines. Christian artists, poets and spiritual writers have devoted their noblest talents to praising her. Numerous families of religious nuns, brothers and priests, and many lay organizations, take Mary as their patroness. Several countries are consecrated to her. Marian hymns are among the most popular in Catholic chant, Marian prayers are those most commonly recited – perhaps after the Lord's Prayer. The rosary is the companion of millions of people in their quiet moments.[1]

The liturgical year is marked throughout by Marian feasts, and Saturday has been Mary's day from the time of Alcuin at the end of the eighth century. Marian celebrations during the liturgical year include:

Advent – her period of expectation
Christmas – December 25th, the flight into Egypt
Purification – February 2nd
National feasts – e.g. Our Lady of Lanka, February 4th
Our Lady of Lourdes – February 11th
Annunciation – March 25th
Holy Week with the Passion, Stations of the Cross, Easter
Pentecost – Mary is present with the disciples
The month of May – Mary mediatrix of all graces
Mount Carmel – July 16th
Assumption – August 15th
Nativity of Mary – September 8th, the Holy Name of Mary
Our Lady of Sorrows – September 15th
Holy Rosary – first Sunday in October
Our Lady of Fatima – October 13th
Presentation – November 21st
Immaculate Conception – December 8th
Loreto – December 10th
Guadalupe (Mexico) – December 12th

Main themes in traditional Marian devotion

The popular understanding of Mary is very much expressed in Marian devotions at her shrines, in the celebration of her feasts and in prayers recited by Christians. Among these, Marian hymns are especially important because they express in music and with feeling the content of Catholic belief regarding Mary. To these may be added popular prayers, such as the 'Hail Mary', 'Remember O most gracious Virgin Mary' (*Memorare*), 'We fly to thy patronage', the *Sub tuum praesidium*, the Angelus and *Regina Coeli*, the 'Hail Holy Queen' (*Salve Regina*) and the Litany of the Blessed Virgin Mary.

The Marian hymns sung by English-speaking congregations in Sri Lanka indicate the type of emphasis given to Marian devotions. Two popular hymnals are the hymn book *Songs for Worship and Praise*, St Philip Neri's Church, Colombo,[2] and the *Hymnal*, Church of Our Lady of Fatima, Maradana.[3]

In these there are nineteen hymns to Our Lady. Seven hymns are in both booklets. Of the nineteen, one is the Magnificat. This contains the radical social message:

> He casts the mighty from their thrones
> and raises the lowly
> He fills the starving with good things
> sends the rich away empty ...
> and scatters the proud hearted.

This song, with its revolutionary import, is not of recent origin. It is attributed to Mary herself in the Gospel of St Luke (1.55), and harks back to the Old Testament. Thus we have a directly biblical song which has a clear reference to God's concern for social justice and integral human liberation.

Of the nineteen, there are two other hymns which have a passing reference to Mary's courage. One is 'All hail to you Mary' – 238 in the St Philip Neri hymnal and 13 in the Fatima Church hymnal:

> When Gabriel had spoken
> You humbly said 'Yes'.
> May we have the courage
> God's word to confess.

Here, her courage is in confessing God's word and refers to Mary's humility. There is no clear reference to the courage in society which Jesus and Mary actually manifested in their day. In the other hymn, 'The wonders he has done for me' (170 in the St Philip Neri hymnal), the second verse reads:

> Through your heart a sword will pass in sorrow
> Opening a mother's love to men.
> Showing us the courage of a woman
> Standing with her Son against all men.

Here there is an appreciation of Mary's courage in standing by Jesus when he was condemned and crucified. A similar theme is explored in hymn 78 in the Fatima hymnal, 'No man can live as an island'.

Other than these three references and the Magnificat, the fifteen other popular hymns have an approach to Mary that does not expressly appreciate her strong adult womanhood. She is not seen as participating in the life-struggle of her son Jesus. His message of radical liberation is totally absent from these hymns.

Mary is presented in these hymns as a humble virgin mother. She is the dearest, fairest, purest, brightest, rarest Madonna. She is a loving, tender, 'gentle, chaste and spotless maid', ever caring, hearing our prayers. Her role is linked with the view that Jesus 'paid the price of our iniquity'. She saves us 'from peril and from woe', 'Whom the Holy Spirit filled with grace', 'Virgin of all virgins', 'Lily of the valley', 'Mystic Rose'.

In these hymns human beings are portrayed as sinful, tossed in a sea of tempests. We plead with her: 'Pray for us sinners', 'None can give them hope but thee', 'Patron in life's brightest bloom, Patron even to the tomb' and:

> When the tempest rages
> She calms the troubled sea.

We sing of ourselves as weak sinners, sick, suffering and asking for help:

> Help us, help we cry to thee
> Soothe those rack'd on bed of pain.

We rejoice in her glories:

> Conceived, conceived immaculate,
> O greater joy for me. (hymn no. 95, Fatima Church hymnal)

This view of Mary corresponds to a traditional theology built around the hypothesis of humanity's fall in original sin, and our inability, as a consequence, to help ourselves. It is a negative view of human beings without the original blessing of God. Mary, on the other hand, is portrayed in the hymn as the rarest virgin, insulated from having to face the normal trials and temptations of life.

As a woman, Mary is shown as tender and loving but not concerned with removing the human-made societal causes of poverty, injustice and the exploitation of women. Her sexuality is emphasized but as the virgin of virgins: ordinary women can hardly emulate her. The emphases given to her physical virginity and her immaculate nature draw attention to sexual morality and preservation from sin and temptation. This derives from a spirituality that stressed the virtues and sins of sexual relations and neglected the other sins of human and social relations, such as selfishness, injustice, exploitation and male domination.

This is quite different from the person of Mary of which we read in the Gospels and the Acts of the Apostles. Her strength of character, her adult womanly qualities in contesting the social evils of the day, along with her son, are not recalled in these hymns, except in the Magnificat, and a few lines of three other hymns.

The hymns also present human beings as weak, dependent, sinful, needing help and tenderness. While this is partly true, they do not present us as having a role to play in the liberation of humanity from the social evils which are part of the cause of our misery. The active virtues of co-creativity on earth and in human relations are neglected. The positive value of human sexuality is not only neglected but even downgraded.

Thus these Marian hymns contribute towards making Christians less concerned with the transformation of society. Christians are encouraged to be dependent on Mary for resolving their individual concerns, but not for bringing about the radical change that the Magnificat announces. This Marian spirituality makes for less socially concerned women and men in the Church.

Sinhala hymns to Mary

Hymns to Mary in Sinhala carry the same message as those in English. In the Sinhala hymnal of Fatima Church there are twelve hymns to Mary. Of these one is the Magnificat with its radical message. However, as one church organist explained to me, though this hymn is sung occasionally, it is seldom that the verses of the latter half are sung because the hymn is particularly long. The Mass or other services would be unduly lengthened if the whole Magnificat were sung. It is, however, sung at Vespers on the eve of Church feasts amid the din and joy of the celebrations.

The other hymns are like the English, though one refers to the cross of Jesus, and another, 'Ridie Vala Gabin', has a reference to the flight into Egypt:

Who was she who made the escape into Egypt
who was she who saves Jesus from the cruel king.

Yet even here the reference is to Mary's protection.

The Sinhala hymns are even more flowery in language than the English ones. The language is beautiful, using alliteration and simple words. The music is attractive and the sentiments are those of praise of Mary, our human weakness and sinfulness, and Mary's maternal care for us – taking us under her mantle. Thus no. 170, 'Mariya Rajiniye', reads:

Mary the Queen and loving mother
You help the weak and the suffering
Looking after them in their distress
O mother of the weak and the suffering
We shall find refuge always
Under your maternal care.

Hymn no. 202, 'Ma Mavni', says it more expressively:

Our dear mother Mary
is light for our blindness,
strength in our weakness,
grace for our sinfulness.

These are all admirable sentiments. The problem is not that they are felt and expressed but that they miss the complementary message of positive human strengths, and Christianity's radical social content. They tend to make the liturgy a complacent exercise. They foster the sentiments of dependence and filial piety but do not move people towards a strong commitment to human values and responsibility, including the remedying of social and political evils. They rather make our Marian piety individualistic, a-social and security-seeking, on the bases of our weakness, sinfulness and fear.

The hymns in the publication *Kithunu Gee* are similar. One hymn in *Kithunu Gee* refers to Mary as protecting us from war and harm, referring to Mary's assumed protection of Ceylon from Japanese invasion in World War II.

The very popular hymn 'Sri Lanka Rani Maniye' is sung especially on Independence Day, 4 February:

You are the glitter of Lanka
You are the hallmark of Lanka
You are the stature of Lanka
You are Queen of Lanka.

The words are beautiful and the hymn has an attractive musical lilt. It does not, however, express the aspirations of the people for freedom or the meaning of Mary's Queenship.

Popular Marian prayers

The universally popular Marian prayers are the rosary, the Angelus and *Regina Coeli*, 'O Queen of Heaven, rejoice', the *Memorare* (Bernard of Clairvaux's 'Remember, O most gracious Virgin Mary'), 'We fly to thy patronage', the 'Hail Holy Queen' (*Salve Regina*), and the Litany of the Blessed Virgin Mary.

When the mysteries of the life of Our Lord and Our Lady are reflected on, the rosary is capable of manifold levels of interpretation. There may, however, be a tendency to recite the rosary in a repetitive manner in which the content of the mysteries becomes less meaningful. The practice of recent decades to relate the recitation of the rosary to the message of Fatima may give it a particular emphasis on the saving of souls from perdition, without much reference to integral human liberation.

The Angelus and the 'O Queen of Heaven, rejoice' are brief references to the mysteries of Jesus and Mary, and a prayer for the glory and joys of eternal life.

The *Memorare*, 'Remember, O most gracious Virgin Mary', emphasizes the same characteristics as the hymns analysed earlier. In it, the protection and intercession of Mary are implored for us who are sinful and sorrowful. Likewise 'We fly to thy patronage'. The sentiments of the 'Hail Holy Queen' are similar: 'We poor banished children of Eve send up our sighs mourning and weeping in this valley of tears ... She is our advocate, O clement, O loving, O sweet Virgin Mary.' All these, including the Hail Mary, intercede 'Pray for us sinners now and at the hour of our death'. There is almost an overarching fear of death and of our sinfulness linking these prayers.

The *Litany* of the Blessed Virgin Mary has been a very popular prayer in churches and in Catholic homes. It was approved for public recitation in churches by Pope Sixtus V in 1589. An analysis of its themes brings out the meaning of the concepts of Mother and Virgin.

Titles associated with Mary's motherhood include: mother of God, of Christ, of divine grace, mother most pure, most chaste, inviolate, undefiled, most lovable, most admirable, of good counsel, of our creator, of our saviour. They relate to Mary's sexual purity and her care and concern for us. There is little or no reference to what she had to undergo as the mother of the human Jesus, who led a very troubled life, especially during his public ministry.

Mary's virginity is recalled and praised. Mary is the virgin most prudent, most venerable, most renowned, most powerful, most merciful, most faithful. Here, too, there is an accent on her biological status, something which is considered as most significant for her virtue, fame and power.

Thereafter there are several titles which are associated with Old Testament prophecies and symbolism, although some seem less meaningful in our time: mirror of justice, seat of wisdom, cause of our joy, spiritual vessel, singular vessel of devotion, mystical rose, tower of

David, tower of ivory, house of gold, ark of the covenant, gate of heaven, morning star, health of the sick, refuge of sinners, comfort of the afflicted, help of Christians. In these, again, we see the themes of veneration, and invocation of help in our troubles. The title 'help of Christians', of course, presents her as particularly concerned with Christians, though she is also regarded as a universal mother of all humanity which is redeemed by her son.

The final set of twelve invocations are to her as queen: of angels, patriarchs, prophets, apostles, martyrs, confessors, virgins and all saints.

Thereafter her special graces of Immaculate Conception and Assumption into heaven are recalled. Finally, she is queen of the most holy rosary and queen of peace.[4]

This litany shows that prayer is very much influenced by the prevailing theology, which, in turn, is significantly influenced by the interests and concerns of the power-holders of a community. There is little or no reference to Mary's Magnificat, with its radical implications, nor to the message of religious and social liberation of her son, for which he gave his life.

The *Hail Mary* is the most commonly recited Marian prayer. Millions of Catholics recite it several times each day. Its first part is from the message of the angel Gabriel to Mary at the Annunciation, in the Gospel of Luke (1.26–38). The second part, 'Holy Mary, mother of God, pray for us sinners, now and at the hour of our death', is again an invocation to her as from poor sinners. This suggests a concept of salvation in which the liberative aspect of the transformation of values, relationships and structures is absent. We are made suppliants, without a motivation for an active participation in social liberation. Since the 'Hail Mary' is the most common personal and public Marian prayer, the absence of a socially liberative dynamic has a significant impact in tranquillizing Catholics. There is no suggestion that this is intended, but it can be the unintended or subconscious effect of a frequently repeated prayer.

The significance of the Hail Mary would have been different if it had included an invocation for Mary's support for radical social change, such as: 'Help us oppressed to bring down the mighty and exalt the humble, to fill the hungry with good things and send the rich away with empty hands' (see Luke 1.52). This, too, could have become a routine like the Magnificat recited at Vespers, but it is possible that a different Marian spirituality would also have been developed through such a prayer.

The *Rosary*, which dates from the Middle Ages, is mainly a recitation of Hail Marys, with a meditation on the five joyful, five sorrowful and five glorious mysteries of the lives of Jesus and Mary. The impact of this reflection depends very much on the understanding of the nature of the mystery of salvation through Jesus Christ. Until recently an understanding of salvation in Christ had little to do with integral human liberation.

Marian apparitions

One example of the way in which Marian spirituality has been evolving in the Catholic Church is found in the apparitions of Mary. Generally the apparitions reveal the conditioning of Christians at a given time and place. For instance, at Lourdes, Mary appears to Bernadette and speaks of herself as the Immaculate Conception, but she does not say anything about the conditions of the working class in France of the day. The apparition occurred during the heyday of the growth of industrial capitalism in Western Europe, and the working class was being severely exploited. Mary as the mother of all, and especially as a woman of the working class, should have felt these social evils to be a grave injustice.

Much less did Mary, appearing in Lourdes, even hint at the enormous harm being done in Africa by French military and economic expansion in the colonial empire. It would be interesting to know whether Mary ever appeared to British Christians to challenge them concerning the British presence in Ireland or in India.

Why was Mary of Lourdes incapable of enlightening French Christians concerning the atrocities being committed in Africa by their compatriots? These atrocities were committed almost in alliance with the Christian Churches. We note instead how Marian spirituality ignored such important aspects of Christian witness. However, if Bernadette had spoken of such things as the rights of French workers or of the African peoples, the shrine of Lourdes would probably not have developed in the manner it has during the last one and a quarter centuries.

Mary appeared in Fatima in 1917, the year of the communist revolution in Russia. The message of Fatima was regarded as a warning against atheistic communism and its threat to the world. At the same time, however, Portugal was exploiting Africans in Angola and Mozambique. Yet Mary seemed to say nothing about the internal and external evils of the ruling Portuguese regime. This Mary, who comes to us in apparitions, and who is accepted by the dominant establishment, is not a liberating Mary. She speaks of sin and prayer and their significance in the Church and world. Such Marian apparitions do not communicate to women the sense of their dignity and rights. Services at Marian shrines are usually dominated by male clergy, and

women are the recipients of advice and benedictions. The consciousness of Mary as an adult lay woman and mother, who participated
actively in the work of Jesus, and in the mission of the early Church, is
not conveyed by these apparitions nor the devotions associated with
them.

Thus Marian devotions still have, by and large, a domesticating
impact on women and the laity. Religious women, too, are not helped
by them to acquire a greater sense of their dignity, responsibilities and
rights in the Church and in society.

The male-dominated, patriarchal, salvation-oriented theology of the
period from Augustine to Vatican II still pervades much of the Marian
piety of Sri Lanka. There are a few changes, but very much more can be
done to present Mary as she is seen in the Gospels, and in a manner
relevant to today's struggles.

Marian shrines

The Marian shrines, which are numerous and popular in Sri Lanka,
have a similar impact. A shrine like Madhu has the effect of bringing Sri
Lankans of different races together, and this can make a valuable social
contribution. But many of the devotions are as described above. The
hymns and prayers at the novenas of Our Lady of Perpetual Succour,
Our Lady of Fatima and the Miraculous Medal encourage largely
individualistic piety.

Marian devotions – hymns and prayers and litanies – do not encourage the laity to penitence characterized by a concern for humanity and
justice. This is quite different from the focus of the Mary of the
Gospels.

Similarly, Mary, who is said to have given the rosary to Christians, is
claimed to have been on their side against the Turks, and she is invoked
as the champion of Christians in the battle of Lepanto as 'Our Lady of
Victories'. It is presumed that she favours Christians, but why should
she be partial to one group – say Europeans? Is she a European or
Christian goddess or really the mother of Jesus who cared for all?

We have, therefore, to examine the Mary of our theology, spirituality
and popular devotions. With a few exceptions, witnessed by the
Madonna of Guadalupe, or the Black Mary of Poland, where people
suffering hardships present her differently, she is portrayed as one who
does not understand the socialist world, nor the suffering imposed by
countries that called themselves Christian in Asia, Africa and the
Americas. This traditional Mary is a Mary of the capitalist, patriarchal,
colonialist, First World of Christendom.

This top-down Mariology leaves Mary to embody the message that the powerful want to hear. It is those who determine and dominate theological thinking who decide on the authenticity of any Mariology.

Mariology might also be analysed in social terms, for it has been developed within a Christian community that depreciated the human, the feminine and sexuality, and did not appreciate liberative commitment to social justice.

Mary has been declared the patroness of many Catholic countries. In Sri Lanka, the national basilica has been dedicated to her. She is honoured as Queen of Sri Lanka. But what is the substance of the message which is expressed in the basilica and in its official teachings and prayers to Mary? It would seem that she is invoked mainly as a protectress in distress, and a healer in sickness. The Madonna was invoked to defend us against the Japanese during British rule, but she was not asked to help our peoples in their struggle for national independence and economic liberation. It may be said that we were saved from the ravages of war. This is true, but it is not understood that the causes of the war were in great measure the imperialist hold of Britain and her Western allies over most of the poor world. It is necessary to consider these issues critically, otherwise we might create our national Madonna and shrines to accommodate the framework of an unjust world order. This is quite against the spirit of the Magnificat.

At present the shrine can help people to understand the root causes of our people's misery, which include the selfishness and exploitation of local and foreign agencies.

The national basilica can thus be a witness to Mary or a counter witness to her. Currently it would seem that little at the shrine is conducive to the triple liberation which the Magnificat proclaims: social, cultural and political. These areas need to be reconsidered in order that the shrine may be faithful to the message of Mary and of the Gospels.

If the national basilica expresses an integral message of liberation from personal and societal constraints and points to full human development, it can be a great inspiration to Catholics, and through them to the rest of the people. For this to happen, Mary has to be presented as a mature, committed woman, incarnate in her country, and participating in her people's struggles for overall liberation and self-realization.

The themes of traditional Marian devotion revolve around:

(1) significant events in her life mentioned in the Gospels;
(2) ecclesiastical definitions and teachings concerning her graces and privileges, such as her Immaculate Conception, virginity, divine maternity and the Assumption into heaven;

(3) the holiness of Mary and the virtues attributed to her: faith, humility, obedience to God's will, love and care for others;

(4) the roles assigned to her in the traditional theological perspective of salvation such as co-redemptrix, mediatrix of graces, mother of all humanity, the hope of those in need.

These events, teachings, virtues and roles are all understood and interpreted against the background of traditional theology, including the Christology, that prevailed in the Church between the fourth century and the modern era up to the end of Vatican II.

The Gospels mention some significant events in her life, especially in connection with the birth, life, ministry, passion and death of Jesus. The graces and privileges of Mary that have been the subject of Church pronouncements have been deduced from the teaching of the Church concerning Jesus Christ. In that sense, throughout the centuries Mariology was derived from Christology, and both of them had a close relationship to the Church's teachings concerning the human condition after creation: original justice, original sin, the fall of humanity from original justice, and the need of a divine redeemer.

Notes

1   Bishop Edmund Peiris OMI, *Marian Devotion in Ceylon* (Chilaw: St Peter's Press, 1948).

This booklet gives a historical survey of the devotion of the Catholics in Ceylon to the Blessed Virgin Mary. It was written by Bishop Peiris as a souvenir of the Marian Congress, Colombo 8–11 July 1948, held to mark the centenary of the Oblates of Mary Immaculate in Ceylon 1847–1947.

He traces the history of Marian devotion over four centuries from the more sustained arrival of Christianity with the Portuguese in the sixteenth century to the proclamation of the 'Most Holy and Immaculate Virgin Mary Queen of Our Island and Our Lady of Lanka' at Tewatte on 5 February 1947. He concludes:

> This was the crowning act of four centuries of unswerving devotion to the Blessed Mother of God – a devotion implanted in the days when the Church was in honour in this country, a devotion that emerged strong from the storm blasts of persecution, a devotion that spread forth its branches in the doubtful sunshine of dawning freedom and now holds the hearts of over half a million firm and loyal Catholics of the Church of God. (p. 96)

2   *Songs for Worship and Praise* (Mclean Printers, no date).

3   *Hymnal* (Maggona: St Vincent's Press, 1986).

4   Cf. C. H. Bagley, 'Litanies' in *New Catholic Encyclopaedia* (Washington, DC, 1967), vol. 8, pp. 790–1.

2

꒰꒱꒰꒱꒰꒱꒰꒱

Mary in traditional theology

The construction of traditional Catholic theology

The development of theology concerning Mary is an intriguing example of how a religious institution can develop its teaching, patterns of worship, lifestyle of members and spirituality from very simple beginnings. It reveals the importance and impact of presuppositions on the course of the subsequent evolution of theology.

Traditional Marian theology was developed in the Catholic Church against the background of its general construct of theology, something which has prevailed from the early centuries until Vatican II, and until the present.

Many elements of Marian theology, especially the defined dogmas, are not contained explicitly in the Gospels, which narrate the life and work of Jesus. Mariology is very much an evolution of subsequent centuries, though beginning with St Irenaeus in the second century.

Parallel constructs of traditional Catholic theology and Mariology

God
↓

Creation	Mary
↓	↓
Adam and Eve in Garden of	The second Eve
Eden in a state of original justice	↓
↓	
Original sin, fall of humanity	Freed from original sin
from grace	Immaculate Conception
↓	↓
Alienation of all humanity from	Holiness of Mary
God, incapable of saving	↓
themselves for eternal life	
↓	

Therefore need of a Redeemer who could reconcile humanity to God ↓	↓
Promise of a Redeemer who has not to be subject to sin and Satan ↓	Mary, mother of Jesus, mother of God ↓
Incarnation of Jesus, Annunciation. Overshadowed by Holy Spirit, birth of Jesus, life and death of Jesus ↓	Co-redemptive ↓
Church to continue work of redemption, by transmitting salvific grace ↓	Mother of the Church Mediatrix of all graces ↓
Pentecost ↓	Mary present at Pentecost ↓
Mission of Church ↓	Refuge of sinners Help of the afflicted ↓
Resurrection ↓	Assumption ↓
Ascension of Jesus	Queen of Heaven

The teaching of the Church has been evolving over the centuries with the proclamation of:

- Mary Mother of God, *Theotokos*, God-bearer: in 431 at the Council of Ephesus
- The virginity of Mary: by Pope Martin I, 649; the perpetual and perfect virginity of Mary before and after the birth of Jesus, Lateran Council;
- Immaculate Conception: in 1854 by Pope Pius IX
- Assumption into heaven: in 1950 by Pope Pius XII.

The development of Mariology in this form is related to the hypotheses of original justice and original sin. Without them there would be no need of a divine redeemer, nor an act of ontological redemption to be offered by such a redeemer on behalf of the whole of humanity. The traditional Catholic doctrine of salvation is intimately linked with its teaching concerning the human predicament as a consequence of the fall. It is on the basis of the fall that Jesus Christ is presented as the necessary, unique and universal saviour. Correspondingly, the involvement of Mary in the salvific function of Jesus Christ is linked to the fall.

The four Gospels do not speak of original justice and the fall of humanity. There are references in Paul's writings which were later developed into the Church teaching on original sin and redemption by Jesus Christ (Rom 5.6–21 and Col 1.13–14). In succeeding centuries the Church taught that humanity was in bondage to Satan owing to the sin of the first parents and that an infinite reparation had to be offered to God for the redemption of humanity. Jesus Christ the God-Man had the function of fulfilling this redemptive task through his incarnation and death.

Since Jesus the God-Man could never be under the dominion of Satan even through original sin, it was argued that he was not born of a human father. Hence the development of the view that Jesus was conceived in the womb of Mary through the 'overshadowing' of the Holy Spirit. Based on the story of the birth of Jesus as told by Matthew (1.18–24), and Luke (1.26–38), and on the hypothesis of salvation in the context of original sin, the Church's teaching on the virginity of Mary was advanced from about the third century onwards.

As Vatican II states, Mary was seen as co-operating in the work of human salvation:

> Being obedient, she became the cause of salvation for herself, and for the whole human race. (Irenaeus, *Adv. haer*. III. 22.4, quoted in Vatican II *Lumen Gentium*, art. 56)

Vatican II continues:

> Hence not a few of the early Fathers gladly assert with him [St Irenaeus] in their preaching: 'The knot of Eve's disobedience was untied by Mary's obedience, what the virgin Eve bound through her unbelief, Mary loosened by her faith.' Comparing Mary with Eve, they call her 'Mother of the Living', and frequently claim: 'death through Eve, life through Mary'.

Vatican II here quotes, in addition to Irenaeus, Epiphanius, Jerome, Augustine, Cyril of Jerusalem, John Chrysostom and John Damascene (*LG*, art. 56). Vatican II and these Fathers attribute virginity not only to Mary but also to Eve in the Garden of Eden – without of course any evidence for it, even if there had been a first couple Adam and Eve.

It was not enough that Jesus should be born without a human father; it was necessary that his mother should be without original sin, otherwise she would transmit that sin to Jesus through procreation. Thus we have the gradual evolution of teaching concerning the conception of Mary in the womb of her mother, Anne, without the stain of original sin, and it was a common belief that Mary was conceived immaculately. This was eventually defined as a dogma by Pope Pius IX in 1854.

From the Church's teachings concerning the Immaculate Conception of Mary, it was argued that she had no inclination to sin. She was free of concupiscence. Owing to this, and her faith in God, she was supremely holy, holier than any human being except her son, Jesus.

Her divine maternity was derived from the divinity of Jesus, and she was proclaimed *Theotokos*, Mother of God, by the Council of Ephesus in 431.

Her Assumption into heaven was asserted on the basis that her body could not bear corruption, as it did not have to pay the 'wages of sin which is death', and because the popular tradition of the Church had believed in this doctrine for many centuries. On 15 August 1950 Pope Pius XII defined the dogma of the Assumption of Mary, body and soul, into heaven.

The role assigned to Mary as co-redeemer is due to her close association with Jesus in his life, work, passion and death. She shared in this redemptive task more than any other person except Jesus. Through her motherhood she is regarded as the universal mother of the redeemed, and of all humanity. By the incarnation, Jesus is related to the whole of humanity. Through her sublime holiness and co-redeeming function she is queen of the universe and of heaven.

Since Mary was closely associated with Jesus in his earthly mission, she loved all humanity with a self-sacrificing love, as Jesus did. She is all-powerful in heaven because she is intimately linked with the Holy Trinity, being mother of Jesus, spouse of the Holy Spirit and most beloved daughter of the Father. She is, therefore, the one who is best placed to help weak and sinful human beings in all their needs. As a loving mother she cares for all. She is our mother of good counsel, and a sure refuge in all our difficulties.

Marian devotions thus venerate her for her spiritual greatness and redemptive role, invoke her as a never-failing source of help and offer her for imitation as the most perfect example of faith, hope, love and obedience to God:

> [Mary] in heaven is the image and beginning of the Church as it is to be perfected in the world to come. Likewise she shines forth on earth, until the day of the Lord shall come (cf. 2 Pet. 3.10), a sign of certain hope and comfort to the pilgrim People of God. (Vatican II, *Lumen Gentium*, art. 68)

Mary and Sri Lanka: the Marian theology of Jacome Gonsalvez (1676–1742)

The beliefs of the Catholics of Sri Lanka depend on the theology of the Portuguese missionaries who first taught them the Christian faith.

During the Dutch period, when Catholics were persecuted in the Dutch colonies, their faith was sustained and nourished by Fr Joseph Vaz and his Oratorian priests from Goa. Jacome Gonsalvez was the greatest scholar among them. He was well versed in Sinhala and Tamil, in addition to Portuguese, Dutch and his native Konkani.

Fr Joseph Vaz entrusted Jacome Gonsalvez with the task of presenting the Catholic faith in Sinhala and Tamil. He was a prolific writer in both prose and poetry. His poetic and prose writings were a principal means of the instruction of Catholics during a period of 150 years. S. J. Perera, writing in 1938 in *Historical Sketches*, records:[1]

> The Poems on the Passion are still widely used, being chanted aloud during Lent in Catholic villages, while the *Veda Kavvya* still holds its place as the greatest Catholic poem in Sinhalese.

In the *Veda Kavvya*, Mary has a prominent place. Verses 75–243 and 382–495 of its 537 verses are mainly concerned with Mary, or form a dialogue between her and her son. Mary is presented in this long poem as 'the Virgin pure in thought and deed, like the moon' (v. 81). She was conceived in the womb of holy Anna, full of grace (v. 83). She is portrayed as a woman of incomparable beauty:

> The sun and moon have flaws: 'tis night on one side,
> The milky ocean too stirs and becomes salty.
> But none of them is like this pure maiden
> Whose beauty is e'er bright and on the increase. (v. 86)

The poem dwells at length on Mary's virtue.

> However much they spoke to that maiden.
> Her affections never turned to carnal pleasures.
> For her thoughts were intent on pleasing GOD alone.
> So she kept GOD in her mind and observed her chastity. (v. 91)

Jacome Gonsalvez then narrates at length the story of the choice of a partner for Mary (vv. 92–112), probably taken from the writings of the Fathers of the Church. Quite imaginatively the poet presents a story to explain Mary's espousal to Joseph and the non-consummation of their marriage. He then explains the angel's salutation and the conception of Jesus in a miraculous way:

> She did not feel even the weight of a cotton lump,
> Nor was there on her lips a craving for special diet.
> There was no longing for pomegranates and mandarins,
> Such desires were like drops of water gliding over Lotus leaves.

> Holy Joseph lived happily with her, but like monks apart;
> Intent on merit she preserved her virginity, both living like hermits.

Seeing this with His divine eyes the Supreme GOD came down from
    heaven
Leaving gladly His celestial throne, to be born from His mother's
    womb. (vv. 131 and 132)

Gonsalvez explains the birth of Jesus from the Virgin's womb:

Like the full moon coming out of the clouds,
Like a jewel taken out of a golden casket,
The Son of God, the Father, illustrious in the three worlds,
The GOD of goodness, issued from the Virgin's womb. (v. 147)

Atonement for the disobedience and punishment of Adam and Eve
(which had been narrated earlier, vv. 64–74) was the reason for the birth
of Christ:

Adam and Eve sinned by their disobedience,
But He desired to atone for it by taking it upon Himself,
And thus to fill the celestial thrones with men.
In this manner, my friend, was Christ,
Our God and Lord born. (v. 156)

The poet chants the idyllic conditions of the holy family:

At that time the maiden mother,
Was in adoration of the divine Babe.
She caressed Him on her hips,
And suckled Him with God-mixed milk.

In the meantime holy Joseph
Took his place on a slide
And placed his head on the sacred feet,
Which were like red lotus buds. (vv. 166 and 167)

And even the animals help to keep the baby warm:

The bull which stood on a side,
Sensing the cold was too much
For the charming divine babe,
Gave out a hot breath from its mouth. (v. 168)

The events of the visit of the three kings, the flight into Egypt, the
return to Nazareth, the visit to the temple when Jesus was twelve years
old, are all imaginatively described. Jacome Gonsalvez was well versed
in the style and idiom of Sinhala and Tamil literature.

At the end of the work is a long dialogue between the mother and
son. Mary is confused and inconsolable at the sight of her son's tortured
body:

'After nine months I brought you forth; you grew up on golden milk.
You prattled sweet words and exhibited charming childish frolics.

Is it right on their part to torture you and kill you thus?
Why have you turned away from me leaving me in unbearable agony?

'Did you not love all mankind and undergo these sufferings!
Did they not admire the soft growth on your cheeks and your beard!
Now these brute beasts have dishevelled and plucked the hair.
God has been patient with them. But. Oh! how can I console myself?'

(vv. 426 and 427)

Several verses thus describe the beauty, innocence and passion of the son and the lamentation of the mother: 'How can I ever be consoled?', 'How can I survive?', 'The Mother prone on the ground weeps in her anxiety and grief':

Recognizing Him from the sign given by that wicked disciple, Judas.
His enemies held Him fast, Him who was so good and loving.
Today, due to the incessant suffering inflicted on Him, His life has
    departed.
The Mother prone on the ground weeps in her anxiety and grief.

(v. 435)

In the ensuing dialogue Jesus gives the reason for his suffering and death:

'You, who were like the wishing-gem, are now one mass of torn flesh.
What are these marks on your navel set on your body like a golden
    image placed on a water-clock?
Son, adorable for beauty of form, tell me now the reason for this.'
'Listen, Mother! this is what I suffered for sinful man.' (v. 486)

The theology of the life, passion and death of Jesus is explained by Fr Jacome Gonsalvez through this dialogue.

His poetry portrays the Jews as responsible for the cruel torture and death of Jesus. Mary is inconsolable at this thought:

'He sustained the earth and showed His power,
But the Jews raged against their Maker
And made him suffer without ceasing.
Seeing this how can I be consoled?' (v. 448)

There is, however, no indication that Jesus died because of his prophetic stands against injustice, exploitation and hypocrisy in his society.

An individualistic and asocial Mariology?

For several generations this theology has been communicated to Sri Lankan Catholics through the catechesis, the liturgy and paraliturgies like passion dramas. Mariology and Christology were linked together in dogmatic theology and consequently in the prayers, hymns and literature of the Church. Prayers, in turn, communicated doctrine. It is only in very recent years that there is a preaching, in some churches, of a more Gospel-oriented explanation of the life of Jesus and Mary.

While Marian spirituality is historically deep-rooted, and geographically widespread among the Catholics of Sri Lanka, its impact is of a rather individualistic and even other-worldly nature. It has not contributed adequately to the understanding and growth of new dimensions of mission and ministry required in our day, something desired by the Popes, too, as I will describe in the next chapter.

Spirituality is influenced by the prevalent theology, and vice versa. Marian spirituality has been developed against the background of the cultural and social life of the people here, especially of the Catholic community.

Marian theology in Sri Lanka has come first from Portugal and in the British period, after 1796, mainly from Southern Europe. Hence there is a great accent on external rituals such as processions and feasts. This type of spirituality readily suits our national temperament, our traditions of external celebration, and dependence on deities when facing difficulties in life, such as in sickness and misfortune. The shrines of saints like Anthony, Sebastian and Jude respond to certain felt needs of all people, beyond the boundaries of religious particularity.

While the Christian mission contributed to the growth of education, the Portuguese missionaries could not develop a theology and spirituality which accentuated justice and non-exploitation, since they were allies of the foreign rulers whom they thought of as providentially beneficial to them. It is not irrelevant that the Portuguese did not encourage a local clergy or religious life in Ceylon, though they were here for well over a century. A theologically well-formed local clergy and religious leadership might have been in greater sympathy with the liberation struggles of the peoples against Portuguese rule.

On the other hand, under the Dutch persecution Catholics had recourse to Mary as a protectress against oppression. The celebration of Church feasts, often dedicated to Mary, was a form of religious opposition to the oppression of Catholics. In later decades Catholics learned to protest publicly against some of the penalties imposed on them. Belgian Oblate and historian Robrecht Boudens has described some of these protests in his book *The Catholic Church in Ceylon Under Dutch Rule*.[2]

There is, thus, an experience of the Catholic community here as defenders of their rights *vis-à-vis* the state. This may be in the sub-consciousness of the community. The beatification of Fr Joseph Vaz may provide an occasion for an active consciousness of Catholic history in this country. It could also be an opportunity for reflecting on the closeness of the Goan Oratorian missionaries in Sri Lanka with the people and with the Buddhist rulers of Kandy, who provided them with a refuge in their difficulties under the Dutch.

In this regard we can understand the limits of theological development under the Portuguese and later under the British. Catholics had to develop their theological reasoning against the background of the dominant theology of the day within a framework of European domination of the colonies, and of the popular religion of the colonized peoples themselves.

Such a theology, when concerned with Mariology, would find it convenient to elaborate teachings and religious practices that related to angels, the Garden of Eden and idyllic figures such as shepherds. They would have been somewhat compromised if they had directed their attention to more earthy socio-political realities, such as Mary's flight into Egypt, her exile, the later challenge by her son, and his companions, of the local religious establishment and of the foreign rulers and their false values. We do not find in classical Marian theology this dimension of liberation from social, economic and political oppression, highlighted in the Magnificat and emphasized by recent Popes. Neither do we find, in Mariology prior to recent decades, an inspiration for the liberation of women from male domination in society or within Catholicism itself.

Now that a new approach to Christology is being derived from the Gospel witness to Jesus' commitment to human life and social justice, a new Mariology is also emerging and can be developed. Thus prayers, meditations and hymns to Mary can be evolved so that prayer life itself bears witness to Mary's radical commitment to human fulfilment and social liberation in this life. This is a task that this generation is challenged to fulfil.

Notes

1 S. J. Perera, *Historical Sketches* (Jaffna: St Joseph's Catholic Press, 1938), p. 139.

2 Robrecht Boudens OMI, *The Catholic Church in Ceylon Under Dutch Rule* (Rome: Book Agency, 1957), ch. VI, 'The growth of Catholic resistance (1732–1762)', pp. 132–57.

3

❦❦❦❦

The need for a renewed Marian theology

The development of doctrine

The development of theology and spirituality in the Catholic Church presents an interesting example of change and continuity, of a claim to infallibility and the fact of the transformation of doctrine and practice. This raises the question of how changes in theology, even in doctrine, take place. Is it always an evolution in the same direction, or are there changes that are a contradiction of a previous position? What are the criteria for such changes? Who is entitled to make them? How do changes come about? How prepared are local Churches for changes that take place in the universal Church? How can we convince ourselves and others that we are holding the same view always and not changing our thinking for reasons which are not of faith and theology?

Is it not a fact that sometimes changes in practice precede changes in thinking and teaching? This is a slow and painful process in which there can be much grief before the new light dawns. This process can be seen in the case of the Church's attitude towards religious freedom.

> For most of the church's history only rarely were Christians able even so much as to tolerate other religions, and they were almost never able to tolerate other forms of their own religion (heresies). Notions of genuine human freedom as a religious right were soundly rejected by Popes Gregory XVI, Pius IX and Leo XIII because in their view these notions were inextricably bound up with indifferentism and rationalism. Nevertheless, in practice, if not in theory, Catholics took a far more tolerant view of Protestants. In this century the rise of totalitarian regimes of both the right and the left, the destruction of two world wars, and growing global consciousness helped religious leaders to focus on human dignity, the inviolable rights of the human person, the nature of human community and its relation to the state, and other issues affecting human solidarity. It was in this context, too, that Popes Pius XI, Pius XII, and John XXIII moved towards the acceptance of the ideals of human dignity and freedom consonant with the teachings of the church.[1]

44

In the nineteenth century the central leadership of the Catholic Church had sustained objections to accepting democracy and liberty even in civil society, especially because of the French Revolution. At that time, authority was said to come from God, so that it could not be from the people. The objection to socialistic demands for societal reforms was even more deep-seated, until the historic encyclical of Leo XIII on the *Condition of the Working Classes* in 1891, and even this encyclical was very much downplayed for several decades.

The changes in the situation of colonial peoples after their independence made the churches reconsider their attitude towards other religions. Now because of much work to raise consciousness in some local Churches, Catholics have changed to be among the foremost defenders of democratic rights and of free and fair elections, as in the Philippines in 1986.

Some recent trends in theology

In the renewal of Catholic theology in the second half of the twentieth century, especially after Vatican II, various issues have been discussed in different regions according to the concerns and needs of particular contexts. Some earlier renewal had taken place in Western Europe, following the Enlightenment, with developments in biblical interpretation and hermeneutics. They reflected on the mission of the Church in the context of European rationalism, modernism, Darwin, Marx and Freud and the growing secularization of the West. They were reaping the fruit of decades of biblical studies based on linguistic, cultural and historical analysis.

In the United States, with its experience of the separation of Church and State, John Courtenay Murray, perhaps the strongest theological proponent of religious freedom in the Church, led the reconsideration of the relationships between Church and State and the need for religious tolerance. He had a primary influence in the formulation of the Vatican II Declaration on Religious Liberty which recognized that the dignity of human beings consists in their responsible use of freedom.

In Germany, Johannes Metz, agonized by the experience of the horrors of Nazism, developed a political theology, emphasizing the need to witness to Christian values in the social and political spheres. Such thinking had a great impact on Western countries and contributed to the growing commitment of Western Christians and Churches to social justice, at least within their own societies.

The East–West cold war, and the fear of nuclear annihilation, motivated groups towards building up the peace movement beyond denominational, religious and ideological boundaries.

North America was foremost in the development of Black theology and feminist theology, both including strands of a liberationist approach.

Black theology was built upon the consciousness of African-American people that they were discriminated against on the basis of colour. They showed how the scriptures, and church practice, had been interpreted to justify White supremacy. They regarded this as a betrayal of the Gospel in a racist manner. They advanced the concept and liturgies of a Black Church. Their theologizing was linked to, and influenced by, the struggles of Black people in the United States, led by Martin Luther King, in a non-violent campaign, and by Stokely Carmichael's development of Black Power. James H. Cone, Gayraud S. Wilmore and Cornel West were pioneers of Black theology.

Black theology later developed in Africa and the Caribbean and was linked with liberation theology, feminist theology and Asian theologies. The struggles against racism, poverty and the Vietnam war, in the United States, led to a re-thinking of Church life and the growth of peace education and non-violent strategies.

Latin American liberation theologians took the discussion much further, with a full-scale elaboration of their liberation theology. Their starting-point for theology was, in addition to scriptural studies, the experience of the social exploitation of a whole continent for several centuries, and especially their domination by the capitalist North. They applied social analysis to theology and spirituality. They stressed the secular and social spheres as arenas for the realization of the values of the Kingdom of God, preached and promoted by Jesus Christ. The praxis of Jesus, with his option for the poor and marginalized, reveals God's concern and will for the liberation of humankind. Liberation spirituality saw the human struggle against oppression as a way of union with God. The life of the Church had, therefore, to be directed towards participation in such struggles, especially through the organization of Basic Christian Communities. The Peruvian Gustavo Gutiérrez, Brazilian Leonardo Boff, El Salvadorian Jon Sobrino and Uruguayan Juan Luis Segundo are among their well-known theologians.

Liberation theology has had an impact throughout the world, even influencing the Magisterium of the Catholic Church so that Christian freedom and liberation are now accepted as legitimate and necessary concerns of the Church.[2]

Feminist theologians brought the dimension of gender analysis to Christian practice and thought in every area of life and study. This is a growing movement which now engages in quasi-universal and radical questioning of almost all aspects of theology and spirituality. The starting-point of feminist theological reflection is an acute consciousness of the systematic exclusion of women from leadership in the life of the Church. Women have been excluded from the study of theology, and hence from teaching and ministry, as well as from administration in the Church.

From this perspective feminists observe that theology and spirituality have been conditioned to legitimize male domination throughout the centuries. Three dimensions of the development of feminist theology are, firstly, the demonstration of an androcentric and misogynist bias in the whole of church life, including scripture and theological tradition. Secondly, feminists try to draw up alternative norms and sources of tradition to challenge these biases. This is a process of deconstructing traditional theology and spirituality. Thirdly, they seek a reconstruction and re-envisioning of theological themes, and life relationships, to free them from prejudices against women.

There are numerous feminist theologians in all the continents of the world, and a variety of theological trends are rapidly developing within this movement. Some radically question whether a male God can be a liberator for women. Thus, Mary Daly repudiates the possibility of the reform of the Christian tradition and seeks a new spirituality. There is also a trend towards a more holistic spirituality that seeks to transcend difference and divisions of gender and makes common cause with the other struggles of humanity today, such as for the preservation of the environment. Marian theology is also developed by several feminist theologians, as will be demonstrated in the latter part of this book.

A theological re-thinking is now developing significantly in Asia and Africa, especially since emancipation from colonial rule. In Africa the accent has been on issues like African culture, family and community values, traditional religions, the place of ancestors, poverty and liberation from discrimination on the basis of race and tribe. Relating to Islam is a dimension of Christian reflection and life in most African countries, also. In South Africa numerous theologians and Church leaders like Desmond Tutu and Albert Nolan contributed to the struggle against apartheid, and to the recent success of the democratic process in transferring power to the Black majority.

In Asia theological thinking is influenced by the realities of poverty, massive populations and religious plurality, in addition to the other dimensions that are bringing about theological renewal elsewhere. Thus the ferment here, especially in South Asia, is very active and leads to much deeper questioning than elsewhere. The nature of the human condition, the understanding of the presence of the divine in the world, the identity and role of Jesus Christ, and the mission of the Church, are all under scrutiny in this environment. Asian theology is being developed in many countries, but especially in the Philippines, South Korea,

India and Sri Lanka. Oppression of caste and tribe is also contributing to the development of liberation theology in India.

Throughout the world there is a growing concern for the *environment and ecology*. The future of planet earth is worrying many – particularly because of the noticeable changes in the climate and the recognized exhaustion of some limited, non-renewable, resources.

Theological processes

In all these theologies there is a process of theological deconstruction and reconstruction including:

(i)   A reflection, by those who are victims, from a lived experience of oppression and marginalization, leading to

(ii) A critical rethinking of the interpretation of scripture and tradition, that was seen as, *de facto*, allied to discrimination on the basis of race, gender, social class and religion;

(iii) Consequent on the experience of these different groups, there has been an analysis of doctrines and authority patterns in the Church, based on gender, race, class and even caste;

(iv) The issues raised in this process include the understanding of the human condition of original sin; gender relations, partly related to responsibility for original sin; the nature of the redemptive process, the role of Jesus Christ and of the Church in human salvation;

(v)   This rethinking of theology includes a re-evaluation of the formation of the clergy and leadership of the Church. Traditionally formation in the seminaries has served the purpose of the continuation of the *status quo* in the Church and society;

(vi) The understanding and practice of spirituality in the Church has failed to challenge discrimination. This approach was helped by the narrow, self-centred, individualistic 'salvation-of-soul' perspective that prevailed in Europe, especially in the modern period after the decline of feudalism. The shift is now to a broader interpersonal and social concern, according to the new perspectives from which spirituality is being developed.

Rethinking theology

In the growth of these new theologies creativity is moving away from Europe, and to some extent from North America also, to the so-called 'younger churches' or the 'Third Church', as Walter Buhlmann calls it. This is especially so in theologies concerning class and non-Christian religions and cultures. In the different stages of this evolution, the

Church authorities have had difficulties in acknowledging the validity and significance of these new movements. The Church authorities are attached to long-standing orthodoxies, which have acquired a sacredness because of tradition, not to mention the advantage to them as the dominant social force.

The process of re-adjustment of thought and life has not been without conflict and much heart-searching within the Churches. The authorities think they must preserve the simple religion of the faithful. The faithful, in turn, have a sentimental attachment to conventional modes of thinking and to the pious practices with which they were brought up, even when these domesticate them to accept a multiplicity of forms of alienation and oppression. The internalization of one's own subjection to the powerful acquires a legitimation and sacredness.

On the other hand, those who are more thoughtful, especially among the younger generation, tend to lose confidence in the entire system and even become 'unchurched'. This happened to the working class in Western Europe and was mournfully regretted, by Pope Pius XI in the 1930s, as the scandal of the nineteenth century. If the Church does not rethink its theology and spirituality in a manner relevant to the present generation and their needs, the Churches will be bypassed as irrelevant. During the past fifty years there has thus been a large-scale 'unchurching' and secularization of people who call themselves Christians in Western Europe. Now not even 10 per cent of the population attends Sunday Mass in many Western European cities, including Rome. Many people are giving up the other sacraments too.

The Catholic priesthood is ageing and decreasing in numbers. Many have left the ministry. Seminaries are largely empty, and many are being closed down or amalgamated into clusters. In the not-too-distant future, the Catholic Church in Western Europe will become a clergyless church, unless some radical changes are introduced to remedy its irrelevance. Likewise, religious life is declining owing to lack of vocations and the increasing age of those remaining. Religious houses are becoming homes for the aged, memorials to a more active past that has no appeal for the youth of today.

The Churches in Asia and Africa have seriously to ask themselves whether, and how, they can avoid such a fate. The more perceptive among Church leaders, such as Bishop Julio Labayen in the Philippines, Kim Chi Ha in South Korea, Samuel Rayan in India, and feminist theologians in every country, are pathfinders seeking new ways forward. Unfortunately, they are still somewhat marginal to the mainstream of the Churches.

Recent Vatican Mariology

Marian theology and spirituality, too, are subjects of this rethinking and growth. To a certain extent, the Popes have led in this process, even though they have serious reservations about gender equality in relation to the Church's ministry. Both Paul VI and John Paul II have shown a warm devotion to Mary, and they have written encyclicals about her stressing both tradition and the need for a changed theology and spirituality.

Pope Paul VI

Writing in February 1974, prior to the International Year of Women, Pope Paul VI called for an updating of Mariology and Marian piety.[3]

He observed the need to adapt and update Marian spirituality for different times and cultures:

> The Second Vatican Council also exhorts us to promote other forms of piety side by side with liturgical worship, especially those recommended by the Magisterium. However, as is well known, the piety of the faithful and their veneration of the Mother of God has taken on many forms according to circumstances of time and place, the different sensibilities of peoples and their different cultural traditions. Hence it is that the forms in which this devotion is expressed, being subject to the ravages of time, show the need for a renewal that will permit them to substitute elements that are transient, to emphasize the elements that are ever new and to incorporate the doctrinal data obtained from theological reflection and the proposals of the Church's Magisterium. This shows the need for episcopal conferences, local churches, religious families and communities of the faithful to promote a *genuine creative activity* and at the same time to proceed to a careful revision of expressions and exercises of piety directed towards the Blessed Virgin. We would like this revision to be respectful of wholesome tradition and open to the legitimate requests of the people of our time.

Pope Paul VI also proposed some principles and guidelines for action:

> It is sometimes said that many spiritual writings today do not sufficiently reflect the whole doctrine concerning the Holy Spirit. It is the *task of specialists to verify and weigh the truth of this assertion,* but it is our task to exhort everyone, especially those in the pastoral ministry and also *theologians,* to meditate more deeply on the working of the Holy Spirit in the history of salvation, and to ensure that Christian spiritual writings give due prominence to his life-giving action.
>
> Similarly the faithful will appreciate more clearly that the action of the Church in the world can be likened to an extension of Mary's concern. The active love she showed at Nazareth, *in the house of Elizabeth,* at Cana

and on Golgotha – *all salvific episodes having vast ecclesial importance* – finds its extension in the Church's maternal concern that all men should come to knowledge of the truth (cf. 1 Tim. 2:4), in the Church's *concern for people in lowly circumstances and for the poor and weak,* and in her constant commitment to peace and social harmony, as well as in her untiring efforts to ensure that all men will share in the salvation which was merited for them by Christ's death.

Among these guidelines he included:

(a) A return to biblical inspiration

Today it is recognized as a general need of Christian piety that every form of worship should have a *biblical imprint* ... texts of prayers and chants should draw their inspiration and their wording from the Bible, and above all that devotion to the Virgin should be imbued with the great themes of the Christian message.

(b) Concern for the liturgy

... What is needed on the part of the leaders of the local communities is effort, pastoral sensitivity and perseverance, while the faithful on their part must show a willingness to accept guidelines and ideas drawn from the true nature of Christian worship; this sometimes makes it necessary to change long-standing customs wherein the real nature of this Christian worship has become somewhat obscured.

(c) Ecumenical concern

Pope Paul VI noted that a convergence of understanding of the role of Mary in salvation could draw together the Churches which have been historically divided by Mariology:

... In the first place, in venerating with particular love the glorious *Theotokos* and in acclaiming her as the 'Hope of Christians', Catholics unite themselves with their brethren of the Orthodox Churches, in which devotion to the Blessed Virgin finds its expression in a beautiful lyricism and in solid doctrine. Catholics are also united with Anglicans, whose classical theologians have already drawn attention to the sound scriptural basis for devotion to the Mother of our Lord, while those of the present day increasingly underline the importance of Mary's place in the Christian life. Praising God with the very words of the Virgin (cf. Lk. 1:46–55), they are united too with their brethren in the Churches of the Reform, where love for the Sacred Scriptures flourishes.

(d) Mary and modern women: feminism

Pope Paul noted that some women are becoming 'disenchanted with devotion to the Blessed Virgin and finding it difficult to take as an example Mary of Nazareth' interpreted traditionally, in comparison with the vast spheres of activity open to modern women who have

equality in the home, in politics, society, scientific research and intellectual life. Paul VI exhorted 'theologians, those responsible for the local
Christian communities and the faithful themselves to examine these
difficulties with due care'.

Thereafter, the Pope offered his own reflections for this task. He
pointed out that the difficulties alluded to above are closely related to
certain aspects of the portrayal of Mary found in popular religious
writings. They are not connected with the gospel image of Mary nor
with doctrinal data. It is to be expected that different generations would
interpret Mary from different socio-cultural contexts:

> The modern woman will note with pleasant surprise that Mary of
> Nazareth, while completely devoted to the will of God, *was far from being
> a timidly submissive woman* or one whose piety was repellent to others; on
> the contrary, she was a woman who did not hesitate to proclaim that God
> vindicates *the humble and the oppressed*, and removes the powerful people
> of this world from their privileged positions (cf. Lk. 1:51–53). The modern
> woman will recognize in Mary, who 'stands out among the poor and
> humble of the Lord', *a woman of strength*, who experienced poverty and
> suffering, flight and exile (cf. Mt. 2:13–23) ... These are but examples,
> which show clearly that the figure of the Blessed Virgin does not disillu-
> sion any of the profound expectations of the men and women of our time
> but offers them the perfect model of the disciple of the Lord: the disciple
> who builds up the earthly and temporal city while being a diligent
> pilgrim towards the heavenly and eternal city, the disciple who *works for
> that justice which sets free the oppressed and for that charity which assists the
> needy*; but above all, the disciple who is the active witness of that love
> which builds up Christ in people's hearts.

The Pope then corrected certain pious attitudes already denounced
by Vatican II:

> ... the exaggeration of content and form which even falsifies doctrine
> and likewise the small-mindedness which obscures the figure and mis-
> sion of Mary ... *vain credulity*, ... merely external practices ... sterile and
> ephemeral sentimentality, ... Careful defence against these errors and
> deviations will render devotion to the Blessed Virgin more vigorous and
> more authentic ... It will ensure that this devotion is objective in its
> historical setting, and for this reason everything that is obviously legend-
> ary or false must be eliminated. It will ensure that this devotion matches
> its doctrinal content – hence the necessity of avoiding a one-sided
> presentation of the figure of Mary, which by overstressing one element
> compromises the overall picture given by the Gospel. It will make this
> devotion clear in its motivation; hence every unworthy self-interest is to
> be carefully banned from the area of what is sacred.
> ... When the children of the Church unite their voices with the voice
> of the unknown woman in the Gospel and glorify the Mother of Jesus by

saying to him: 'Blessed is the womb that bore you and the breasts that you sucked' (Lk. 11:27), they will be led to ponder the divine Master's serious reply: 'Blessed rather are those who hear the word of God and keep it!' (Lk. 11:28). While it is true that this reply is in itself lively praise of Mary, as various Fathers of the Church interpreted it and the Second Vatican Council has confirmed, it is also an admonition to us to live our lives in accordance with God's commandments. It is also an echo of other words of the Saviour: 'Not every one who says to me "Lord, Lord", will enter the kingdom of heaven, but he who does the will of my Father who is in heaven' (Mt. 7:21), and again: 'You are my friends if you do what I command you' (Jn. 15:14).

With such a renewed Marian theology and spirituality

... Contemplated in the episodes of the Gospels and in the reality which she already possesses in the City of God, the Blessed Virgin Mary offers a calm vision and a reassuring word to modern man, torn as he often is between anguish and hope, defeated by the sense of his own limitations and assailed by limitless aspirations, troubled in his mind and divided in his heart, uncertain before the riddle of death, oppressed by loneliness while yearning for fellowship, a prey to boredom and disgust. She shows forth the *victory of hope over anguish*, of fellowship over solitude, of peace over anxiety, of joy and beauty over boredom and disgust, of eternal visions over earthly ones, of life over death.

Pope John Paul II

The present Pope has emphasized the spirituality of Mary's commitment to justice and the liberation of the weak and oppressed, especially through his reflections on the Magnificat:[4]

... At the same time, *by means of this truth about God* the Church *desires to shed light upon* the difficult and sometimes tangled paths of man's earthly existence. Following him who said of himself: '(God) has anointed me *to preach Good News to the poor*' (cf. Lk. 4:18), the Church has sought from generation to generation and still seeks today to accomplish that same mission.

The Church's *love of preference for the poor* is wonderfully inscribed in Mary's *Magnificat*. God 'has cast down the mighty from their thrones, and lifted up the lowly, ... filled the hungry with good things, sent the rich away empty, ... scattered the proud-hearted ... and his mercy is from age to age on those who fear him.'

Mary is deeply imbued with the spirit of the 'poor of Yahweh', who in the prayer of the Psalms awaited from God their salvation, placing all their trust in him (cf. Pss. 25; 31; 35; 55). Mary truly proclaims the coming of the 'Messiah of the poor' (cf. Is. 11.4; 61:1). Drawing from Mary's heart, from the depth of her faith expressed in the words of the *Magnificat*, the Church renews ever more effectively in herself the awareness that *the truth about God who saves,* the truth about God who is the source of every gift, *cannot be separated from the manifestation of his love of preference for the poor and humble,* that love which, celebrated in the *Magnificat,* is later expressed in the words and works of Jesus.

The Church is thus aware – and at the present time this awareness is particularly vivid – not only that these two elements of the message contained in the *Magnificat* cannot be separated, but also that there is a duty to safeguard carefully the importance of 'the poor' in the word of the living God. These are matters and questions intimately connected with the *Christian meaning of freedom and liberation.* Mary is totally dependent upon God and completely directed towards him, and, at the side of her Son, she is *the most perfect image of freedom and of the liberation* of humanity and of the universe. It is to her as Mother and Model that the Church must look in order to understand in its completeness the meaning of her own mission.

Cardinal Ratzinger

The Vatican Congregation for the Doctrine of the Faith, with Joseph Cardinal Ratzinger as Prefect, has issued two documents on liberation theology. The first in August 1984 was rather critical of liberation theology, and underlined the danger of Marxist influences in its teaching and praxis.

The second, *Instruction on Christian Freedom and Liberation,* issued in March 1986 after a deeper study and wider consultation, stressed the need for freedom and liberation. These, it is asserted, have an ecumenical dimension and belong to the traditional patrimony of the Churches and ecclesial communities. The *Instruction* invites theologians to develop theological thinking from different and new situations; from liberative praxis, as well as from a reading of the scriptures in the light of the experience of the Church itself:[5]

> Similarly, a theological reflection developed from a particular experience can constitute a very positive contribution, in as much as it makes possible a highlighting of aspects of the Word of God, the richness of which had not yet been fully grasped.

The conclusion of the *Instruction* is a reflection on Mary, 'the most perfect image of freedom and of the liberation of humanity and of the universe', and on her Magnificat, 'with its liberating effects upon individual and social existence':

> Pastors and all those who, as priests, laity, or men and women religious, often work under very difficult conditions for evangelization and integral human advancement, should be filled with hope when they think of the amazing resources of holiness contained in the living faith of the people of God. These riches of the *sensus fidei* must be given the chance to come

to full flowering and bear abundant fruit. To help the faith of the poor to express itself clearly and to be translated into life, through a profound meditation on the plan of salvation as it unfolds itself in the Virgin of the *Magnificat* – this is a noble ecclesial task which awaits the theologian.

Thus a theology of freedom and liberation which faithfully echoes Mary's *Magnificat* preserved in the Church's memory is something needed by the times in which we are living. But it would be criminal to take the energies of popular piety and misdirect them toward a purely earthly plan of liberation, which would very soon be revealed as nothing more than an illusion and a cause of new forms of slavery. Those who in this way surrender to the ideologies of the world and to the alleged necessity of violence are no longer being faithful to hope, to hope's boldness and courage, as they are extolled in the hymn to the God of mercy which the Virgin teaches us.

My thinking in the next two chapters endeavours to articulate a Marian spirituality and theology that is biblical, ecumenical and relevant for the women and men of today in their struggles for meaning, justice and love.

Notes

1 John Linnan CSV, 'Liberty, religious' in the *New Dictionary of Theology* (Bangalore: TPI, 1993), pp. 578–9.
2 Congregation for the Doctrine of the Faith, *Instruction on Christian Freedom and Liberation* (Vatican City, 1986).
3 Pope Paul VI, Apostolic Exhortation *Marialis Cultus*, 'To Honour Mary', arts 24–39 *passim*; 56.
4 Pope John Paul II, *Redemptoris Mater*, Encyclical Letter on the Blessed Virgin Mary in the Life of the Pilgrim Church, art. 37.
5 Joseph Cardinal Ratzinger, *Instruction on Christian Freedom and Liberation*, Congregation for the Doctrine of the Faith (Vatican City, 1986).

4

Mary: a mature adult woman

Mary in the scriptures

There are only a few references to Mary in the Gospels and the Acts of the Apostles. Of these, some are of a rather imaginative and symbolic nature, such as the infancy narratives, with the stories of angels, stars, Oriental visitors and perhaps even the killing of the innocents, and the flight into Egypt. They were written, perhaps, about eighty years after the events they describe.

The two evangelists, Matthew and Luke, present the events of the infancy of Jesus in ways that are difficult to reconcile with each other. Thus, Luke does not report the visit of the Magi, the massacre of the innocents by Herod, or the flight into Egypt. Luke's story mentions the purification of Mary and the Presentation in the temple in the verses following the circumcision and naming of Jesus a week after his birth. Thereafter 'they returned to their home town of Nazareth in Galilee' (Luke 2.39).

In Matthew's narrative, Joseph is the key actor. It is to him that the angel appeared before the birth of Jesus, to warn him concerning the plot of Herod to kill the baby Jesus, and later to recall him to the land of Israel.

We have to accept, with modern scholarship, that much of the material concerning the birth of Jesus is a way of presenting his infancy in a symbolic manner. The evangelists are also concerned to show that Jesus was the Messiah awaited by the Jews. Hence they write details which are, as it were, a fulfilment of the prophecies of the Old Testament concerning the expected Messiah. As Matthew writes, 'Now all this happened in order to make what the Lord had said through the prophet come true' (Matt 1.22).

Whatever their historicity, the infancy narratives had, and still have, a deep impact on the lives of Christians. Many consider them as an actual record of events. They can, thus, be significant for popular reflection and meditation, always remembering their generally symbolic nature.

On the one hand, therefore, we can think of Mary as portrayed by the Marian dogmas of the Church – the sinless, spotless, virgin mother ultimately assumed to heaven as a particularly privileged person. On the other hand, when we reflect on Mary as presented in the Gospels and the Acts of the Apostles, we see her as an ordinary woman of her time who went through the process of living in very difficult circumstances.

The Gospels have very few references to Mary. More important than these, however, is the whole life of Mary with Joseph and Jesus, her relatives and the small community of Jesus' followers during his lifetime, and shortly afterwards. Most of it is not written and we have to use our imagination, and, therefore, we are subject to correction.

Mary was living at a time of imperial rule, of the exploitation of the poor, of women, and of her race, by the Romans. It was a time of intense social upheaval and even conflict in her country. It is within this context that we have to think of the life of Mary and the events mentioned in the Gospels.

The Annunciation

If we accept the traditional perspective of Mary as virgin mother, we note a problem. How would society accept her? What would Joseph's reaction be? This was a time when the Law of Moses, including the death penalty for adultery, could still be invoked.

Even without a virginal conception, Mary could have had difficulty accepting the announcement concerning her future child, that he was to be the Messiah expected by the people. It would have meant also that the child would have had to undergo much suffering. It is likely that Mary was terrified by such an extraordinary vocation. Her *fiat* can be understood as a courageous, positive acceptance of a call to bear responsibility among her people. Her whole future life was a carrying out of the consequences of such a calling.

While most spiritual writers have interpreted Mary's *fiat* as a sign of her submission to God's will in respectful docility, some feminist theologians have stressed that God was dependent on a woman for the carrying out of the divine plan of redemption. God's action is seen as an example of respect for the mutuality of relationships, even between the creator and the creature. How much more, then, should there be mutuality in human relationships between women and men?

The visit to Elizabeth

A few months later, we see Mary going through the countryside to visit her cousin Elizabeth, who had conceived a child in her old age. Mary was performing a personal, loving service. This is still done in Oriental families by a mother when her daughter conceives. Mary remained for about three months with Elizabeth. Here she prays in the prophetic tradition. Her prayer is the Magnificat: 'My soul glorifies the Lord.' She announces the promises of God to her people. Perhaps we are so accustomed to reciting it that we do not often think of the content of its message. In the context of Old Testament prophecies, Mary proclaims the liberative message of salvation promised by God to the people.[1] She speaks of the deeds being realized by God:

> 'The arrogant of heart and mind he has put to rout, he has torn imperial powers from their thrones. But the humble have been lifted high. The hungry he has satisfied with good things, the rich sent empty away.' (Luke 1.51–53)

We can see in this a threefold strategy for action: first in the sphere of consciousness; second, of political structures and power; and third, in the distribution of economic goods. In modern terminology, it can be said that Mary proclaims *a cultural revolution* in which the proud-hearted and the haughty are rejected in favour of poor, simple, lowly people; *a political revolution* in which power passes from the mighty to the mass of the people; and *an economic revolution* by which the hungry and the starving receive good things, instead of their being monopolized by the rich, who are sent away empty.

We see here a total reversal of values and structures. It is, undoubtedly, a radical message of the sort which can be read in the work of revolutionary prophets of different ages. The pity, however, is that the Christian tradition has succeeded in domesticating Mary so much that she is known as the comforter of the disturbed, rather than as a disturber of the comfortable. Her words can be an inspiration for radical action for changes of consciousness in people and in the structures of societies. The Magnificat reveals how she reconciles social radicalness with personal service, a revolutionary message with interpersonal love. This is a powerful and attractive combination of practical action, deep reflective prayer and personal concern.

Fortunately, modern theology, especially liberation theology, sees in the Magnificat a spiritual support for the struggles of the poor and the oppressed for freedom and justice. This places Mary on the side of the needy, the weak and the exploited. She has been a great inspiration to Christian movements for social transformation throughout the world.

Mary, a young mother

The birth of Jesus

The next recorded event in the life of Mary is the birth of Jesus. She travelled with Joseph from Nazareth in Galilee to Bethlehem in Judaea, a distance of about ninety miles. This would have been a journey of several days when she was in the last stages of pregnancy. It shows a physically strong woman, with great powers of endurance, rather than a gentle Madonna such as we see portrayed in the paintings of Raphael, Lippi or Leonardo da Vinci. She was a tough, ordinary woman of the people. When she came to Bethlehem for the census, there was no place for her in the inn. She was rejected by the well-to-do householders of the day. They would, evidently, have seen her condition but had no sympathy for her. She must have suffered much because of this refusal; she would have felt the unkindness of the rich. She had to choose a very poor place for the birth of her child. The one who thought in terms of the Magnificat must have suffered deeply, within herself, at this treatment of the poor. We can think of her, there, as undergoing the trials and hardships which many people in the slums of modern cities have to suffer every day.

These are the things which the Bible speaks of concerning the nativity. They are rather hard facts of life. The theological tradition, however, has been very much more concerned about trying to find out whether the birth of Our Lord left Mary a virgin or not, though there is no clear evidence about this in the New Testament writings. Preoccupation with such factors has tended to make of the nativity a sort of preternatural phenomenon, in which Mary's sharing in human suffering and the anguish of childbirth, in the context of social rejection, are neglected or forgotten. What the Gospels present, however, is the story of a mature, adult woman facing some of the most difficult problems of womanhood and motherhood, and thereby sharing their common trials. It is necessary to rediscover these facets of the story in order that the life of Mary may have more meaning for ordinary women who also undergo such trials.

Shepherds

At the visit of the poor shepherds, who were spending the night in the fields, taking care of their flocks, Mary hears the message they had received from the Angel: 'Peace on earth . . . ' (Luke 2.14).

The shepherds told Mary of their expectations of the child and 'Mary remembered all these things and thought deeply about them' (Luke 2.19). The Gospel stories show Mary as a very reflective and thoughtful person who was deeply interested in the future of her child – as any mother would be.

The Presentation

We see her next at the Presentation of Jesus in the temple forty days after his birth. She makes the offering of the poor, two turtle doves (Luke 2.22–24). The family belongs to the poor, the *anawim* of whom the Magnificat speaks.

Luke records that the prophet Simeon and the prophetess Anna announced to Mary the suffering that she herself would have to undergo: a sword would pierce her heart. She was, therefore, made painfully aware of what she had to accept in future as the mother of Jesus. We can imagine her having a premonition of her own sufferings. The Presentation is often interpreted merely as an act of obedience to the Jewish rites of the day, neglecting the significance of the old man and old woman. Motherhood is not an easy thing. It is a painful process not merely at the moment of birth, but right through life. The mother suffers in the life of her child, and rejoices in her child also. Mary was made vaguely aware of what was in store for her. She had, once again, to make an option to participate in the redemptive, liberative work of her son. It is only a strong, loving, mature woman who can accept having a sword pierce her heart – and go through life with it (Luke 2.39–40).

Flight into Egypt

Alongside the adoration of Jesus by the shepherds is the visit of the wise men from the East, the Magi. At their return by another route, Herod unleashed his fury. He felt threatened by the birth of an alternative leader of the people. Mary and Joseph, having duly received warning, had to flee to Egypt – a long journey along desert roads, which even today are difficult for people to traverse. They had to retrace the steps taken by their forebears in departing from Egypt. Mary would have had to suffer the trials of this journey in the hot sun with an infant.

Perhaps she had to suffer still more the mental anxiety caused by the massacre of the innocents under Herod. She would have seen that innocent children were killed, and families reduced to mourning, because of the jealousy of Herod for her son. The holy family were political exiles, fleeing their country to safeguard the life of their child.

Mary's action is a common phenomenon that people engaged in radical liberation movements have to face today, as we have seen in the

case of political exiles. She experienced the hatred, jealousy and venom
of the political rulers of her time. She felt the brutality and savagery of
the soldiers who carried out the commands of Herod. From the time of
Jesus' birth she was inevitably involved in political issues.

Herod preferred to kill the innocent children rather than see a threat
to his power. He did not enquire into the nature of the Kingdom the
new Messiah would establish. Political power generally reacts thus,
nervously, violently, cruelly and oppressively. Even today the powerful react thus. The rich are afraid that the children of poor people will
take their thrones and privileges.

Hence the enormous effort of the rich to plan the families of the poor,
instead of reforming themselves and their wasteful ways. Hence the
Herodian approach of the rich who promote the compulsory sterilization of poor women and men, and compel them into situations where
aborting a child may seem a necessity. The murder of the innocents, by
Herod, was a prototype of the way the rich and the powerful deal with
the poor whom they consider a threat to their privileges. Mary experienced this hatred and cruelty in her own life. She had to face it bravely,
sadly and even cunningly. Her approach was the mature and courageous one of a woman who knew her mind.

In the story of the flight into Egypt Mary was a refugee and an exile
in that land. The family returned to a place where the Jews had been
slaves for several centuries. Joseph had to be a *migrant worker*, a non-
national to whom the most menial tasks are given even in our own day.
Hence, for years, Mary, along with Joseph, would have experienced the
tribulations of being a foreign worker in Egypt. In this, too, she experienced personally the problems which many underprivileged people,
even in rich countries, have to face. They are the 'Third World' inside
rich countries. During this time the holy family would have had to wait
anxiously for their return to Palestine, their homeland. They had to
keep track of events at home and await a favourable time to return.
Mary's exile was again related to a political factor and she shrewdly
awaited the death of Herod before returning to her native land.

It is unfortunate that popular devotion to Mary does not do justice to
these experiences of Mary – the incarnation, the visitation, the nativity,
the Presentation, the flight and exile in Egypt – as a poor, courageous
woman. It is in these stories that Mary foreshadows the trials and
struggles of women of our own times too.

The middle-aged Mary

In her life at Nazareth, Mary was identified with her people. She lived
like one of them, running a household and contributing to its livelihood

(Luke 2.39, 40). She was not a solitary recluse in some walled-off convent, but rather an ordinary woman given to the tasks of daily living.

In the temple the young Jesus reveals to Joseph and Mary the nature of his calling. He speaks to them of obedience to the Father concerning his mission among the people of his time. It is said that Mary did not understand. She was even worried that Jesus had apparently treated them disrespectfully. She listened. She contemplated his words in her heart. She would have considered his future life in which her own life would be involved (Luke 2.41–51).

Other than in Matthew chapters 1 and 2, the Gospels, perhaps deliberately, present more of Mary than of Joseph. She, perhaps, had a major say in the affairs of the family and in the formation of Jesus. We are not told when Joseph died. The Gospels lost track of him, whereas Mary is mentioned up to the time of the post-Pentecostal Church. She was, perhaps, the bread-winner of the family after the death of Joseph, and may have contributed even prior to that. She would have begun to be involved in the work which Jesus considered was his mission. The loss of Jesus in the temple, and his indication to Joseph and Mary that he had to be busy about his Father's affairs, can be understood as one of the stages in his progressive dedication to his mission. Even at the early age of twelve, he indicated to them that he had a mind and a work of his own. It is most likely that, having shown his prowess in Jerusalem, he would have continued to concern himself with the problems of the people of his area.

It is unthinkable that Jesus would have lived a merely hidden life for the first thirty years of his earthly existence. A progressive growth of his involvement and commitment is much more likely. As he advanced in years he is said to have grown strong in the Spirit: 'As Jesus grew up he advanced in wisdom and in favour with God and men' (Luke 2.52). This growing in favour cannot be merely a passive life of submission to his parents, nor of being lost in the wilds or the desert. He must have practised what he was to preach later. Otherwise his life itself would have been a counter-witness to his people; and so it would be to us. The parable of the Good Samaritan could not have been related by an authentic leader who had remained for thirty years unconcerned about the lot of his people, while they were subjected to imperial rule and exploitation by the local religious and political leaders.

The character of Jesus would naturally have attracted people to him. People must have come often to Jesus, and Mary, and discussed various issues, even before he engaged himself more fully in his public life. We can thus deduce something of the lifestyle that Mary lived in her house with Jesus; how his openness would have meant the openness of her own home to all sorts of people of good and bad repute. Thus, even in the very early stages of his life, Mary would have had to undergo a process of education in relating to the people that gathered round Jesus. These included publicans, tax-gatherers, sinners and prostitutes. We can rethink this life at Nazareth as one in which there was a gradual evolution in which his mission became clearer and his action developed.

Mary as a loving Oriental mother must have concerned herself much with the thoughts, activities and lifestyle of Jesus. She must have wondered why he was living in the wilds, like a vagabond, without a house to call his own, a pillow for his head. Mary would have wondered why Jesus was not settling down to a married life. She may have often asked herself, as Oriental mothers still do, whether she should arrange a marriage for Jesus. She would have had to try to understand why Jesus preferred to be celibate. She must have shared with him her anxieties for his future when she would be no more. She must have had the desire to have grandchildren of her own. He, too, must have often told her that he had to be about his Father's work. He may have told her that he did not expect to be able to live very long because of the opposition of powerful people to his message. If he remained unmarried, it was not because he did not love any woman, but rather because he wanted to give himself fully to his cause. He would, humanly speaking, have anticipated a troubled life and an early death, which would not have enabled him to provide for a family. Whatever it was, this sort of issue must have provided for Mary opportunities for her own growth in maturity. She would have increasingly shared her son's concerns. She would thus have experienced a process of internal liberation which was to lead to a continuing sharing of his work and struggles.

The Jewish people were in a situation of oppression. There was a resistance to the Roman occupation and their collaborators. It is natural that Jesus, Mary and the group meeting with them would have discussed these matters, as happens even today in similar situations. The struggle grows gradually. It is important to ask ourselves how Jesus became such an extraordinary person with such a unique message. Did he suddenly acquire it by an infusion of grace, was he born with it, or did it grow gradually? Did he have discussions with Mary concerning the nature of religion and the sacred texts? They might have talked over the situation – what were they to do with the Pharisees, the Sadducees and Zealots? As Jesus grew up he would have had to decide about these issues.

When John the Baptist was beheaded because of his strong challenge to the powerful, Jesus proclaimed his own message of liberation. Jesus and John would have known each other well, and perhaps been associated in their teaching. It is said:

> When he heard that John had been arrested, Jesus withdrew to Galilee; and leaving Nazareth he went and settled at Capernaum on the sea of Galilee ... (Matt 4.12–13)

This may have been because it was not safe for Jesus because of his association with John.

When John was beheaded Jesus came forward. Here was a group in which, when one is killed in their mission, another carries it on, though with a somewhat different emphasis. Inevitably, Jesus would have discussed this with Mary, who would have participated in his difficult decision. Jesus would have said that he had to continue his work. He would have discussed with her violent and peaceful methods. Mary, too, would have watched what was happening in her society and to her loved ones, including John the Baptist, whom she knew from his birth.

Mary would, also, have had the challenge of trying to understand the attitude of Jesus towards the religious practices and leaders of the day. She probably had to go through a process of understanding the deeper meaning of the religious teaching of Jesus. He emphasized the religion of authenticity and sincerity. We may presume that Mary did not need such a process; that she, too, intuitively supported the teaching and approach of Jesus.

Mary would have participated in the process of Jesus proclaiming his extraordinary message and the very teaching of Jesus would have made Mary reflect. The religion or spirituality that Jesus proposed is universal. When Jesus said 'Whoever does the will of my heavenly Father is my brother, my sister, my mother ... ' (Matt at 12.50), he was responding to a man who brought a message that his mother and brothers were outside wanting to speak to him. In Luke 11.27 Jesus replied to the woman who called out from the crowd 'Happy the womb that carried you and the breasts that suckled you', 'No, happy are those who hear the word of God and keep it'. These instances would have made Mary think about the meaning of life itself. Jesus would not have addressed his teaching to Christians or Roman Catholics only! The teaching of Jesus is not primarily about Christianity or the Church, but about the Kingdom of God, which is universal.

The thinking of Jesus about the essence of spirituality, about the nature of prayer which should be in spirit and in truth, would have been a cause of much discussion and debate in the society of his day. His attitude towards formulations of prayer and external rituals was profoundly liberating and radical, and all that 2,000 years ago:

'Not everyone who calls me "Lord, Lord", will enter the Kingdom of Heaven, but only those who do what my Father in heaven wants them to do.' (Matt 7.21; Mark 12.40)

His 'woes to the rich', and his teaching on the obligations of rulers and the burdens imposed by lawyers on the ignorant, were of exceptional spiritual wisdom then, and also today (Matt 23; Luke 11.39–52).

Mary would have pondered these things in her heart. She would have seen how Jesus was being misunderstood or rather misrepresented by so many, especially the powerful and the unjust. In this she would have suffered much as any mother, especially an Oriental mother who is very attached to her children, even today.

She would most probably have participated in the very evolution of this message. The mother and son must have often spoken of these things. It is even possible that Mary herself helped the young Jesus to understand the meaning of life. She may have told him of the unkind and oppressive nature of the society in which he was born as an outcast. She might have told him of the killing of the innocent children, and of their long flight and exile in Egypt. Would it be wrong to think that Mary contributed to the growth of Jesus' thinking? His sensitivity towards people would have been learnt in the home of Joseph and Mary.

Mary would certainly have had a share in the elaboration of the programme of Jesus' teaching. He would have discussed with her the risks involved. This would be normal between a mother and son, and more so in an ideal family.

If, however, we hold that Jesus was God from his babyhood, and that he had the fullness of knowledge and virtue, then such a relationship may not have existed between them. If this were the case, Jesus would then have told Mary not to worry about his enemies and the Romans, for he was sure of rising on the third day, if he were killed; and further, that in the future they would be remembered in all the continents of the world, and even Pilate would be spoken of only because of him! In such a situation the relationship of mother and son would have been quite different.

In an ordinary human family, which I think the holy family was, Mary would have had many worries. She would have been concerned about her son: was he wise and prudent? Was he getting into unnecessary trouble? Where would all this lead? These questions would have been her constant preoccupation during the last three years of Jesus' life. If Jesus were the only child, Mary's concern would have been even more intense.

Nonetheless we find Mary following Jesus in his public life, especially when he got into trouble. She would have seen how he cleverly escaped on several occasions, sometimes by a devastating retort, sometimes by disappearing from the crowd. We can imagine how mothers are worried when their sons take up radical positions in revolutionary situations, as was the Palestine of those days. Jesus was on the wrong side of the law, and even of the religious establishment. Large crowds followed him. This itself was upsetting to the authorities and consequently dangerous for Jesus. Mary, who had seen how John the Baptist was beheaded, would have been very worried about Jesus. She was a sorrowful mother.

But she may also have even encouraged him, by being with him and by being supportive of his views. Her holiness and closeness to God would have helped her understand the profundity of the message of her son. It seems to me that reflections such as these are more significant than speculation concerning her preservation from original sin or her being a virgin, for it is such situations that mothers have to face in the troubled circumstances which are so widespread in the world today.

Mary would have achieved a liberation in her religious consciousness; she could have come to understand and live a form of sanctity in the midst of active commitment to people and public affairs. This was to follow the example given by Jesus, her son. Thus the growth of Mary in her spiritual life would have to be understood in a manner very different from what is often written about the stages of spiritual growth. Mary reconciled deep recollection with an active commitment, along with her son, and thus 'grew in grace with God and man', along with Jesus also (Luke 2.52).

In the whole process she would have been torn between her love and care for her only son and her own consciousness of the demands of integral human liberation and social justice. As her son gave himself more fully to his public life, this dilemma must have been heightened within her. In living it through she came to a position that was ennobling for her too.

Mary shared in the public life of Jesus

In the marriage feast at Cana, Mary is actively present with Jesus and his disciples. She is participating in a secular event. She notices the embarrassment of the hosts. She invites Jesus to use his extraordinary powers to help out in the situation. She, therefore, knows already of his miraculous powers. In her solicitude for others, she launches Jesus on the road towards manifesting himself as a new spiritual leader. To come to such a position, Jesus and Mary must have had a deep understanding between themselves as to his work. The servants of the household show their acceptance of the word of Mary to do whatever Jesus says. This is a single event, but it is likely that Mary was associated with Jesus throughout his public ministry. She had by then grown to a new degree of maturity, accepting responsibility as a public person, as the mother of Jesus (John 2.1–12).

Some of the rejection of Jesus was connected with an attitude towards his family which was well known at Nazareth:

> When they heard him they were amazed. 'Where did he get all this?', they asked. 'What wisdom is this that has been given him? How does he perform miracles? Isn't he the carpenter, the son of Mary, and the brother of James, Joseph, Judas and Simon? Aren't his sisters living here?' And so they rejected him. (Mark 6.1–6; Matt 13.53–58; Luke 4.16–30; John 6.42)

Luke mentions the teaching at the synagogue at Nazareth, where Jesus announced his mission of the liberation of the oppressed (Luke 4.18):

> When the people in the synagogue heard this, they were filled with anger. They rose up, dragged Jesus out of the town and took him to the top of the hill on which their town was built. They meant to throw him over the cliff, but he walked through the middle of the crowd and went his way. (Luke 4.28–30)

It is most likely that Mary would have known of this attempt on the life of Jesus.

The threats to his life were linked to his teachings as well as to it being known that he was the son of Mary. His brothers and sisters were known, though the names of the sisters are not mentioned by the evangelists who speak of his brothers.

We meet Mary again occasionally in the Gospel story, for example, when someone informs Jesus that his mother is among the crowd and more particularly at his trial, on the road to Calvary, and at the foot of the cross. Mary followed Jesus in his public life at least from a distance. She would have been challenged to accept his lifestyle, his message and his relationships.

Mary would have noticed Jesus actively contesting the social and religious values of the time that considered women to be inferior, unclean, and unsuitable as companions for a religious man. The life of Jesus contradicted this understanding.

Luke testifies to this, not least in the story of the sinful woman in the house of Simon the Pharisee:

> She stood behind Jesus, by his feet, crying and wetting his feet with her tears. Then she dried his feet with her hair, kissed them and poured perfume on them. (Luke 7.38)
> 'You did not welcome me with a kiss, but she has not stopped kissing my feet since I came.' (Luke 7.45)

Luke then mentions the names of several women who

> travelled with Jesus through towns and villages, preaching the Good
> News about the Kingdom of God. The twelve disciples went with him
> and so did some women who had been healed of evil spirits and diseases:
> Mary who was called Magdalena ... and many other women who used
> their own resources to help Jesus and his disciples. (Luke 8.1–3)

These were women of some means who had made the decision to
accompany Jesus on his mission. Some were known to have been
possessed by evil spirits.

Since Jesus' lifestyle was one in which he contested the social,
cultural, economic and political values of his time, Mary would have
had to think out her own values. She would have had to accept the
misrepresentations made by people concerning him: that he was a
person of low repute, mixing with sinners, tax-collectors, prostitutes,
insurgents and Zealots, that he was upsetting the people and rousing
them to challenge the established values of the times, and perhaps even
to question the political leadership. She would also have suffered in
seeing him travelling long distances with people on foot, and not
having a house of his own.

She would probably have had still more difficulty as she saw her son
getting into trouble with the religious leaders of the day, the Pharisees,
Sadducees, High Priests and governors. She would have noticed Jesus'
involvement in the divisions and polarizations of society, partly
because of his own teaching. She would have been apprehensive about
his safety as she observed the leaders trying to trap him on different
occasions. Therefore, Mary could not have been indifferent to the social
issues of the time. If she were, she would not have been with him in his
public life until the end, and beyond that, with the apostles in the early
Church! We may, therefore, conclude that, perhaps more than anyone
else, she understood the meaning of the life and message of Jesus. She
would have realized why he was giving up his life and why he was
refusing to collude with the wrongs of the leaders of the day.

By this time the relationship between Jesus and Mary was such that
she understood that for him his mission was of paramount importance.
He placed service to the people before the interests of his family. His
family members were worried about him. They even feared that he was
insane.

In the Gospel of Mark there are two passages separated by ten verses.
The first, Mark 3.20–21, mentions the problem seen by the members of
Jesus' family

> Then Jesus went home. Again such a large crowd gathered that Jesus and
> his disciples had no time to eat. When his family heard about it, they set

out to take charge of him, because people were saying, 'He is gone mad'.

In the second passage, Mark 3.31–35, Mark says 'Then Jesus' mother and brothers arrived'.

In the first passage it is not clear whether Mary too thought Jesus was beside himself. As Raymond E. Brown remarks, this would be

awkward after the Lucan and Matthean infancy narratives wherein Mary knew who Jesus was from his conception ...
    Luke and Matthew omit the first part of the Marcan scene and have no such awkward suggestion.[2]

The family members were evidently deeply concerned about what Jesus was doing: 'He and his disciples had no time to eat.' They would have been at least surprised that their brother or cousin was having such an extraordinary impact on people. His behaviour was such that they were worried about his sanity. He was challenging the values of society, keeping company with sinners and at the same time claiming an intimate relationship with God whom he called 'Abba, Father'. Some claimed that Beelzebul the chief of the demons was in him (Mark 3.22).

Whether Mary agreed with her relatives is not directly recorded. But at least she accompanied them. They must have discussed the apparently strange behaviour of Jesus with her.

In this situation Mary would have been very concerned. The people and Jesus' relatives were suspecting that something was terribly wrong with him. If Mary understood the mission and identity of Jesus, she would have been upset that the others thought he was mad. If, on the other hand, she did not have a clear understanding of him, she would have worried – as any mother would – about her wayward son, who seemed dangerously close to being possessed by the Devil and likely to be manhandled by the mob or powers that be. Her relatives would probably have had to persuade Mary to accompany them to speak to Jesus and to call him away from his apparently unwise and risky mission. The response of Jesus is: 'Whoever does what God wants him to do is my brother, my sister, my mother' (Mark 3.31–35; Matt 12.46–50; Luke 8.19–21).

Jesus not only refuses to be called away from his mission, he uses the occasion to explain his understanding of his family of discipleship, which is more important than being a physical blood-relation. Jesus indicates the higher calling of discipleship in response to the word of God.

Mary can be regarded as the one who responds most fully to the call of spiritual communion. That is the deeper meaning of her *fiat* at the

Annunciation, when she heard the word of God calling her to the special task.

If we do not assume that Mary had a knowledge and consciousness of Jesus as God, or God's specially chosen messenger, we need to think in more human terms of the agony of a mother whose son appears to be in serious psychological and political trouble. We could then imagine Mary experiencing the sufferings of millions of mothers who see their children, even as adults, involved in risky political enterprises in times of civil war, insurrection, non-violent protest movements and campaigns considered illegal by political and military authorities. These are very common throughout the world today.

One of the consequences of the development of a top-down Mariology is that Mary is not thought of as a human mother of a human son, who lived in very ordinary human circumstances and faced situations similar to those faced by millions of contemporary mothers and children. This is the damage done by the traditional interpretation of Mariology that makes Mary more of a heavenly being, conversing with angels, than an ordinary woman of the people.

The conversations of Jesus and Mary can be better understood in the context of such a human Mary. Jesus and Mary talk to each other or meet:

- at the finding of the child Jesus in the temple,
- at the wedding feast at Cana,
- during the public ministry of Jesus when his family comes to take him away,
- at the foot of the cross.

At the temple Jesus is apparently a problem for Mary and Joseph: Mary is perplexed: 'My son, why have you done this to us? Your father and I have been terribly worried trying to find you.' He replies: 'Why do you have to look for me? Didn't you know that I had to be in my Father's house?' But they did not understand his answer (Luke 2.48–49).

It was part of Mary's maternal cross to be 'terribly worried' about Jesus. Yet Jesus seems to rebuke her – as twelve-year-old children seem to do today. The story shows her as an intensely human mother who had missed her son for three days. Jesus seems to be too mature for his years – asking questions of the Jewish teachers and giving 'intelligent answers'. The story as narrated is consistent with the idea of an extraordinarily precocious child.

At the wedding feast at Cana Jesus also seems to be telling Mary not to interfere in his programme: 'You must not tell me what to do, my time is not yet come' (John 2.4). The relationship between Mary and the adult Jesus is intriguing. Mary seems to know his mind, whatever his words, or she has so much of an influence on him that she can persuade him to advance his timing. Whatever it was, there is evidence of an understanding between the mother and son.

The third meeting, which has been discussed in detail already, was when Jesus insisted on discipleship as the criterion of membership of his new family.

Finally, at the foot of the cross, this relationship is sealed: the beloved disciple, representing all his disciples, and his mother, a mother of all. Neither is mentioned by name by the fourth evangelist, who alone narrates this incident, which is of enormous importance for the future.[3]

Mary as a mature and ageing woman accepted the changed relationship. She co-operated in Jesus' liberative action. She shows a way in which older women, including widows, can participate in personal and societal liberation.

At the trial of Jesus

Mary was with him. In the last days of his life she, too, was in Jerusalem. It was an emergency situation. These were times of unrest and rebellion, as the historians indicate. The plot against Jesus was gathering momentum. He was betrayed by a combination of Roman soldiers, Jewish priests and one of his apostles. She would have witnessed the apparent triumph of the previous week, when the people cried 'Hosanna' to Jesus. But when he was captured, there were few followers. We can try to appreciate what she would have had to endure during these days. Doubtless her son would have spoken to her of his decision to continue his public challenge to the leaders of his time. Even the apostles tried to dissuade him from going to Jerusalem, but he decided that it was time for him to take risks. It is perhaps only a mother whose only son is condemned to be executed who might understand Mary's plight. The apostles ran away when he was captured, but Mary must have followed her son. She would have been aware that he was tortured, and of the unjust and unfair trial to which he was subjected.

The night of his imprisonment and torture must have been terrible for Mary. The son whom she had safeguarded for so long was now in the hands of his enemies. She must have suffered at the thought of the way he would be treated by the cruel leaders and soldiers. Her sensitive nature would have increased her sense of pain. Her helplessness before the imperial rulers, their native collaborators and the religious leadership must have caused much distress to her. Instead of the mighty being thrown down from their thrones, the innocent one was tortured.

On the way to Calvary she met him. Their words are not recorded, but she certainly suffered with him and on account of him. He was under pressure to abandon his message, to discontinue his mission and thus save his life but he did not compromise, nor do we read of her asking him to compromise in order to satisfy Pilate and be released. She did not suggest a second exile in Egypt. On the contrary, she was with him in his decision to go unto the end. For, as he said, 'Greater love than this no man hath, to give up his life for his friend' (John 15.13).

Mary and women in Jesus' passion

Mary and several women were very close to Jesus in the last days of his life. All the evangelists record this:

> His friends had all been standing at a distance; the women who had accompanied him from Galilee stood with them and watched it all. (Luke 23.49)

> A number of women were also present, watching from a distance; they had followed Jesus from Galilee and waited on him. Among them were Mary of Magdala, Mary the mother of James and Joseph, and the mother of the sons of Zebedee. (Matt 27.55–56; Mark 15.40–41; John 19.25–26)

At the moment of his supreme sacrifice the women, led by Mary, stood with Jesus. It is noteworthy that at the most difficult and trying moment in the life of Jesus, most of his male companions seem to have fled, or have watched from afar, except for John. Other predecessors of the Bishops and of the Popes did not measure up to this occasion.

Mary, with Mary of Magdala and the other women, stood at the foot of the cross. Perhaps there was less danger for them from those who killed Jesus. They participated most closely in the sacrifice of Jesus on the cross. This is the first and real Eucharist – the unique sacrifice of the New Testament. The Eucharist is much more than the Last Supper. It is important to remember this in connection with the restriction of women from the Christian priesthood.

Mary stood at the foot of the cross

Stabat Mater dolorosa. When Jesus said 'I thirst', and the soldiers gave him a sour drink, his mother's heart must have felt an intense pain and sadness. She was unable to help him in his last moments. She suffered the anguish of so many women who are unable to help, even in a small way, to alleviate the sufferings of their dear ones at the hands of torturers and executioners. She experienced the powerlessness which is the lot of the majority of exploited and marginalized people in almost all countries of the world. How many mothers, wives, sisters suffer like her today, when arbitrary rule is increasing, and the condition of political prisoners is so cruel in countries which call themselves democracies? She was steadfast in making the ultimate sacrifice for her only child. He was offering his life for a cause: the integral liberation and salvation of his people and of humankind. She participated in the sacrifice. It must have been the most demanding act of faith in the promise of God and in the unorthodox teaching of her son. She must have been tempted to ask whether any good would come from such a death. She too suffered because of the action of false informants, soldiers, officers of the law, the High Priests, governors and the mob, as he was being stripped, spat on and jeered at.

On the cross her son was identified with criminals and insurgents. A law-breaker was preferred to him and he was rejected by the vast majority of the people who had benefited so much from him. We can imagine the depth of Mary's suffering in the trial and death of Jesus. We can also imagine her trying to understand the meaning of these events. The causes of his death were clear, namely the jealousy and hatred of the political and religious leaderships of the day. Knowing his innocence, the integrity of his life, the sublime quality of his message, the authenticity of his witness and the peaceful nature of his methods, she would have suffered all the more to see how he was being dealt with cruelly by the mob, and the strange combination of Roman and Jewish leaders.

Jesus, too, would have suffered much at the prospect of leaving his ageing mother alone on earth. He tried to provide for her by asking his beloved disciple John to look after her, but the death of Jesus meant that Mary had to face the problems of loneliness (John 19.25–27).

Usually, Oriental parents look forward to spending their old age with their children and grandchildren. Mary had to sacrifice her son for the liberation of others, and in the process she was left alone. The feeling of being alone in the world is a terrible suffering for anyone. Perhaps it is greater for an ageing woman, who begins to realize her own physical helplessness. Struggles for liberation are very demanding on our human nature, especially in times of arbitrary despotic rule. While Mary suffered in the agony of her son, she must have felt, intensely, her own sense of losing the one for whom she had lived, and who had cared so much for her. Jesus' love and concern for others may indicate his even greater love for his mother. Their deep attachment to each other must have made this parting acutely painful and sad. Mary could have said 'greater love than this no woman hath, to offer the life of her only son for the liberation of others'. Her courage and strength of character under such circumstances can be an inspiration, especially to women, to bear the cross of loneliness, not least in old age.

Redemptive suffering, however noble it may be, is painful for those involved, for those in prison and those out of it; for those who die and those who survive. Jesus and Mary must have suffered because of their love for each other. Jesus also shows how in such suffering the small group, or community, is very important. Mary is entrusted to John, and John to Mary. The community of liberative action endures beyond the grave. This relationship of Mary and John can be deeply significant for other small groups and communities that dedicate themselves to human liberation under difficult circumstances. When one is taken to prison, or killed, the others share the responsibilities for their family. This is a common situation in many countries today.

Mary remained faithful to the end

Mary did not run away as most of the apostles did. She identified with her son until the end, in the moment of his apparent failure. In this way she acted as a strong, mature person giving herself totally to a cause, and making the supreme sacrifice of her own son and only child. Since we know that throughout her life she contemplated God's word in obedience, we are justified in thinking that she was aware of the cause of his death. In challenging the false value systems of his time, he affirmed the rights of all and acknowledged God as opposing the abuses of the leaders.

She would have suffered much to see her only son so treated. His very innocence would have made her suffering even more poignant and painful. She would have experienced once again the harshness of the law, of the authorities, of the ruling élites. She would have seen how treacherous the religious leadership was, how the fear of the Romans affected Pilate. The very jeering of the crowd calling for Barabbas, instead of Jesus, would have made her think of the ingratitude of the crowd, the disloyalty of many. Peter's denial must have pained her deeply. Only John and her women companions stood with her at the foot of the cross. This was a moment of supreme tragedy for her. His life seemed a total failure, and she was going to be left alone – except for John.

There is a sense in which Mary is the one who offered the life of Jesus as a sacrifice. Jesus is the one who dies; dying is difficult. Offering one's own son and continuing to live in a hostile environment is even more demanding and heart-rending. She offers the first sacrifice of the life of Jesus – born of her flesh. She is the first priest of the New Testament, along with Jesus, offering the flesh of her flesh. She participates in the first and foremost sacrifice of the New Testament.

We see, here, her strength of character, her convictions, her perseverance. She did not try to persuade Jesus to compromise with the powers that be, and come down from the cross. She did not think it better to persuade him to come to terms with the ruling establishment, and spend the rest of his life quietly. This would be the thought of most mothers who want to save the life of their son. Even when Peter, and most of the apostles, ran away, Mary and the women, with John, stood firmly, resolutely loyal to Jesus to the end and beyond the grave. The first of the Popes and Bishops ran away in the moment of danger, but these women, led by Mary, remained by the side of Jesus – dead or alive. She believed him, and in him.

Mary shows herself strong and determined to face all the insults of a mob, the opposition of the religious and political leaders and the local and foreign powers. She is at this stage a mature, ageing woman, who has gone through many bitter experiences of life. She had risked much to save the infant Jesus by fleeing into Egypt. From the crib to the cross she is present. Now she cannot save him.

Resurrection

It was the women who found that Jesus had risen. When they related the events to his followers, they did not believe them. Jesus then appeared to the eleven, and reproached them for their incredulity and dullness, because they had not believed those who had seen him risen from the dead (Mark 16.11–14). The Jerusalem Bible translates 'dullness' as 'obstinacy'.

In Luke, it is recorded that when the women told the apostles about the risen Jesus, 'the story appeared to them to be nonsense, and they would not believe them' (Luke 24.11).

In the Lukan text, on the road to Emmaus, Jesus, unrecognized by his disciples, tells them 'How dull you are! How slow to believe all that the prophets said' (Luke 24.25).

This reaction of caution perhaps reveals a healthy scepticism. It is perhaps revealed in the way the future Pope and Bishops reacted to the women's experience: 'Nonsense!' The Emmaus story records 'some women of our company astounded us'.

This is a significant aspect of the resurrection narratives. Women were not only present at the death of Jesus. They waited on him. They were the first to witness the resurrection. The men, on the other hand, at best stayed at a distance and were slow, dull and obstinate in believing the women's experience of the risen Lord. It is important to reflect on this.

There are other narratives, like that of the apostles in the Garden of Olives, where they fell asleep. They could not watch one hour – even at this solemn moment of Jesus' life. When Peter was challenged by one of the housemaids: 'You were there too with Jesus the Galilean', he denied it: 'I know nothing.' When another maid asked him, again Peter denied Jesus: 'I do not know the man.' The third time Peter denied with curses ... then the cock crew ... (Matt 26.69–75).

These texts show how close the women were to Jesus in those last days. Mary followed Jesus. Her sacrifice was the greatest and most painful. Yet today men claim to have control over the eucharistic sacrifice which is a principal function of the Christian priesthood. We have a selective use of scriptures. When it is claimed 'Thou art Peter and on this rock ... ', why do we neglect the other texts, 'before the cock crows you will disown me three times' (Matt 26.75), or 'Get behind me Satan'?

The women seem to have been more faithful to Jesus through the darkest moments and days of his life. The men became convinced and courageous only after receiving the outpouring of the Holy Spirit.

After the death of Jesus, when the small group of disciples were in great anxiety and difficulty, not knowing what their future would be, Mary was with them: 'All these were constantly at prayer together, and with them a group of women, including Mary the mother of Jesus, and his brothers' (Acts 1.14). This was the time leading up to Pentecost. Mary was with them, undoubtedly a central personality, one who was consoled by them, and they were strengthened by her deep conviction of the goodness and correctness of her crucified son.

Neither the New Testament nor any other source gives reliable information of the further course of her life and her death.[4]

We can reflect on the perseverance, courage, determination and fidelity to Jesus' teaching that would have animated this group around Mary. They would doubtless have recalled the essentials of Jesus' message: Love one another. If you love one another, even if you die you will live. The early Church had to face misunderstandings and the risk of death. Mary would have seen the apostles and disciples proclaiming the message of Jesus and consequently facing difficulties. She would certainly have been painfully aware of the killing of Stephen. Here was the mother of Jesus staying firm with the small group, despite threats, arrests and killings.

Mary bears witness to a hope that is beyond death, for she perserved in the cause after the death of her son. She was conscious of his mission, identified with it, and, after his death, was perhaps the mainstay of the cause for which he died. Jesus died for the integral liberation of all and we may deduce that Mary too was courageous, consistent and selfless in her participation in the same cause. At the foot of the cross she took the risk of supreme failure, of losing not only the cause, but also her only son. She had the courage to face public shame and jeering.

When everything around her seemed to be crumbling, when all that she had been living for seemed to be ending with the death of her son on the cross, Mary remained steadfast as a mature, level-headed, adult woman. Her faith was tried in the crucible of suffering. Her suffering was perhaps more mental and psychological than physical. She knew that Jesus was innocent. She knew he believed in his message. Yet she saw society condemning him. She saw him ostracized, rejected. She suffered because of the false values of the times; because of the difference between personal goodness and social rejection. The exploitative rulers and hypocrites won the day. Everything seemed to end in the grave. She hoped beyond hope. Jesus must surely have explained to her the meaning of his saying 'he who dies will live'. She is the first, and closest, sharer in the death/resurrection experience of Jesus.

It is of very great importance for the understanding of Mary that her whole life be re-thought in relation to that of Jesus and their common task, in which they had different roles but a similar commitment. We see in her, therefore, a woman who was not concerned merely with the individualistic promotion of her family and of her child. She was not trying to save money or goods. Her concern was not to make a beautiful home for him. She understood Jesus as one living for others, asserting a religion of personal freedom, and contesting the injustices of his day.

We can thus imagine the sort of woman Mary was in real life. It is this sort of woman who should be central to Christian spirituality. Mary belongs to the whole of humanity as a strong, dedicated woman and mother: one who was the closest associate of one of the greatest spiritual leaders of humanity. She was a mature, adult woman who was able to face life's problems along with Jesus. She was able to take up strong positions beside Jesus against all forms of exploitation. This portrayal of Mary is more faithful to the New Testament than the Mary of traditional Christian theology and spirituality.

Mary has to be liberated from traditional theological speculation which has made her a woman who is not female, a woman who does not know what it is to be human, who does not go through the birth pangs of bringing forth Jesus, who does not know sin, who does not feel the trials of human existence.

Mary, in heaven, would perhaps be sad at the sort of attention Christians give to some of her bodily characteristics and at their neglect of her entire life's relationship with Jesus in his mission. She may be even more sad that, for so long, Christians did not appreciate why Jesus had to suffer and give his life in the social conditions of his time.

The most important realities concerning Mary are not so much that she is immaculate, a virgin, and in what form she is mother of God, but that she was intimately associated with Jesus of Nazareth, flesh of her flesh, in the beginning of the new community. This new community was to carry the message of human liberation and fulfilment in loving one another, sharing what we have and building a new humanity. In this, Mary is an example to all humankind.

The Church's preferential option for the poor is wonderfully revealed in Mary's Magnificat:[5]

'My soul magnifies the Lord,
and my spirit rejoices in God my Saviour,
for he has looked on his servant in her lowliness.
For behold, henceforth all generations will call me blessed;
for he who is mighty has done great things for me,
and holy is his name:
and his mercy is from age to age
on those who fear him.
He has shown strength with his arm,
he has scattered the proud-hearted,
he has cast down the mighty from their thrones,
and lifted up the lowly;
he has filled the hungry with good things,
sent the rich away empty.
He has helped his servant Israel,
remembering his mercy,
as he spoke to our fathers,
to Abraham and to his posterity for ever.'
(Luke 1.46–55)

Notes

1 1 Samuel 2, 'The Song of Hannah'.
2 Raymond E. Brown SS, *Biblical Reflections on the Crisis Facing the Church* (New York: Paulist Press, 1975), p. 89 including note 79.
3 Ibid., pp. 101–4.
4 John L. McKenzie, *Dictionary of the Bible* (London: Geoffrey Chapman, 1965), p. 552.
5 Pope John Paul II, *Redemptoris Mater*, 'The Mother of the Redeemer' (Vatican, 1987), pp. 72, 76.

5

❧❧❧❧

Mary and society

The traditional Mariological dogmas are in many senses not adequate for understanding Mary in relation to society. In many ways they have been used for domesticating Mary, women, religion and spirituality. We have to try to understand Mary in relation to what Jesus represented. A holistic approach is necessary because there would have been a very close relationship, and friendship, between Jesus and Mary. This would be natural in an ideal family. We should also remember Joseph in this, for he is perhaps one of those most discriminated against and marginalized by theology.

Mary and Jesus

We may think that Mary had an understanding of Jesus. They grew up together. We can imagine a partnership between Jesus and Mary. At some stage Jesus would have had the leading role, but Jesus died young, and Mary continued to be with his group of followers.

In order to reflect on Mary and society we should not begin with the traditional dogmas of a top-down Mariology: Immaculate Conception, virginity, Mother of God, Assumption and Coronation. We should, rather, begin with Jesus and his work for, more than anyone else, Mary lived for Jesus. Her life was linked to his.

Having reflected earlier on what the Gospels say of Mary, we need to consider Jesus in relation to his mission of integral human liberation. Mary participated in this task, perhaps even helped to evolve his thinking, lifestyle and way of presenting himself to the public.

The message of Jesus

Jesus was principally concerned with the Kingdom of God, a rule of righteousness. He formed a community for this purpose – not primarily a Church. The principal teaching of Jesus is that God is Love and that we must love one another. That is the sum and substance of the Law and the commandments. It is more important than all the books of theology. It is also the core of the teachings of the other religions. This love must express itself in action. 'I was hungry, and you gave me food' (Matt 25.35). The mission of Jesus as set out in Luke 4.18 is 'to announce the good news to the poor ... to liberate the captives ... to set free the oppressed ... '.

Jesus did not claim to be God in such a way as to be 'consubstantial with the Father', 'hypostatically uniting two natures in one person', 'the second person of the blessed Trinity', 'transubstantiated and present in the tabernacle'. These are not words Jesus used. Jesus taught the love of God for all, and that we must move away from selfishness to other-centredness, towards sharing in love, and thus being fulfilled. That is the beginning of the Kingdom of God on earth.

Jesus invited people to be converted to the values he preached, a conversion from:

death	to	life through death to self
darkness	to	light
error and ignorance	to	truth, knowledge, consciousness, awareness of self, others and God
selfishness	to	unselfishness
injustice	to	justice
hatred and prejudice	to	love, including love of enemies, peace, *shalom*, forgiveness
greed	to	sharing
profit-seeking	to	need-serving
pride	to	humility, service
privilege	to	equality, empowerment of all
abuse of power	to	power being service
patriarchy	to	mutuality, partnership
hierarchy	to	community, reciprocity
domination	to	participation
isolation	to	co-operation, communion
indifference and apathy	to	caring, concern, empathy, commitment
unfreedom	to	freedom
hypocrisy and dishonesty	to	honesty, sincerity, authenticity.

Jesus' mission was not the presentation of the highly intellectual dogmas of an abstract theology, but a practical call to the conversion of all people from evil, avarice and injustice to love, sharing and communion ... *koinonia, diakonia*. This is the content of what I understand by integral liberation.

This is what Jesus taught, very often in parables. He did not propound dogmas and theological definitions. His method was to teach by witnessing to his message in his day-to-day life. He was more concerned with setting up a community than with an institution or a hierarchy.

The personality of Jesus

Jesus was loving and strong, affectionate and courageous. Because of his love and concern for others, he took up public life. He challenged the institutions, systems, norms and taboos of his day. Nothing was beyond his critical examination, or too sacred to be challenged. No authority was too great to be contradicted. He questioned the assumptions of society and of the religion of the time.[1]

Jesus was an extraordinary person. We can also think of Mary as an extraordinary woman, the woman who gave birth to Jesus and brought him up to be this exceptional person. I do not think Jesus began life with the fullness of knowledge. He made some mistakes, for example about the end of the world. I do not think that we need to assume that Jesus had the fullness of knowledge, and the beatific vision, even at the end of his life. Otherwise his agony and death would hardly be such a great sacrifice, since he would have known that he would rise again on the third day.

It is most likely that Mary participated in the growth of Jesus. They would have discussed many issues together. Those who bring up children, and teachers of religion, know how children question their elders concerning the meaning of life. Jesus' questioning of these things would have meant that Mary had to respond to them. Or it may be that Mary herself inspired some of this, then heretical, thinking. Especially when we think of the Mary of the Magnificat, the exile and refugee, it is not difficult to think of her also having such views on life and society.

Jesus and interpersonal relations

Jesus' approach to others was characterized by openness. In a society in which there were many taboos and much social discrimination, Jesus accepted and respected everyone as a person. He broke through the taboos of the time because of the love of God, and because of his deep understanding of the human condition. He did not conform to the limits imposed on him by the social restrictions of the time, preventing communication across social classes, religions, races and sexes. He was loving towards all, and yet strongly critical of what was wrong in society, including the exploitation of the weak and the poor.

Jesus had an outgoing approach, and an openness towards community, mutuality and partnership. This included people of both sexes. He was remarkably close to women – both those considered good and those with a bad reputation, like the woman taken in adultery. Women, in turn, were much attached to Jesus, as the Gospels record. They were those who were most faithful to him: Mary of Magdala, from whom he had formerly cast out seven devils, was loyal to him even beyond death, and was favoured by being the first to meet the risen Lord (Mark 16.9).

Rosemary Ruether sees a particular significance in the relationship of Jesus and Mary Magdalene. It has an even more meaningful message in the context of the struggle for women's dignity and rights:

> The Mary who represents the Church, the liberated humanity, may rather be the repressed and defamed Mary of the Christian tradition, Mary Magdalena, friend and disciple of Jesus, the first witness of the resurrection, the revealer of the Christian Good News. Blessed is the womb that bore thee, the paps that gave thee suck? Nay, rather blessed is she who heard the Word of God and kept it (Luke 11:27–28).[2]

The relationship of Jesus with Mary Magdalene was one of love, trust, loyalty and mutuality which went against the social norms of the day and persevered beyond death and the tomb.

Jesus and liberation in religion

The spirituality of Jesus was not that of the traditional religion of the time which included rituals, long prayers and taboos. His understanding of religion was one of interiority, sincerity and authenticity, of honesty, freedom from greed and from seeking for power and pleasure. His concept of holiness was one of self-giving in other-centredness. Spirituality was not merely a matter of an external authority or a sacred text telling people what had to be done. He was supremely free and honest in his search for the true and the good.

He taught that the Spirit is in each human being, and that each has to respond to an inner call; there is no need of an external teacher. He was liberated and liberating with regard to women. He was friendly and relaxed with them. They cared for him. The people disregarded by society were respected by him (Matt 23.8–9; John 16.13).

Jesus criticized the clergy of the day. They in turn found him a danger to religion and to their alliance with the imperial rulers. They therefore plotted against him and wanted him killed. For Jesus, religion was not concerned with ostentatious practices. He presented a spirituality that was profoundly attractive, challenging and, in a sense, akin to the aspirations of men and women of modern times.

Jesus and social liberation

Jesus promoted social liberation. The wealth of society was to be for all.
He was in favour of resource-sharing. The person who had two coats
had to give one of them to someone in need. He was hard towards the
rich, whom he required to share their wealth. He did not spare them.
On the contrary, after a meal at the house of Zacchaeus, the host had to
give away half his wealth, and repay fourfold whatever he had unfairly
taken. Jesus knew how difficult it was to convert the rich. He spoke to
them in a direct way, for example in the 'woes' to the rich and lawyers,
and in his condemnation of blind guides and whitened sepulchres
(Matt 23.1–36; Mark 12.38–40).

Jesus and political liberation

Jesus' stand on political liberation is quite clear. For him, power had to
be a service. He was against élitism, against discrimination and inequality. He demanded love of everyone, including enemies. He promoted a
genuine reconciliation and peace that respected all. He was opposed to
the exploitation of his people by the ruling classes and the Roman
imperialists. He was killed as one who might be the King of the Jews:

> But the crowd shouted back. 'If you set him free, that means you are not
> the Emperor's friend. Anyone who claims to be a king is a rebel against
> the Emperor.' (John 19.12)[3]

All these examples show Jesus presenting a new approach to interpersonal relations, social life, the world and religion. Mary would have
been aware of these developments. Jesus and Mary would have discussed them like any ordinary, loving, mother and son. They decided to
face together the risks involved in such beliefs.

It is possible to imagine that Mary did not understand or approve of
Jesus, at least at some stages of his life. Even then she would have had
to interact with him and perhaps suffer much in doing so.

A principal element in Marian spirituality would be a recognition of
Mary's partnership in the mission of her son. She shared in the life,
message and work of Jesus and the Jesus community.

Mary in the early Church

Soon after Jesus's death, Mary was present at the centre of the Jesus
community. In the Acts of the Apostles it is recorded:

> All these were constantly at prayer together and with them a group of
> women, including Mary, the mother of Jesus and his brothers ... (Acts
> 1.14)

In the young Christian community, Mary's presence is especially mentioned. She would doubtless have been a key personality in this group as the one closest to Jesus.

In the Acts of the Apostles we see how much the life of this community was characterized by persecution. They were opposed as they contested the false values of society and religion. Acts mentions how they were arrested (Acts 4.3), and when they were freed: 'they went back to their friends and told them everything that the chief priests and elders had said' (Acts 4.23).

Stephen, before he was stoned to death, related at length the story of the Exodus – the liberation of the people by God through Moses. Stephen announced how God was concerned about the oppression of the Jews in Egypt, and how God heard their groans and sent Moses to rescue them (Acts 7.34). Stephen drew a connection between the liberation from Egypt and his own situation. The Jewish leaders had killed or persecuted all their prophets (Acts 7.52).

Acts records violent persecution and plots against the lives of the apostles (Acts 9.23). Herod beheaded James (Acts 12.2). The early Church had to face many difficulties. The apostles were suspected, threatened and persecuted. The women were with them, supporting them in word and prayer and perhaps also helping them to hide (Acts 12.12).

It is possible to imagine Mary, the mother of Jesus, as a bedrock of strength and understanding. In times of trouble and oppression, men get into trouble. They even take up arms, though not in this case. Many women remain steadfast at the side of those in trouble. We know this from modern experiences of oppression and peaceful resistance.

Property in common

This group of Jesus' followers was one in which everything was held in common. If the words were not so often used pejoratively we might call it a sort of 'socialistic' or 'communistic' society. They shared their goods.

> The whole group of believers was united, heart and soul; no one claimed for his own use anything that he had, as everything they owned was held in common. The apostles continued to testify to the resurrection of the Lord Jesus with great power, and they were all given great respect. None of their members was ever in want, as all those who owned land or houses would sell them, and bring the money from them, to present it to the apostles; it was then distributed to any member who might be in need. (Acts 4.32–35)

Mary appreciated this approach to economic and social life. She would have been a principal participant in it, for this is how the earliest disciples of Jesus understood his message and lifestyle. A theology of Mary has, therefore, to be developed in terms of liberated interpersonal relations, a community which shares its goods, and a spiritual teaching of interiority, sincerity and social justice.

We can think of the group made up of Mary, Joseph, Jesus, John the Baptist, the brothers of Jesus, the sons of Zebedee, the women, Mary of Magdala, the mother of the sons of Zebedee, Mary of Cleopas, Peter, John and Andrew as part of a small community that had been evolving over a period of time. In a society in which hierarchy and patriarchy were normal, a new type of community evolved based more on sharing, partnership and bearing witness to a liberating message.

Mary was very much, perhaps, the mother in this situation. She would have been keeping the group together. In Jesus' lifetime, her home would have been a place where many discussions took place. They would have gathered together to mourn the death of John the Baptist, who would have been very close to the family.

We can think of this community as a group that was bonded together in struggle, in arrests, in persecution, in death and in joy. It was a new community which was also attractive. In it there was a dignity for people. It was not money-seeking or power-hungry. It did not accept the inequalities of the day. It was a counter-culture to Jewish and Roman societies. We can imagine the sort of relationships and understanding that would have existed in the community. Mary, the mother of Jesus, would have had a close relationship with Mary of Magdala who had been attached to Jesus in life and beyond death.

The roles of women and men in the Church today could be studied in relation to what they seem to have been in the life of Jesus and in the early community. Women had a very important and primary role in that society. It was not hierarchy that constituted it. Participating in communicating a message, and building new communities of faith and life, in self-sacrifice, were the principal tasks of the early disciples.

Models of Mary

Contemporary theology sees, better than that of previous generations, that there are numerous ways of understanding God and human destiny. Within Christianity we discern different models of Christ, as well as of the Church. The Church of the first disciples, the persecuted Church of the first three centuries, the Church reconciled to the Roman Empire, the Church of feudal Europe, of capitalism and European imperialism, of the years following World War II – each has had its concept of Jesus Christ, of his role and identity.

Likewise, we can see different understandings of Mary through the ages, and even in the four Gospels there are different accents. As Raymond E. Brown remarks, since there are many fewer historical data concerning the life and personality of Mary than even of Jesus,

> She lends herself more freely than Jesus does to a symbolic trajectory
> . . .
>
> In later ages the Church constantly turned to Mary to meet the ever-changing aspects of Christian discipleship, translated into terms of virtue and piety. In the Constantinian period, when the threat of martyrdom had passed and the ideal of carrying one's cross was beginning to find expression in asceticism, Mary became the model of women who were withdrawing into the Egyptian desert to lead a cenobitic life. Both Athanasius and a Coptic document that appears in the proverbs of the Council of Nicaea[4] describe Mary as a perfect Egyptian nun who ate and slept only when her body demanded it, modulated her voice, shut her eyes when dressing and undressing, avoided her relatives and even other women who spoke of the things of this world, and who made progress every day.
>
> In the Middle Ages Mary became the fair lady of the knights, 'Our Lady', the symbol of chaste love. In the Renaissance she became the tender mother caring for her spiritual children.
>
> In this century she was exalted as part of the Holy Family, that model family of Nazareth which was the Church's rebuttal to divorce and lax morals. And most recently she has been hailed by the American Bishops as the model of the liberated woman. One cannot historicize all these diverse and even contrary pictures of Mary; but in having her assume these symbolic roles, the Church has been contemporizing the ideal of Christian discipleship. The Church has been diagnosing a way in which Christians of various times needed to hear the word of God and keep it. As Pannenberg says, 'It is quite understandable why the Church saw itself and its faith-relationship to God and to Christ expressed in Mary rather than in some other figure'.[5]

To this list I might add the models of Mary presented by feminist theologians, especially those of North America, and the Latin American liberation theologies of the 1970s and 1980s.

Elizabeth A. Johnson, of the Catholic University of America, has made an interesting hypothesis that Mary's image has been developed historically as a female representation of the divine, precisely because the 'feminine' has been excluded from the mainstream Christian perception of God as Father, Son and Spirit. The patriarchal bias of Christian theology has made God more a powerful creator, and a just judge, than a loving, caring, tender, nurturing being. God has been made, theologically speaking, according to the image of man, and a patriarchal concept of maleness as tough, aggressive and dominant, and thus the so-called 'feminine' dimensions of warmth, concern and love have been diminished.

Corresponding to this figure of the male God, there has been an interpretation of Jesus, also, as a male who could not bring an element of maternal affection to the Christian understanding of the divine, even though he called God 'Abba', 'Father', and spoke of being like a mother caring for her little ones.

Human beings, however, have a need of the loving care associated with a nurturing mother. The 'womb love' of a mother is missing from most theological presentations of God, especially because of dualistic understandings of matter and spirit, human and divine, natural and supernatural, which are still prevalent.

Within this framework, popular religion, and even theology, has given to Mary a quasi-divine position.

> Female images of God, arguably necessary for the full expression of the mystery of God, but suppressed from official formulations, have migrated to the figure of this woman. Mary has been an icon of God. For innumerable believers she has functioned to reveal divine love as merciful, close, interested, always ready to hear and respond to human needs, trustworthy, and profoundly attractive, and has done so to a degree not possible when one thinks of God simply as a ruling male person or persons.[6]

Elizabeth Johnson shows how Mariology over the centuries has developed this aspect of Mary, and how it was an 'excellent missionary strategy in a world where female duties were so highly honored'.[7] From this perspective she surveys ten representative positions of well-known theologians, including Jean Daniélou, Edward Schillebeeckx, Yves Congar, René Laurentin, Elisabeth Schüssler Fiorenza, Virgil Elizondo and Leonardo Boff.

Leonardo Boff develops a concept of a closer relationship between Mary and the divinity. Boff puts forward the hypothesis that 'the Holy Spirit had made her his temple, sanctuary and tabernacle in so real and genuine way that she can be regarded as hypostatically united to the Third Person of the Blessed Trinity'. He compares this to the assumption of the human nature of Jesus by the second person of the Trinity, the Logos.[8] Boff's hypothesis reveals another way in which theological imagination may be developed, within the construct of a general Western Christian theology of the relationship of God and humanity.

As Elizabeth Johnson suggests, such an exaltation of Mary can indicate a dimension missing from the doctrine of God in traditional Catholic theology, something which has been heavily conditioned by patriarchal thinking. The human qualities of tenderness and mercy which are often called 'feminine' should also help enrich our concept of the divine.

We must be careful, however, not to make Mary into an image of the ideal 'feminine' which might exclude the qualities of courage, energy and creativity required for the programme articulated in the Magnificat, of social transformation. The division of 'masculine' and 'feminine', and attributing male qualities to God and the 'feminine' to Mary, is bad both for the divinity and for Mary. A more holistic approach is required with regard both to God and to Mary.

I would also ask whether this way of interpreting God is not linked to the interpretation of the human predicament described in Genesis and God's supposed judgement on humanity. If the 'feminine' bowels of mercy or 'womb love' were also seen in God, she would not conceivably have condemned all humankind to being deprived of the goal for which it is created. Thus, the original sin of Western Christian theology is seen to have repercussions even for this issue. Latin American liberation theologians, like Leonardo Boff, operate within the framework of the hypothesis of the fall of humanity. But those of us from a multi-faith context have to question more deeply in order to purify the very idea of the human–divine relationship in this hypothesis.

The other Asian religions, like Hinduism and Buddhism, do not have a concept of the eternal damnation of any human person. In this, do they not incorporate better the different dimensions of the Absolute, as in the Trimurthi of Hinduism? The three faces of God are portrayed as creative, destructive, and reconciling and loving: the last being indicated by a feminine face.

Mary and the liberation of women

A message is coming from women's movements throughout the world, that in modern society, too, women need liberation to be their true selves and to develop as fully realized human beings. This accords with my experience when I see so much goodness and potential suppressed and repressed in most societies.[9]

I have described in the preceding chapters how a traditional Marian devotion, and Marian theology, have been associated with, and partly responsible for, the oppression of women. The image of Mary was made to fit into the stereotype of the dominated, patient woman, and this Marian model itself fostered a concept of holiness linked to the subordination of women to men, and of the poor and weak to the wealthy and strong.

Nonetheless, the current development of Mariology throughout the world is contributing to the liberation of women. Feminist theologians, some of whom have been referred to already, have helped immensely in this process. They are pointing out the silence and neglect concerning women in the Bible and in tradition.[10] Some have shown Mary participating as an equal person in the life and work of Jesus. Others have contributed by the critique of traditional interpretations of Genesis and the concept of original sin.[11] Still others have interpreted Mary's privileges as indicating a woman's autonomy and independence of men, or, even, God's dependence on a woman's consent for realizing the divine plan for humanity.[12]

Latin American liberation theologians have contributed to this discussion through their overall approach to theology, including the use of social analysis and the rereading of the scriptures from the point of view of the weak and the oppressed. Their re-thinking of Christology and the accent on a bottom-up Christology has a corresponding and salutary impact on Mariology, since the two are so closely linked together.

Ivone Gebara and Maria Clara Bingemar's *Mary, Mother of God, Mother of the Poor*[13] makes use of a new hermeneutical perspective, through which the authors suggest a Marian theology built upon the people's actual experience. They lead us to grasp God's revelation in woman. In the midst of people trying to establish the justice of the Kingdom, the figure of Mary arises, heir to the hopes of the poor and at the same time giving new impulse to those hopes.

I attempt in this book to offer a reflection from a Third World situation in which, in addition to poverty, women's exploitation and social injustice, there is also a plurality of religions and cultures, and a considerable degree of secularity. Hence I have had to approach the issues of Mariology with a critique of theology that has further implications for Christianity as a whole.

I am presenting a Mariology in which the human Mary is seen as participating in the mission of Jesus, a mission characterized by openness to all humanity. I am, therefore, proposing a more open Mariology, related to a more open Christology, required and inspired by a Sri Lankan context.

Within this approach I include women's struggle for full humanity. This is particularly necessary in Asian countries where women are the new proletariat of the socio-economic system that is being foisted on our peoples.

Reflection on the liberative message of Jesus, and the participation of Mary and other women in it, can be an inspiration for the liberation of women, particularly in developing women's consciousness of their rights and dignity. Understanding Mary's role and identity in a more human manner can motivate all the disciples of Jesus to join in the struggle necessary for the realization of women's rights in a world-system in which they are exploited for profit, pleasure and power.

Women and priesthood

One of the important areas in which the rights of women need to be realized is within religions themselves. There has been a general tendency for men to control power within religions, not least by restricting clerical status to men. Christianity is a principal example of a religion in which women were refused priestly ordination. The Catholic Church is, in this respect, perhaps one of the main bulwarks of male domination, and one which uses theology as the basis of this domination.

Since women are banned from the priesthood, and since power in the Church is controlled by the clergy, women tend to remain under-developed in the Church. They have less access than men to theological education, administration of the sacraments, decision-making on matters of doctrine and morals, and less access to financial resources and the freedom that flows from these powers. Women have an uphill task in asserting and obtaining their rights in the Church.

The right of women to priestly ordination is one of the main issues concerning women's rights in the Christian Churches. Some denominations have already ordained women as priests. A woman, Barbara Harris, was consecrated bishop in the Episcopal Church of the United States. This has been a considerable challenge to the Churches since Barbara Harris is a black woman, who has also been divorced.

The Catholic Church still does not accept the priestly ordination of women. Discussions on this issue relate to particular understandings of priesthood. It is difficult to demonstrate that Jesus Christ established a male priesthood like that currently in the Church. However, Jesus did set up a community of disciples who were to continue his message and ministry. In so far as the priesthood implies leadership in the community, we have to ask what are the goals and means used by that community. The Jesus community was to be one of love and service, of self-giving and self-sacrifice even unto death.

In such self-giving, women shared fully in the mission of Jesus. Mary, as I have already indicated, was the one who was closest to Jesus from before his birth until after his death. She was found worthy to bear Jesus in her womb and she offered her son on the cross. Would she not have been worthy to fulfil the functions of Christian priesthood, such as presiding at the Eucharist, and sharing in teaching the doctrine of Jesus, and the administration of the community? If she was worthy of Bethlehem, Jerusalem, Cana and Calvary, was she not worthy to preside over the breaking of bread and the sharing of goods? A well-developed Mariology can be one of the best supports for the cause of the equality of women and men in the Church at all levels, including the priesthood.

In any community or organization some leadership is necessary. In the spirit of Jesus that leadership has to be one of service, as indicated in Mark 10.42–45. Jesus said 'follow me', 'take up your cross and follow me'. This service is a human service. It is not a biological service in which gender is important. In the community of Jesus, women had significant roles, as I have indicated earlier. There is no reason why women cannot fulfil a role of leadership in the Church. Many of the limitations placed on women in the Church are linked to the interpretation of particular texts by patriarchy and in a Christian community influenced by patriarchy, in which men had leadership.

To resolve this issue it would be necessary to ask questions about the origins of priesthood in the Christian Church, and about the place of Bishops and of the papacy. But, in the early community of Jesus, if there was anyone who was close, intimate, participating and sacrificing with Jesus, it was Mary. This was not only as a mother before birth and in his lifetime, but also after his death. Those who know of liberation struggles know how much women can be part of these struggles. They can sustain commitment even when some are killed in the process. Among those Mary knew well, John the Baptist was beheaded, Jesus was crucified, Stephen was stoned to death, and later the other disciples were killed. Mary, as long as she lived, would have been one who was central to, and steadying of, the group.

If the Church is to be the continuation of this community of Jesus, I do not see why women cannot offer the sacrifice and announce the message of Jesus. I put forward my view in Sheffield, in the United Kingdom, in 1981 at the World Council of Churches' consultation on 'The Community of Women and Men in the Church' thus:

> There is no reason: biological, psychological, pastoral, theological or spiritual, why we cannot have a yellow, brown, black or white woman Pope.

The papacy is a function in which gender is not significant. The functions of the Pope are similar to those of a head of state or of a spiritual community. Many women have been great spiritual leaders throughout history. In the Catholic Church, several women have been founders, and inspiring administrators, of religious orders.

Priesthood is a spiritual function and not a biological one. But, in a society in which power has been exercised by men, and the texts of the

scriptures have been written and are interpreted by men, such discrimination against women is not surprising. With regard to the papacy, the
very election process is one in which only elderly men can vote, so it is
understandable that only men became Popes. By a similar process of the
selection of Cardinals, we have had Italian Popes for many centuries.
We should not be so naive as to attribute divine origin to an ecclesiastical practice which can be explained in this way.

Since women participated fully in the Jesus community, there is no
reason why they cannot share in leadership patterns, including the
priesthood. Current theological stances against the ordination of
women are partly due to a top-down theology. The argument is: Jesus
is male, therefore only men can represent the divine principle in the
Church.

But the world is growing up, and the women are growing in consciousness. The experience of women is important and should not be
neglected or regarded as nonsense, as the women's experience of the
risen Christ was described by the apostles. We men should be careful
not to be incredulous, dull or obstinate in relation to the competence of
women to serve the Christian Churches (Mark 16.11–14; Luke 24.11).

What we need is a new understanding of the Church as a community
of women and men, based on partnership, mutuality and reciprocity. In
it, it is not the body or gender that is important, but the human person.
Functions in the Church have to be allocated according to competence,
talent and calling.

The US Catholic Bishops are preparing a pastoral letter in which they
say that sexism is a sin, and that anyone who wants to be a priest should
be free of sexism, that is, they should not consider women to be inferior
to men. This represents a considerable change in the Church. The US
Bishops are in dialogue both with their women's movements and with
the Pope. Time will settle this issue.

Mary and social liberation

Mary supported Jesus in opting for the poor. The Church today is
coming to share this position. Pope John Paul II in his recent encyclical
Social Concern of the Church, emphasizes this option. Mary recognized it
in her life – not least at the birth of Jesus, when she was rejected by the
people of Bethlehem because she was poor.

Neither Mary nor Jesus would have been naive about the need for
social change, as evidenced by the parable of Dives and Lazarus. How
difficult it was for Dives to change, as it was for the rich young man
called to follow Jesus. Mary can be an inspiration for the social struggles
of our times. She can understand the desire for a society that is not based

on class distinctions. She has had experience of property held in common. In this she shares in the prophetic background of the Jewish people. It was also Mary's experience in the early Christian community. Her own house would have been the place where Jesus began such a practice.

The teaching of Jesus is radical in this respect, and Mary would have understood it better than anyone because of her own poverty and experience of oppression by the powerful. Christianity, an underground movement, was a radical social force for nearly three centuries, till it became part of the dominant social system at the conversion of Constantine. Thereafter, theology was diluted and the cutting edge of the gospel was blunted.

Mary and political liberation

Mary would have been conscious of the significance of political factors and their implications for the life of her people. She had to attend for the census, because of the decree issued by the Emperor Augustus. The killing of the innocent children was because of Herod's fear that a political Messiah was born, not because of the birth of a divine child. After the nocturnal flight into Egypt, Mary had to be sensitive to the political events in her country. It was only when Herod was dead that she could return home. When in exile, her political sensitivity and sense of political injustice would have been sharpened.

The family returned to Israel: 'hearing, however, that Archelaus had succeeded his father Herod as King of Judaea, he [Joseph] was afraid to go there. And being warned by a dream, he withdrew to the region of Galilee; there he settled in a town called Nazareth' (Matt 2.22–23). Mary would naturally have been involved in this choice. Thus her domicile once again was decided by political factors. That is how the holy family came to live in Nazareth. The infancy narratives, whatever their historicity, communicate a powerful message concerning the effects of politics on the life of the holy family.

Mary saw how John the Baptist grew up to be a young man of radical opinion. The two families of Mary and Elizabeth and their relatives and friends would have had long discussions about the sad condition of their people. They would have been concerned about the different political opinions of Jews who collaborated with the Romans, and of others, like the Zealots, who wanted to fight them. Both John the Baptist and Jesus promoted non-violent approaches.

John preached a radical message through a radical lifestyle, with deep social and political consequences:

'Whoever has two shirts must give one to the man who has none, and whoever has food must share it.' (Luke 3.11)

To the soldiers who asked him 'what are we to do?' John counselled:

> 'Don't take money from anyone by force or accuse anyone falsely. Be
> content with your pay.' (Luke 3.14)

Luke comments that the crowds followed him as he preached a radical
message.

> People's hopes began to rise, and they began to wonder whether John
> might be the Messiah. (Luke 3.15; Matt 3.1; Mark 1.1–8; John 1.19–28)

John referred his disciples and other enquirers, such as the Jewish
authorities in Jerusalem and the Levites (John 1.19), to the one who was
to follow him, whose sandals he was not good enough to untie. Mary
would have known the close connection between John and Jesus, and
the socio-political implications of John's message. John and Jesus had
different lifestyles and approaches, but substantially the same message
of socio-economic-political liberation, accompanied by a powerful critique of the dominant political leaders.

Mary would have been deeply distressed at the arrest of John the
Baptist, something which would have been a traumatic experience for
Jesus and Mary. Matthew writes:

> When he heard that John had been arrested, Jesus withdrew to Galilee;
> and leaving Nazareth he went and settled at Capernaum on the sea of
> Galilee in the district of Zebulun and Napthali. (Matt 4.12–13)

Jesus had to withdraw because he was closely associated with John
who had rebuked Prince Herod,

> over the affairs of his brother's wife Herodias and his other misdeeds.
> (Luke 3.19)

It was after the arrest of John that 'Jesus came into Galilee proclaiming the gospel of God'. His cousin was arrested and beheaded, and so
Jesus decided to come out into the open in Galilee. This would have
been an important and difficult decision for both Jesus and Mary. Jesus
would have known that he was courting trouble. It is said that soon
after this the

> Pharisees began plotting against him with the partisans of Herod to see
> how they could make away with him. (Mark 3.6)

Mary would also have been very conscious of the political dangers
Jesus was facing. She would have been concerned about some of the
options the Jewish people were considering, taking up arms like the
Zealots. She would have understood Jesus' option, but also known that

some Zealots were among his entourage. All this is evidence that Mary would have been deeply involved in the political troubles of the time. Her son, her nephew, her cousins and the sons of her friends were all involved in trying to decide the fate of her people. Mary was not a person who lived a secluded life, away from the troubled area of politics. Her family was in the thick of it, and it is from within such a context that Jesus made his choices and preached his message.

Difficulties for Jesus arose from a combination of the socio-economic and religio-political forces in that situation, for the support that the religious leaders gave to the imperial rulers meant there was an intimate link between the religious and the political systems. A critique of the superficial religiosity of the day meant also an attack on their allies – the political powers.

Mary witnessed how Jesus was captured and killed by a combination of the religious, political and military powers. The burial of Jesus and the guard set at his tomb involved the political authorities. Thereafter, the life of the early Christian community was closely bound up with the attitudes of the political rulers wherever they went.

Mary knew the teaching of Jesus concerning political power, and its legitimacy only as service to the people. She saw the cruel abuse of power affecting her people and her own family. She was, therefore, not indifferent to politics. She was deeply involved in it, as Jesus was, in a liberative and fundamentally non-violent manner.

Marian spirituality can and should carry a liberating message into the political arena, something which is especially required in today's world, where the conditions of exploitation and domination are similar to those of Jesus' time.

Mary and the liberation of men

When Mary is interpreted in order to promote the domestication of women, this interpretation has, also, a corresponding impact in making men less fulfilled in their genuine humanity. The liberation and self-realization of women and men are interrelated and interdependent. Thus, traditional Mariology has had an unfortunate impact on men as well as women, in encouraging men to be more dominant.

A reaffirmation of the strong and mature personality and message of Mary can have the impact of humanizing men also. It can help them to understand the capabilities of women, and to be more truly themselves by developing their potentialities as mature adult people. A transformed imaging of Mary can inspire men to help draw out the best in women. Both women and men can then regard themselves as positive co-creators of each other and of the society in which they live.

Women who are motivated to follow the Mary of the Magnificat can help men also to be more committed to the overall transformation required by that ideal. Then women and men can together contest the evils of the dominant trends in our society, which enthrone selfishness and self-seeking. They can co-operate in overcoming the deadly sins which beset our civilization – pride, covetousness, lust, gluttony, envy, anger, sloth – or, in the Hindu–Buddhist way of expressing it, *loba, moha, dwesha, thanha*.

In a more particular sense, it may be said that the liberation of men lies in being freed from these deadly sins in relation to women. Men need to free themselves from attempting to dominate, to cure themselves of pride in the superiority of masculinity. It also requires an acknowledgement of the equality of the sexes and of their mutuality and partnership in the common enterprises of life. The Marian proclamation that God will put down the proud in their conceit is applicable to contemporary men in many of our social and interpersonal situations. We need to focus instead on the relationship of Jesus and Mary, and of Jesus with other women, which modelled a sense of equality, respect and understanding.

In order to achieve this, the virtues of humility and service must be sought by both men and women. Service must be mutual, and not interpreted as if it were only women who serve, while men are to be the beneficiaries.

We can reflect, likewise, on each of the deadly sins and the corresponding values of the reign of God – love, truth, freedom, justice, equality and peace. These are all applicable to both men and women. The liberation of men, as males, lies in eschewing vices and being inspired by the virtues in their attitudes towards women. Seeing Mary as a strong, adult woman associated with Jesus can be a motivation for men to acquire the virtue of respecting all women as equal with men in dignity and rights as human beings.

Mary of the Third World

In most of Asia and Africa today we need a model of Mary that also relates to our presently exploited, neo-colonized, Third World context. Our local rulers, authoritarian if not despotic, are often the Pilates and Herods of modern multinational empires.

Perhaps the historical Mary of Nazareth may be closer to this reality than many other models of Mary which were often explicitly or implicitly utilized for patriarchy, hierarchy and domination. The contribution of feminist theology to Mariology can be of universal value in so far as sexism is a universal phenomenon. Feminism has, however, to consider the other forms of domination, just as Third World theology, in general, has to consider male domination within the Third World context, also.

The Marian spirituality I am proposing would be deeply, and desperately, concerned with the present situation in the world where the condition of the poorest of the poor is worsening in both relative and absolute terms. Mary, as the mother of Jesus, and a universal mother of all humanity, would be concerned most with those who suffer so much physically and psychologically.

A Marian approach to the Third World would be inspired by the perceptions and practical responses implied in the Magnificat, of feeding the hungry and exalting the humble. Marian devotion and Marian shrines throughout the world might, thus, be invited to look at the present international situation, to understand the causes of the growing gap between the affluent and the poor, and to take steps to remedy the situation.

The military expenditure of Third World countries has increased fivefold between 1960 and 1986. Arms imports have grown from 1 billion to 30 billion dollars. It will be clear that while arms exports are mainly from rich countries, the arms imports and use are mainly in poorer countries. Much of the foreign aid received by poor countries goes back to the arms exporters of the rich countries. Thus foreign debt is directly related to the arms industry and consequent deaths in the Third World.

Since 1945, the poor countries of the world have been the arena of 124 wars. Although these wars were in the Third World, intervention by major military powers was frequent, and often covert.

War deaths were heavily weighted towards Asia, and the Far East in particular. Asia contains 55 per cent of the world population but has suffered 70 per cent of war deaths. In Asia the civilian death total has risen from half the world's deaths in the 1950s to three-quarters of total deaths in the 1980s.

Deaths in war represent only a fraction of human loss. Those seriously injured, and the loss to property, incomes, production and natural resources, increase the burden of war significantly.

A Marian spirituality influenced by the Magnificat would reflect seriously on this situation of so much human misery. Unfortunately, many devotees of Mary reflect little on the causes of conflicts, both local and international. Not a few of them are producers of, and traders in, weapons of destruction.

The effects of war on the Third World have to be considered in relation to the rest of an international economic system that is also exploitative of poor people and poor countries.[14] The Third World

might even be called, as Susan George suggests 'dominated countries'.[15]
    Alongside the cost of the arms race:

- 500,000 mothers die in childbirth,
- 600,000,000 women of child-bearing years suffer from nutritional anaemia;
- 2,900,000,000 people lack the simple sanitary facilities essential to health;
- 525,000 people annually have been killed and 1,200,000 have been injured on average in wars since 1945;
- 3,500,000 children die annually of dehydration, something easily and cheaply preventable;
- 4,000,000 children die annually of six diseases preventable cheaply by immunization.

This is an appalling social balance sheet. Yet it does not include the record of suffering because of other causes, such as the destruction of nature and the pollution of the environment.
    International poverty could be eradicated in a short time if the human community had the will to do so. If Marian spirituality led to such a commitment to change, it would have an immense impact on the world, since many dominant powers are countries containing many people who are devotees of Mary.
    In Asia and Africa we need to develop a Mariology that, while incorporating the best of other theologies, is also concerned with issues such as challenging the local élites and the marginalization of the masses. This would mean looking at: patterns of development, especially their impact on women, debt, human life, torture, human rights; economic, political, social, cultural and religious domination and liberation; and IMF/World Bank policies of structural adjustment. Asia can particularly contribute to developing a Mariology that is global and relates to the planetary theologies which are emerging.

Mary and world justice and peace

The planetary dimension of a Marian spirituality suitable for today might take into account the fact that traditionally Mary is regarded as queen of the world, queen of humanity, mother of all humankind. These are appellations given to her by the institutional Church and the popular Church and they have relevance to the one-world situation of today.
    Marian spirituality which takes seriously the Magnificat must involve an approach which declares that the goods of the earth are for

everyone. The primitive communism of the early Christian community must be reconsidered in our situation and times. The goods of the earth are not for the particular nations that possess them at present. They are not merely for big transnational companies which can dominate and exploit peoples. The mere accumulation of capital should not ensure the right to buy more and more lands and assets and exploit them for maximum profit. On the contrary, the challenge of the Magnificat is to bring about changes in the political and economic order that would see to it 'that there is no one in need' and that, in a meaningful sense, 'everything is held in common' (Acts 4.32–35).

When Pope John Paul II visited Bolivia, he drew attention to the great poverty and inequality there – one-quarter of the children die of malnutrition. Our world is one in which many die of hunger while there are vast accumulations of resources among others. There is enough food for all. The mountains of butter in the affluent countries must be redistributed to those in need. Methods must be found to enable this to happen. The unjust world system leads to the deaths of millions of innocent children each year. These deaths echo the killing of the male children of the Jews by Pharaoh, and the massacre of the innocents by Herod. Fear of the populations of Asia and Africa leads White 'Christian' nations to promote family planning, including sterilization and abortion, instead of sharing food and resources.

Technologies must be developed which provide meaningful employment for all. If there is involuntary unemployment, worthwhile avenues should be provided for fulfilling leisure. These technologies, the availability of goods, and of leisure, and human freedom for everyone, is a demand which is at the heart of all world religions also.

The big companies which dominate the world economy today are a means by which the principalities and powers are profit-centred and mammonic. They own the power of decision-making and of influencing people's views and values. They control much of the information media. They influence the values of women in a manner quite different from a Marian spirituality, presenting women as consumers and as objects for pleasure and sex.

Arms production, the arms trade, and the militarization especially of poor countries, perpetuate wars in the Third World. It is important to remember that the existence of nuclear weapons, as well as the production of conventional arms, helps create wars in poor countries. At present, both the rich capitalist and the rich socialist countries are involved in promoting wars. They both benefit from arms sales and may even hope to have a political advantage from the further weakening of Third World countries. At present much of the arms production is based in Europe and North America, while the wars are fought in the poor countries of the South and the East. Through the sale of arms the powerful of the world help aggravate local conflicts everywhere. This in turn can keep Third World countries locked in internal conflict, and weak.

Another important focus for international relations is in the realm of finance. The indebtedness of poor countries is growing, and becoming an unbearable burden. These structures of debt are in marked contrast to the way of life of Mary and the early Church, where 'they held everything in common'. Within the Torah it was asserted that debts were to be cancelled and lands restored to their owners every few decades in special years of Jubilee.

Drought, famine, hunger, malnutrition, unemployment and political repression in poor countries are related to the excess of food in the rich countries. Unfair terms of trade make the situation worse for the poor and the weak.

The values of Jesus and Mary, of peace and justice, should be applied to international relations also. Marian theology and spirituality can contribute to the promotion of these values. In so far as she is considered the Mother of Humanity and the New Eve, it is possible to regard Mary as one who is concerned with the care of nature, the preservation of the environment and the building of a suitable home on earth for all humanity. The movements for the care of the earth and of the environment can gain inspiration from Mary as one whose Magnificat suggests the resources of the world should be for all.

Mary's words in Cana in Galilee, 'They have no wine', and 'do whatever he tells you' (John 2.2–5), can be applied to international relations when people have no food and no drinking water. The sensitive Mary would notice this and ask us to do whatever 'he tells you'. The path presented by Jesus is a way to resolve the great inequalities in the world. It is the way of unselfishness and sharing, which is also the message of all the world religions.

Mary's Magnificat (Luke 1.46–56)

The Magnificat of Mary expresses beautifully and powerfully the integral liberation for which Jesus and Mary stood. The song of Mary bears a strong resemblance to the canticle of Hannah in 1 Samuel 2.1–10. In the Magnificat, Luke brings out Mary's great faith and lowly dependence on the merciful God. Her lowliness has been turned into fruitfulness and because of this all human beings can have hope.

God appears in the Magnificat as the mighty one, and divine power is exercised primarily in caring for the needy. God's holiness is shown in mercy and in 'stretching out his mighty arm'. The fulfilment of God's promise is in coming to the help of the needy and the oppressed.

Mary speaks of a threefold revolution that is brought about by God – a cultural, political and economic revolution. Pope John Paul II also refers to this in his recent encyclical on Mary.

'He has shown strength in his arm and scattered the proud-hearted.' This statement of revolution is of a cultural nature. The arrogant of heart and mind are put to rout. 'The mercy of God is from age to age to those who fear him.' Mary's words are powerful here. They are even more expressive than most of the teaching of Jesus. Significant aspects of our cultural values, our educational system and our media of communication are debased through making people proud, greedy or vain. A transformation is needed in our media.

It is a challenge to the disciples of Jesus to develop the means of an alternative culture that places a value on the human person and human dignity. It requires us to combat all forms of cultural domination and discrimination, and to work against racism, sexism, casteism, classism and religionism. The call is for humility and respect, for the equality and dignity of all to be made the principles on which public policies are decided at local, national and international levels.

'And cast down the mighty from their thrones.' The politically mighty, those who are dominating their countries and the world system, will be put down. By contrast, humble people will be lifted up. They will possess the land meant for them. This is the language of the liberation of all the oppressed – those oppressed because of gender, race, class, and the economic inequalities of the world. It is the language of a Marian spirituality with an incisive cutting edge and challenge.

Mary's declaration that 'God will fill the hungry with good things and send the rich empty away' indicates that there is an economic aspect to the radical changes envisaged in her prophecy.

This transformation is the *leitmotif* of the scriptures, and places Mary in the prophetic tradition of Judaeo-Christianity.

Mary's Magnificat also gives a distinct social content to holiness. The promise of God is to come to the help of the needy – 'to Abraham and all his descendants for ever'.

In traditional theology, both the understanding of God and the presentation of Mary did not adequately indicate the thoroughly radical nature of the divine intervention in human history. Holiness has to do with a total transformation of society in order to accord with the divine plan. The Magnificat points to an inspiring combination of faith in God, and humility, with a radical commitment to total revolution.

Marian spirituality

Marian spirituality should, therefore, inspire the disciples of Jesus to bring about such changes. An analysis at national and international levels would be required for this to happen. Social analysis, and an understanding of the deeper causes of human power and pride, must go hand in hand with commitment to change for the benefit of the needy.

In countries like Sri Lanka, the Marian shrines could be a focus to communicate a radical message for the realization of the people's aspirations for a meaningful life. The shrines must come to communicate clearly an understanding of the social forces operating in the country, if the message of the Magnificat is to be realized in our time.

Marian spirituality should endeavour to bring about new inter-personal relations in which people are respected for themselves, implying a respect for the human body and sexuality. Woman is not to be discriminated against. There should be a partnership of women and men in the family, in society and in the Church.

Jesus and Mary refuse to discriminate on any grounds, including class, ethnicity or race. Marian spirituality should inspire us to work towards a new society, and a new world order, that would embody the values of Jesus and Mary, values which, in fact, are also the values of the other world religions.

A renewed Church must face the challenge of developing such a spirituality. The Church is called to be a spiritual community derived from Jesus. The Churches can be a blessing to humanity if we are not exclusive, narrow-minded, ghetto-like, spiritually proud and exploitative; if we do not claim control over God and over the treasuries of grace. To be such a blessing the Churches should be free of sexism, including the belief that men have special privileges, such as a power of forgiving sins, which women do not have. Christianity itself has to be transformed so that it comes to acknowledge that God can speak through different texts, leaders, organizations and languages.

Strategies for transformation

In order that the Churches are able to come together to build this new society of equality and plurality, we have to think strategically.

Popular religious expression, which is so important in the Churches, needs to be developed in such a way that Mary is understood as the woman and mother who was alongside Jesus in evolving and promoting his message and community of integral human liberation. It was a community of partnership, honesty and authenticity, and one which contested all that was wrong and unjust.

The realization of this community is possible, in so far as people's movements emerge in our countries to struggle for their real needs and rights. These movements can see Mary as a woman in the struggle of her people for a new type of relationship, and a new understanding of spirituality. In this, she paid the price of sacrificing her son, Jesus.

The Marian shrines and places of apparitions can be induced to proclaim this message of an integral Marian spirituality. Marian hymns, prayers and litanies need to be rewritten to communicate the liberative message of Mary. Her images and paintings should bring out the strong, working-class character of Mary, who went through life sharing in the mission and struggle of Jesus.

This is the task before us, to help liberate Mary to be the woman she was and, in turn, women need to liberate themselves to be truly themselves and partners in building a new world. The experience women have of oppression and domination can help them to understand and empathize with what others are suffering, what workers and people of the Third World are suffering. Women of the First and Second Worlds can then understand more clearly the great burden placed, today, on Third World women especially in the Free Trade Zones, as migrant labour, in the tourist industry, in the plantations, factories and urban shanties. These women are a great mass of the much-exploited world proletariat in the present neo-colonial world economy. In response, strategies of analysis and action for change must be considered integral to our spirituality.

There is a need for women who are aware of their dignity and responsibility in the struggle to be connected with the other peoples of the world. We have seen this, to some extent, in the United States in women's protest against the US policies in Nicaragua. Likewise, women need to develop their own strategies for achieving an appropriate place and power in the Church. Such changes do not come about merely because of prayer or theology. Women must develop and use their women-power. The Churches depend on women. If for two weeks women did not contribute to Church funds unless women's rights were accepted, there would be an immediate impact on the power-holders. Or if women contributed instead to funds which supported women's emancipation – Mary's pence instead of Peter's pence – they could have more effective power as women-Church. These are non-violent methods that need to be developed.

Women-power, thus built up, needs to be linked across the world. If women all over the world had taken action against apartheid in South Africa, there would have been a change sooner. Women and men can join in such strategies.

The liberation of women, as I have suggested earlier, can also help in the true humanization of men to be themselves, understanding their humanity as partners in a common enterprise of building family and society.

The universality of the Church can be of great value and help to humanity, in so far as we are a community following the way of Jesus and Mary and of the New Testament. In the struggle for the new humanity, we can be one of the best-organized communities in the world. The authority of the Church can then be of real service to struggling peoples. To a certain extent the papacy is moving in that direction. We must encourage the Pope in this. Women can help to educate him and the Bishops when they tend, like the apostles, to be 'dull and obstinate'. This is a role which women performed from earliest times according to the New Testament!

There is thus a great task, opportunity and challenge for us all to participate in the building up of the new Christian community, in the service of a renewed human community inspired by Jesus, Mary and all the great spiritual leaders of humanity. Christians need to ally themselves with all people of good will and movements for desirable social change. Mary can inspire such alliances, since she is the mother of all humanity.

Mary, queen of martyrs

Following the way of Jesus and Mary led to the martyrdom of many in the first centuries of Christianity. Mary herself shared in the suffering, sorrow and sacrifice involved in the martyrdom of John the Baptist, Jesus, Stephen and perhaps some of the other disciples. Such deaths were due to the opposition of the powerful of the day to the message, and life, of these religious radicals who wanted a complete transformation of personal and societal relations.

In recent decades the martyrdom of Christians is once again becoming a common feature, when they opt for the liberation of their peoples. Such martyrdom is due to their opposition to the exploitative structures and relationships in their societies. The countries of the Third World are the principal areas of such martyrdom. This is because it is in Latin America, Asia and Africa that the repression of those who oppose the exploitation of the poor is the fiercest. For those in the Third World, Christian spirituality is, today, understanding that the call of discipleship is a call to follow the path of the cross, as Mary had to do in her life.

A conscious option for the values held by Jesus and Mary leads to various forms of marginalization in secular society, and not infrequently within the Church too. The forms of martyrdom vary according to the risks involved. The modern Church is being renewed by the suffering and death of many such martyrs.

An overall re-thinking

In this context we need a reconsideration of Mariology within an overall re-thinking of theological issues such as: what is human salvation; how is God related to humanity and salvation; how is salvation open to all; what is the relationship between the Creator and creation; who is Jesus; what is the meaning of redemption in Jesus; what is the nature and mission of the Church? It is within a framework which addresses these issues that we can place Mary's relationship with the human race, the Church and each of us, as well as with God.

The essential teaching of Jesus is that the love of God and of neighbour are one, and the fulfilment of the will of God. Truth, love, sharing, freedom, justice and peace are the core values of the Kingdom of God preached by Jesus. It is within such an understanding of Christology that we can understand Mary.

Historically, Mary's role developed within a perspective of divine–human relations, and of Christology, in which the Church controlled the sources of grace, and the clergy held the keys to the Kingdom of Heaven, within a male-dominated partriarchy. In that theology, the other world religions were marginalized. Within such a theology, Mary found her place as the woman who gave birth to Jesus, and both Mary and Jesus were used to ensure the continuation of the dominant social system.

Such an understanding of Mary is unacceptable. It is not in accordance with the Gospels. It militates against the aspirations of the majority of the human race for liberation and fulfilment. It is not acceptable to Protestantism and so cannot contribute to inter-Christian ecumenical relations. It is also unacceptable to women today, come of age and seeking their place of equality in dignity with men, in all spheres of life. This is not a Mary who can respond to a world seeking justice, and in which the vast majority of people are not Christians.

I am questioning the traditional dogmas as a whole construct, because piecemeal adjustments authorized by the Euro-American Church establishment, or its theologians, are inadequate. A more thorough re-thinking of Marian theology and spirituality is needed at the theoretical level, as well as in practical Christian living.

Just as Jesus has to be liberated, as Kim Chi Ha says in his play *The Gold Crowned Jesus*,[16] in order to respond to real life, so Mary needs to be liberated. She needs to be known for who she was and is. It is from such a perspective that we are called to understand her as a loving mother and sister of all, a woman among women, a human being among us, one who faced the difficulties of life united to Jesus for a better humanity. In understanding her in this way, we can contribute to the liberation of Mary to be herself, and encourage her devotees to be better disciples of Jesus and better human beings.

Notes

1 Albert Nolan, *Jesus Before Christianity* (Maryknoll, NY: Orbis, 1977).

2 Rosemary R. Ruether, *New Woman New Earth* (New York: Seabury, 1975), p. 59.

3 Tissa Balasuriya OMI, *Jesus Christ and Human Liberation*, Quest 48 (Colombo: CSR, 1976).

4 Hilda Graef, *Mary: A History of Doctrine and Devotion* (London: Sheed & Ward, 1963), pp. 50ff.

5 Raymond E. Brown, 'Understanding Mary' in *Biblical Reflections on Crises Facing the Church* (New York: Paulist Press, 1975), p. 107.

6 Elizabeth A. Johnson, 'Mary and the female face of God', *Theological Studies* 50 (1989), pp. 500–26.

7 Ibid., p. 507.

8 Leonardo Boff, 'The maternal face of God' in *The Feminine and its Religious Expressions* (San Francisco: Harper & Row, 1987), p. 93 – quoted by Elizabeth A. Johnson, op. cit., p. 515.

9 Tissa Balasuriya OMI, *Original Sin and the Christian Mission*, CRS Pamphlet 40 (Colombo: CSR, 1990).

10 Elisabeth Schüssler Fiorenza, *In Memory of Her: A Feminist Theological Reconstruction of Christian Origins* (New York: Crossroad, 1983).

11 Phyllis Trible, in her lectures at the Conference on 'Community of Women and Men in the Church', Sheffield, 1981.

12 Mary Daly, *Beyond God the Father: Towards a Philosophy of Women's Liberation* (Boston: Beacon, 1973), pp. 81–92.

13 Ivone Gebara and Maria Clara Bingemar, *Mary, Mother of God, Mother of the Poor* (Maryknoll, NY: Orbis, 1989).

14 Tissa Balasuriya OMI, *Planetary Theology* (New York: Orbis, 1984), chapter on world system, 'Foreign debt – is there a way out?' – cf. *Logos* (Oct.–Dec. 1989).

15 Susan George, *How the Other Half Dies: The Real Reasons for World Hunger* (London: Penguin, 1978), and *Ill Fares the Land* (London: Penguin, 1990).

16 Kim Chi Ha, *The Gold Crowned Jesus* (Maryknoll, NY: Orbis), p. 66.

6

❧❧❧❧❧

Presuppositions in theology

What are presuppositions?

In so far as religions present perspectives concerning other-worldly realities – such as life after death or the nature of the divine – accepting them belongs to the realm of faith. They propose beliefs which cannot be rationally or experimentally verified by human knowledge. The propositions of religions are accepted either because of the authority of a person in whom there is confidence and trust and/or as presuppositions that form the basis of the teaching of a religion. Presuppositions are accepted or assumed as true by a community or religious group even if they are not verifiable.

At the foundation of all the religions that propose meta-cosmic perspectives on human life there are some assumptions or presuppositions that are taken for granted. They cannot be demonstrated as necessarily true to human reason but are accepted in faith; they are, as it were, the implicit working hypotheses of the religions.

Explanations that religions give about birth, growth, health, sickness and cause of death can be verified. Sociological factors, such as the distribution of food, housing and employment; and psychological realities such as love and friendship, joy and sorrow, can be enquired into by these human disciplines. We can, also, have consciousness of right and wrong, of virtue and vice, of fulfillment and frustration, of acceptance and rejection, of power and powerlessness, of justice and injustice. Regarding these there may be, and there are, differences of opinion, but they are verifiable by human experimentation and reflection. The moral teachings of the religions are developed on the basis of such a consciousness among the people of a given community.

Presuppositions are generally not called into question within the group that accepts them, unless they are found to be disadvantageous to them. They are ingrained in the life of a people and become part of their cultural heritage. For centuries the Bible story of creation in six days was unquestioned by almost all Christian people until scientific data seemed to contradict it. People, generally, acquire a certain uncritical approach towards the presuppositions on which their religious and cultural life is based.

Presuppositions exist at different levels of the evolution of a religion or faith. They may concern the founder and his or her teachings, the texts which contain such teachings, or later elaborations by the religious community built up around the founder, and the original core message of the founder. These different levels of presupposition do not have a uniform claim to the loyalty of the followers of a religion. The core values, and foundational teachings, are generally derived from the religious experience of the founder. The later elaborations are influenced by the course of history and the particular evolution of a religious community. Even a founder's teachings are conditioned by the culture of that time, though generally they tend to be more universalistic, at least in their basic intuitions.

Evolution of theologies

Many elements contribute to the evolution of a theology. The vision of the founder is interpreted according to various factors, such as the culture of a people, the myths that give a people its identity, philosophies, popular religion and its cultic practices, group interests and ideologies, and other factors. Hence, it is necessary to try to understand the origin of the content of teachings that constitute a theology and the beliefs that form part of a religious faith. They do not necessarily all derive from the founder.

The theology thus developed tends, in turn, to become part of the tradition of a people; and it acquires a certain credibility or sacredness in the community. Thus the Adam and Eve story became so significant a part of Christian theology, as well as of folklore, and a help to the ideology of patriarchy. The relationships of races, social classes, sexes and castes, as well as religions, are deeply influenced by the stories believed by them about each other.

In the pluralist world in which we live, different explanations are given about the ultimate realities by the various religions and philosophies. The Confucianists, Hindus, Buddhists, Christians and Muslims, rationalists and Marxists each have their own interpretations based on the presuppositions with which each of them begins. Each one's culture and philosophical system supplies a medium through which to present particular explanations to adherents and the rest of the world.

Different views, or presuppositions, concerning history also influence a people's thinking and culture. The Oriental view of history is cyclical rather than linear. In Hinduism and Buddhism, this life is only one stage in a vast cycle of birth and death and rebirth. The cycle continues until all reach ultimate liberation in Nirvana or Moksha. The Christian view of human existence is more linear; this life determines someone's ultimate eternal destiny. This is the Judaeo-Christian-Islamic tradition.

Systems of logic differ between the major cultural groups. The Western system of logic is based on the principle of contradiction: what is is, and is not its opposite. It is linked to a tendency to be exclusive of opposites. It makes a dichotomy of true and false, not leaving room for the excluded middle. Its view of history is linear. The Oriental logic is more inclusive and harmonizing. It tries to hold together opposites in a wider whole.

Religious beliefs have a special content concerning the concept of the divine, either affirming, denying or ignoring the existence of a supreme transcendental being. Among those who believe in a God, there are differences of outlook concerning the nature of the divinity and its impact on the universe and on human beings. For some, God is impersonal, for others, God is a person, and even a trinity of persons. Some claim to have a special message from God handed down to them and indicating the path to salvation for humankind. Others reject the very idea of a God as an illusion, a figment of the imagination of religious-minded people. Some think talk of God is even a dangerous alienation of human beings from a concern with the transformation of the unjust realities of the world. For some, God is unknown and unknowable. The reality beyond this life, they say, is something about which humans can only be silent as before a mystery. Still others claim a mystic, intuitive, contemplative experience of God that is unique and incommunicable.

On the basis of differing interpretations of reality, different peoples have built their philosophical systems and their religious or secularist views of life. Based on these perspectives, communities of belief have been set up, ways of life organized, institutions developed, rites and rituals established and popularized. From generation to generation these are communicated and promoted. The secularists and Marxists, too, have their beliefs, their rituals and their heroes. Within each group, in so far as a way of thinking is similar, and the presuppositions are accepted, there is a continuity of tradition that forms a part of their culture.

Inter-religious dialogue and presuppositions

In the dialogue of religions and ideologies that is now developing, it is to be expected that at a certain stage the question of differing pre-suppositions is considered. How can we cope with them? Can they coexist? Can people compromise by being tolerant towards them all? Are they contradictory? If so, can they derive from the same divine source? Can we develop criteria for critically evaluating presupposi-tions, theologies, and ideologies themselves? A genuine dialogue of religions requires that we relate to one another at this level too, for the dialogue is deepened and may become enlightening for all involved.

There are different levels of dialogue among the religions. The easiest, and presently fairly common, level is in co-operation in social service and social action. This level of activity is deepened by religious services, such as for peace. A study of religions is a still further level. This is a more rare phenomenon as yet, and tends to be confined to scholars. Nonetheless, all these are an advance on the centennial isola-tion in which religions existed and functioned.

In the longer term, and at a deeper level, people are beginning to ask more serious questions about the conflicting views of the religions on the ultimate realities, and on their perceptions of each other.

There are also questions that arise in a special manner for Christians from cultures which are not European. These Christians live in an environment that is, at least, bi-cultural. Their normal life is in the culture of their country with its religions, their presuppositions, beliefs, cult and community practices. As Christians, their theology is based on another set of presuppositions, beliefs, cult and community life. Are they to think the latter is correct, from God and the whole truth, and that the former is not so?

The Churches have moved to the position of accepting that Christian-ity is open to all cultures. Western culture is not now regarded as an essential element even in Latin Christianity. The Christian faith can be expressed in terms of other cultures. This is uncontroversial if it means translating the Bible and the ritual of the Church into local languages, or even changing the dress, art, music, architecture and lifestyle of Chris-tians in these countries. Much of what is referred to as the incarnation, adaptation or inculturation of the Church in Asia and Africa reflects this thinking.

It is also possible to find a measure of agreement among Christians who opt for the social liberation of their peoples from economic and political domination by local élites, foreign rulers or transnational corporations. Christians in the so-called developed and developing countries may agree on this if their societal option is in favour of the liberation of the oppressed. This is perhaps the most important area of agreement that Christians and people of other religions should work towards, to bring about a world of justice with peace. The 'Justice, Peace and Integrity of Creation' programme of the World Council of Churches seeks such an agreement on principles and action.

More serious theological questions, however, arise if we go further and try to relate the presuppositions of the religions, and the perceptions each religion has of itself and of others, about the ultimate realities of the meaning and destiny of human life. In this, we have to go deeper than the external expressions of culture, and ask whether the stories, myths, interests and philosophical presuppositions of a people have gone into the making of its religious thinking and theology.

In order that theology may be more faithful to its foundational charism, spiritual experience and the core values of a religious community, it is necessary to discern the elements of a given theology that relate to its source. What are later additions to this core may have been made by succeeding generations. This process of discernment enables us to clarify the type of faith that a believer is required to give to a particular thesis or teaching of theology, or practice of religion. All the teachings of a religion do not merit the same type of faith – some of them are directly from the founder, others are elaborations by successive generations who are members of the religious community.

From this perspective, we can ask what elements prevalent in Europe, and among the Jews prior to their acceptance of Christianity, have also entered into the present mixture that is Christian theology. It is also important to ask whether the disciples of Jesus from other continents and cultures should distinguish between a purely Jewish or European, or North American, culture and what is of Jesus Christ in modern, Western Christian theology. It may be possible to identify specifically Christian content – or what comes from Jesus of Nazareth – in terms of the philosophy, culture, stories, myths and even rites and rituals of very different contexts.

These are very difficult questions. We would have to begin by first trying to discuss what is required of all of us in Christian theology, and what is its particular clothing in Jewish and European world-views, philosophy, culture and popular religion which predated the conversion of these people to Christianity.

It is important to distinguish between the faith due in Christianity to what Jesus teaches, and to what the Churches have subsequently developed as interpretations of his teaching. The direct teachings of Jesus can be regarded as the communication of his primordial spiritual experience. Of course, we depend on the Gospels for information concerning this teaching, for the core values of the discipleship of Jesus

– which is what Christianity should be about – are also in this teaching. It is remarkable that there is hardly anything that is divisive of religions in his teaching. Rather it is a call to an interiority of life and a love of neighbour in union with God.

Our acceptance of Jesus as a supreme teacher, as one showing a path to deliverance from sin, and union with God, is based on faith. It can also be corroborated by personal experience of a life guided by the teachings and example of Jesus. But ultimately, the acceptance of the person of Jesus as our guide in life is a response of faith in him. That he is intimately united to God is also a matter of faith. In this light we accept the Gospels, the New Testament and the Bible as divine revelation. While the core message, concerning the way human life is to be lived, is subject to experiential verification, many elements of Christian theology are developments based on presuppositions accepted by Christians in different communities or Churches. Significant questions are to be asked, like: in what way is Jesus united to God? To what extent and in what way is the Bible inspired? The Church's answers to these questions can claim only a faith that is due to the Church in her teaching power. They are not necessarily answers directly from Jesus.

Many of the later conflicts among the Christian Churches, and many differences of opinion among theologians, concern these secondary or derived conclusions which themselves reflect presuppositions. Likewise, difficulties in inter-faith relations have been concerned with secondary presuppositions and teachings that have tended to make Christianity normative, exclusive and dominant.

In order that Christian theology may make a positive contribution to the integral development and liberation of all humankind, it is necessary for us to clarify these issues. We will, thus, be able to distinguish what is the essential teaching of Jesus and what are later elaborations. This may have the effect of purifying Christian theology and may help the people of our time appreciate the basic teaching of Jesus, which is what Christians consider the core of their faith.

This process is likely to be a difficult one, since Christians are accustomed to consider many teachings as belonging to the tradition of the Church and hence part and parcel of the Christian faith. It is a process likely to be misunderstood, and even misinterpreted. We need, however, to investigate critically the content of theology – precisely in order to discern the core of the faith from its less essential elements. In order to achieve this we should try to establish some norms of critical evaluation that have a foundation in the teaching of Jesus and/or in the common sense of humanity. I will call them 'principles of critique'.

Validity of presuppositions

A presupposition is assumed to be true, is taken for granted: it is not necessarily the subject of proof and rational argument. To the one who believes in a presupposition of religion, it has a validity and a truthfulness based on faith or confidence in the credibility of the one who proposes or presents it. It can be borne witness to by living according to its teachings or demands. It can be inspiring and meaningful to the one who accepts it.

It is, however, not necessarily true for others, nor is it necessarily seen as true by them. Other people would not feel obliged to accept it in faith. They can, however, respect the faith of a believer, particularly when it leads to good both for the believer and for others.

Even within the same religious tradition, such as in Christianity, there are certain presuppositions that are accepted by all, for example that Jesus is the supreme teacher and that he gave his life in fidelity to his teaching. There are other claims by some Churches that are not accepted by others. Thus, teaching concerning the infallibility of the Roman Pontiff is a point of division for the Churches. There are other issues on which Christian Churches have divergent views also, like the nature of original sin, grace and redemption. There can even be fundamental differences in the interpretation of commonly accepted texts such as the Bible.

The issues are even more profound when we have different religions presenting totally different sets of propositions. There may be a similarity at certain levels – as in the core values or in their application to a concrete situation – but the total thinking within one religion may be organized in a different manner from the thinking in another. Thus Christian theology and Buddhist religious thought, or philosophy, may agree on certain common values and applications, but the constructs of thinking, and their expression, are quite different from each other.

So long as these religions are practised by people in different contexts, there may be no issue concerning their interrelation. But when they are lived by different groups within the same country, or region, their interaction is important. The situation is worse if they lead to religious conflicts, as in the communal conflicts in some Asian countries. If one religion claims a right to dominate the others, or claims a unique and privileged path to salvation, the relationships among the religions may lead to much conflict, as the history of the past few centuries attests.

While recognizing that religions are based on particular presuppositions, we need to develop criteria and methodologies for dealing with their interrelation. A first consideration would be that the presuppositions of one religion are not necessarily more valid than the presuppositions of another religion. Both are assumptions about things concerning which there can be no proof. We can, of course, see from their impact whether each or both lead to human fulfilment. When evaluating religions we should not compare the theory of one with the practice of another, or the best of one with the worst of another. The saint of one religion should not be compared with evil-doers who happen to be in another tradition.

We must be prepared to recognize assumptions as assumptions, and having a validity only to those who accept them. We can, however, study the implications of different sets of assumptions or theological positions. A religion which acknowledges the equality of all races before God would have a different impact on history from one which has a concept of a chosen people who are favoured by God, especially if such favours are understood as a right to domination. Clearly, in such an analysis it would be necessary to examine the impact of an ideology which may influence the interpretation, and expression, of the core values of a religion.

Is it possible to develop some critical principles for evaluating all presuppositions, and consequently all theologies that depend on them? Or, at least, within each tradition, can such principles be evolved? It is my contention that within the Christian tradition it is possible to evolve a critical principle that would be valid, at least in its application to interpretations of Christian theology. If it is rationally convincing or in keeping with the core values of other religions and persuasions, it may have a validity for them also.

The presuppositions of a religion may be related to a myth or myths. A myth is a narrative concerning fundamental symbols which are vehicles of ultimate meaning. A myth tries to express, through symbols, ultimate reality, which transcends both the capacity of discursive reasoning and expression in ordinary human language.[1] Thus, the creation story in the Bible has the character of a myth: it contains an implicit truth which is communicated through the narrative to those who accept it.

A myth should not be taken literally, as if it were historically attested and not a story. Theology may be built around a myth, and much would depend on the interpretation given to it and its message concerning the ultimate realities.

The influence of ideology

Mariology, like all theology and spirituality, is influenced not only by the teachings of the religious founder, and the presuppositions of the founding community, but also by the interests of the group that evolved Christian thinking. When thinking is developed to foster the interests of a group, it is called an ideology. Those in power in a society tend to develop thought patterns that will legitimize their power and help them to remain in power. This is a common human tendency that affects all power-holders.

Those in power are not generally satisfied with exercising power through physical control over the people by means of the machinery of legal and political power, including the armed forces. They often wish to win over the minds of their subjects. This is why rulers develop ideologies to promote their authority, and seek an intellectual justification for their power:

> Every ruling oligarchy of history has found ideological pretensions as important a bulwark of authority as its political power.[2]

Religious establishments also tend to evolve their religious thinking and teaching in such a manner that they help them to establish and maintain power in the religious community. This may be a conscious or unconscious influence on them. Normally, they do not develop doctrines that would disempower them. Likewise, it is true that religious founders teach that power must be a service ('If any one of you wants to be great he must be the servant of the rest' (Mark 10.43)) but those in power are inclined to reflect that their own being in power is the greatest service to the community. Thus the Bishops in the Vatican Council, while agreeing to a limitation of their term of office, fixed their retirement at 75 years of age. And the Pope who is called 'the servant of the servants of God' is not yet prepared to limit the life-long tenure of the papacy by fixing a retirement age. Niebuhr suggests that:

> All human knowledge is tainted with an 'ideological' taint. It pretends to be more true than it is. It is finite knowledge, gained from a particular perspective; but it pretends to be final and ultimate knowledge.[3]

The Catholic Church, which has exercised both spiritual and political power for centuries, over whole civilizations, may therefore be particularly susceptible to making its theology an ideology, that is, making its religious teachings suit the interests of the power-holders in the Church.

In considering the development of theology we have, therefore, to keep in mind that throughout almost all its history of over 1,500 years, the authority for the evolution of theology has rested with male clerics who, in the Catholic Church, have also been celibates. Further, until this generation, they have all been Europeans or the descendants of Europeans in other countries such as the United States and Latin America. Thus, there is a strong likelihood that Catholic theology has been evolved for the furtherance of the interests of the male Euro-American clergy.

In analysing a theology, or doctrine, it is necessary that there be a hermeneutic of suspicion. Since 'ideological taint' is a common human phenomenon, it is to be expected in all theology, including mine. In Mariology we should keep in mind the suspicion that it is possible, likely, and even probable, that male clergy would foster a theology that would preserve their interests and power in the religious community. Further, since the Church experienced an era of feudalism, followed by European domination over most of the world, Mariology, with the rest of theology, is likely to be tainted with the ideology and interests of the dominant powers in Europe, and, later on, of the European imperialist and capitalist domination over others.

When the interpretation of a theology concerns issues about which we can have no empirical evidence, and about which we cannot come to conclusions from rational investigation, there is even more room for the influence of ideology. That is, the interest of the controlling group may have a major impact in conditioning the growth of a theology. Then, whatever is in the interest of the power-holders may be proposed as faith.

Myths or narratives which are pointers to the ultimate realities may themselves be taken as literal truths. Their interpretation too may be such as to serve the power-holders in the community. Once this route of theological development has been entered into, tradition, which is considered a source of revelation, can buttress ideological positions, and perpetuate them as divinely revealed truths.

It is, therefore, very important that an endeavour be made to distinguish myth or narrative from historical fact, presuppositions from revealed doctrine. Many of the limitations of theology in the previous centuries were due to the Genesis story of the creation and fall of humanity, interpreted rather literally as historical data revealed by God. This mythical narrative contains elements of truth, and an important spiritual message concerning the human predicament, but it should not be taken as the literal truth.

> Christian theology has found it difficult to refute the rationalistic rejection of the myth of the Fall without falling into the literalistic error of insisting upon the Fall as an historical event. One of the consequences of this literalism, which has seriously affected the thought of the Church upon the problem of man's essential nature, is the assumption that the perfection from which man fell is to be assigned to a particular historical period i.e. the paradisiacal period before the Fall.[4]

When theology advances and propagates doctrines with an ideological bias, there is a tendency for them to become ingrained in people so that prejudice develops. This can be seen clearly from the impact of the Garden of Eden story on the attitude of society towards women.

Since a myth is a narrative that endeavours to communicate an aspect of ultimate or transcendent reality, in relation to the origin, destiny and meaning of human life or for a community, it leaves considerable room for fantasy and imagination. This is true of the biblical story of creation, or popular stories of ethnic origins, like St George and the dragon, or the arrival of Vijaya and his followers from India to Sri Lanka.

Precisely because of this literary form, the subsequent interpreters of the myth have an opportunity to exercise their imagination in explaining and developing the myth. When the interpretation of a myth is made by the power-holders in a community, it is likely that they use their power to safeguard their interests.

In Christian theology the original mythical presentation of the beginnings of the universe, and of human life, have been the subject of interpretation in later centuries by the ecclesiastical authorities. These, in turn, have claimed authority on the basis of divine inspiration, and the power given to them by Jesus Christ. These interpreters have also been, at the same time, male clergy, feudal lords and, later, medieval political rulers, for example in the Holy Roman Empire. It is, therefore, necessary to exercise a critical judgement about the evolution of the myth into religious teaching, and later even the defined dogma of the Catholic Church.

This process reveals a combination of myth interpreted by the authorities becoming Church tradition, which itself is then given a quasi-divine sanction, through being considered a source of revelation.

It is in response to this process that modern thinkers, such as Rudolf Bultmann, have developed the concept of demythologizing in order to try to separate the real import of a myth from its later expression.

The role of imagination in theology

Some of the foundations of traditional Mariology are derived from the mythical stories of the Old Testament, and of the New Testament, developed rather imaginatively into theology, and, at times, dogma. This need not be a problem if the doctrines had no unfavourable impact on people and communities.

But, in Mariology and Christology, they have had disastrous consequences for the understanding of the relations of the sexes and of religions. The Adam and Eve story has been a foundation of the ideology of male domination; Mariology is linked to it, since Mary is presented as the second Eve. Both Mariology and Christology, as they have been historically developed, are closely related to the myth of the fall of humanity and its consequences in original sin and in the development of a particular type of redeemer needed by humanity. This in turn has led to exclusivist and intolerant teachings and attitudes by Christian theology and 'Christian' powers, such as the European colonizers of Asia, Africa, the Americas and the Pacific in the past five centuries.

There is much room for imagination in Mariology, because the content of the teachings of traditional Mariology have been concerned with things about which we do not have verifiable information, or which are beyond the capacity of the human mind to understand and comprehend.

Examples of this are:

- the conception of Mary and the relation of divine grace to her from the first moment of conception;
- the conception of Jesus by Mary through the 'overshadowing' of the Holy Spirit;
- the 'perfect and perpetual virginity of Mary';
- Mary as 'mother of God';
- Mary's bodily Assumption into heaven;
- Mary's role as mediatrix of grace and coredemptrix of the human race.

Nonetheless these have been, and are, highly developed in teaching and preaching concerning Mary. Once again, these doctrines show signs of the vested interests of the interpreters.

There are very different explanations of the origin of Eve from Adam, but generally in favour of the priority of the male. Varying interpretations are given to the condition of Adam and Eve before the alleged 'fall' also. This is spoken of in general Catholic theology, as the state of original justice, something about which we cannot know anything by reason or experience. The Genesis narrative itself does not describe it, except briefly, and idyllically. It is later writers who refer to the action of the first parents, in the myth, as a grave sin against God's commands. The concept of original sin, as expressed in Catholic theology, evolved over centuries of Christian experience, with Augustine, then through the Middle Ages, to the definitions of the Council of Trent in the sixteenth century.

The differences between Catholics and Protestants, and even among Catholics and among Protestants, show what varieties of interpretation are possible. Each view presents an explanation of the state of original justice, the nature of the 'fall', its consequences, and correspondingly a concept of redemption. While we know from experience that human fallibility and mortality are combined with the desire for good and for immortality, we cannot know the historical origins of this predicament. But different theories, or hypotheses, propose varying views about the condition of humans at a time chronologically prior to the 'fall' in an earthly paradise. Is not what is said about that state and stage very much a matter of theological imagination, for example Adam and Eve not being subject to concupiscence or death?

Yet these doctrines led to conclusions about the nature and necessity of the grace of Christ and of the Church, for the salvation of every human being. Thence, it was easy to conclude – as the Churches did – that the other religions were not salvific. Vital theological questions were answered on the basis of conclusions derived from the inter-pretation, over time, of a mythical story. Clearly, each succeeding generation in the Church could give the authority of tradition to the interpretations of their predecessors in the faith.

The graces and privileges of Mary are deduced from presuppositions assumed on the basis of the creation myth, and its later reinterpretation especially by Paul. These, in turn, led to the proclamation of Jesus as son of God and Mary as mother of God. The Immaculate Conception of Mary depends on the concept of the state of original justice and original sin in Catholic theology.

Teaching on the holiness of Mary, unparalleled by any other human except Jesus, is also deduced from these doctrines. This holiness is interpreted in such a way as to fit into the power system of the Church. J. F. Murphy in an article on the 'Holiness of Mary' in the *New Catholic Encyclopaedia*[5] writes:

> Traditionally, therefore, the Church has always attributed to Mary any grace that has been granted to a lesser saint, either in its own form or in some more eminent and fitting manner. Certain graces, of course, could not be directly bestowed on Mary. The priesthood, for an instance, was not appropriate for Our Lady *as a woman*, but the divine maternity brought her the local, not simply the sacramental presence of Christ's body [italics added].

Such theological elaborations show how the theologian's imagina-tion can be guided, and tainted, by the prevailing law of the Church. The conditions of the disciplinary law of the Church are said to be binding on Mary. In fact, it seems easier for God to be responsible for a virgin birth, and a divine-human being, than to have a woman priest. This shows how the presuppositions, prejudices and prevailing ideo-logy of an age can influence the imagination of theologians and Church teachers.

J. F. Murphy continues his explanation of Mary's holiness by relating it to sacramental life:

> Since the Sacraments were instituted as a chief means of growth in grace
> for the Christian, the graces gained by Our Lady would be immense,
> since she was prepared to receive the Sacraments with ideal dispositions.
> Of course, not all the Sacraments were necessary in the case of Mary;
> Some she could not even validly receive.[6]

It is interesting to note how later-developed sacramental theology is
applied to Mary with retrospective effect and Church discipline is made
binding for Mary. She could conceive the physical Jesus in her womb,
but her gender denies her making Jesus sacramentally present at the
altar. This is a prime example of how far ideology and prejudice can
condition theological developments.

Developments in theology concerning the virginity of Mary, and the
role of Joseph in the holy family, are another area in which the
imagination of preacher and writer, as well as of ecclesiastical teachers,
has had much leeway. Who can know, after the time of the apostles,
whether Mary was a virgin even after the birth of Jesus? Yet because of
a desire to affirm a certain perspective on holiness, there has been a
trend to attribute perfect and perpetual virginity to Mary, even when
the scriptural evidence itself is of doubtful import, as I will discuss
later.

These considerations reveal that it is important to adopt a hermeneutic of suspicion, in order to try to evaluate the impact of myth,
ideology, imagination and prejudice in the evolution of dogmas. This is
particularly necessary in contexts in which dogmas have a divisive
impact on a pluralist society, or deflect the attention of Christians from
the important issues of human community and the core message of the
gospel.

A twofold criterion for evaluating Christian theologies

While appreciating the innumerable and unfathomable benefits Christian theology has brought to many millions of human beings, for nearly
two millennia, we can and must evaluate it. This is so especially in
relation to some of the drawbacks of the Christian tradition, both for the
sake of believers themselves, the Church, and for inter-faith relations,
especially in Asian countries.

From a Catholic perspective, the sources of Christian theology are the
Bible and tradition. Both these should be subject to critical evaluation.

The Bible contains a core teaching of love and unselfish service which
is truly meaningful and redeeming for all humanity. This teaching is
part of the primordial religious intuition, inspiration, experience and
example of the Jewish people in the Old Testament, and of Jesus and his
disciples in the New Testament.

However, there are many elements in the Bible which are less praiseworthy, or even indefensible, especially where they impinge on the rights of human beings. Thus, the Book of Deuteronomy calls for the total extermination of the seven nations that will be inhabiting Canaan when Israel occupies it (Deut 7.1–5; 20.16–18). The Israelites are to 'utterly destroy them' (Deut 7.2) and to 'save nothing' that breathes (Deut 20.16). Before the interests of Israel, the chosen people of God, the lives of these others do not count.[7]

Likewise, in the tradition, too, there are different interpretations of texts which have led to conflicts among Christians, and teachings of the Church that have been intolerant and harmful to others – particularly concerning other religions or women.

Given this situation, how can there be a valid principle for the critique of theologies and their sources – Bible and tradition? I propose a twofold principle – one negative and one positive – both flowing from the love command of Jesus, which is the core of his message.

A negative principle

Any theology that is authentically derived from God in Jesus must be loving, respectful and fulfilling for the whole of humanity of all places and times. This is the nature of the God revealed in the fundamental inspiration of the Bible, especially by Jesus the Christ: God is Just. Hence, any element in a theology that insults, degrades, dehumanizes and discriminates against any section of humanity, of any time or place, cannot be from God in Jesus. If these elements are present in Christian theology it is an unjustifiable intrusion by later theologies and should be exorcized from the body of acceptable Christian theology. As Jesus says, 'By their fruits you will know them'. Fruits of hate and insult cannot come from Jesus or God.

This provides a principle for the purification of prevailing and predominant Christian theology. If there are such degrading elements in a theology, their source must be searched. Perhaps they are an illegitimate inference from an acceptable source, or else the source itself may reflect a presupposition that is not justified or justifiable. In the latter case, that source itself must be very critically analysed and evaluated. We must be careful not to attribute to God what is of mere human elaboration.

Through the application of this principle, a good deal of the traditional construction of Western Christian theology will have to be reviewed.

A positive principle

Since we believe that all that is good in the world comes from God, we can also draw the inference that everything that is truly humanizing and ennobling in any religion or ideology is also ultimately from the divine source, and must be respected as such.

God wills the happiness and fulfilment of all individuals and peoples. We can conclude from this that the more a theology is contributing to genuine human self-realization and fulfilment, the closer it is to the divine source: that is, it helps the resolution of the personal problems of individuals as well as improving the societal relations of groups.

This principle of critique is, in the first instance, a rational and an ethical one. It can, therefore, be presented and applied to any religion or ideology. It is, at the same time, based on the central teaching of Jesus Christ. It tries to take the core message of Jesus seriously and make it the touchstone of good theology. Should not all Christian theology have this as its guiding principle?

This principle of critique affirms God, as revealed in Jesus Christ, who is a God of love, who cares for all irrespective of any divisions, even of creed. It is an affirmation of the centrality of universal love, a concept which can be made a measuring rod of the authenticity of any sacred text, Church teaching, or practice.

Clearly these criteria will seem both simple and exacting. But that is what the gospel of Jesus was and has to be. He was, himself, in favour of purifying the religion of the day. He struggled against wrong interpretations of the Law and the Prophets which had ended in imposing unnecessary burdens on the mass of the people in the name of religion. The teaching of Jesus is very much concerned with a moral life inspired by the love of God. The dogmatic definitions of later Christianity are not found, as such, in Jesus' teaching. At the same time, much of the simple evangelical teaching of Jesus is not given a sufficiently significant place in dogmatic theology.

These criteria need to be worked out in practice, and they would be subject to differences of opinion. But the principles, as such, would seem to have a validity in relation both to the teaching of Jesus and to human rationality. They give us a way of applying the key value of the Jesus gospel to theologies that claim to derive from him. That helps us liberate Christian theologies from presentations of God that are unfaithful to Jesus' teaching, for example, of God as intolerant, partial and cruel, or fostering inhumanity, dehumanization and the exploitation of human beings. They thus constrain us to explore more deeply into the origins of certain theological teachings, which cannot be from God, or God in Jesus, and are purely of human sectarian sources.

This approach of critically evaluating theologies may seem, at first sight, a weakening or dilution of the Christian faith. This is not my intention. What is desired is not the diminishing of faith in Jesus the Christ, but a purifying and deepening of it, and that in the contemporary context of a one-world situation, and of religio-culturally pluralistic societies. Such a critical dialogue can help relativize what is not certain in theology, and give more attention to what is the core message of the faith in God communicated by Jesus.

While the particular presuppositions and some conclusions, of religions and theologies, may tend to divide the followers of those religions, the core message of religions, concerning human life and human fulfilment, can help bring peoples together in mutual understanding, and respect, and in common action for the good of all. This can be a better, deeper and more lasting basis for inter-faith cooperation at all levels, including social justice and human liberation. Such a dialogue can help disengage the core message of Christianity from its encrustation in a particular culture or even theological school. The faith in, and discipleship of, Jesus can then be seen in clear perspective. It can perhaps be harmonized with the core message of the other world religions – if these too can be understood in their essence beyond their particular religio-cultural expressions.

The two principles I have just outlined – exclusion for negativity, and approval for positive contributions to human fulfilment – give us two valuable approaches for the evaluation of religions, including the present theology and the tradition of the Churches.

The Bible and tradition are both to be subject to the norm of excluding what is degrading to human beings. Jesus himself challenged the Law, as expressed in the Old Testament, for example concerning the teaching of Moses regarding divorce (Mark 10.5). Jesus spoke forcefully against those who scandalized or had contempt for little children: 'See that you do not despise one of these little ones' (Matt 18.10). Jesus did not accept the ritualistic religion of the past, or respect for the Sabbath irrespective of human need. The supreme freedom of Jesus, in dealing with the Old Testament, was for the genuine freedom and fulfilment of human beings, as children of God. He tried to free his people from their prejudices concerning other peoples, as witnessed by the parable of the Good Samaritan. Universal love and forgiveness are fundamental to his reinterpretation of the scriptures.

A critical purification of theology

When we find that some Christian teachings have been harmful, injurious and degrading to human beings, or have given legitimacy to grave injustice, we should institute a critical re-examination of such theology. This is required for the good of the Church itself. Jesus embarked on this in his day. He was critical of what passed for religion but was harmful for people. The reform of the Church has come about through such self-critique. When the Church was unable to accept and integrate such criticism, there were ruptures in the life of the Church, as at the time of the Protestant Reformation. It is only in our day, after over four and a half centuries, that Catholics are beginning to acknowledge that there were several valid criticisms in the work of reformers like Martin Luther. The failure of open and frank communication within the Church at that time was disastrous for Christians, because the Church was badly splintered, and whole communities were at war with each other for several decades, even centuries.

This principle can be very helpful in evaluating the presuppositions and content of Western Christian theology which has been considered and presented as universal for all humanity. We may also suggest that what leads to conflict and the death of human beings for religious beliefs cannot be from God and Jesus. Thus, if two religions have had long and violent conflicts, it is an indication that some of the presuppositions, and even some of the teachings, of these two religions may have elements which are not from God but are expressions of human selfishness and perhaps of ethnic aggrandizement.

Presuppositions derived from one world-view or culture may not be mere presuppositions if the corresponding theology is limited to peoples who draw their inspiration from the same culture. European men will not normally find difficulty in accepting Adam and Eve as the first parents of all humanity, and the story of the Garden of Eden is not such a tragedy for them, since the teachings of the Church provide them with a way out of their predicament through the Church itself. Other peoples, however, including European women, may not necessarily accept this story and its consequences.

A doctrine evolved in one context, in which it is harmless, may have damaging effects in another situation. Thus, Christian theology which has been developed in a situation of relative isolation, like Europe during the Middle Ages, may have to be re-thought when the Church finds itself in a plural context of different religions and social systems. The exclusiveness of some of the assertions of Christian theology may be understandable in the circumstances of Western European Christians, for Europe was isolated from most of the rest of the world for several centuries when Islam separated Europe from Africa and Asia. This situation lasted from the seventh or eighth century till about the middle of the fifteenth century. By then Christians had come to regard Europe as the centre of the world, and the other religious beliefs known to them were regarded as of the infidels and enemies. These Europeans practised theology in a context in which all the people with whom they were in regular, peaceful contact had the possibility of being Christians. Hence a theology that considered baptism essential for salvation was not regarded as harmful or inconvenient and could go unchallenged for centuries. Different historical situations, like large-scale secularization, or religious pluralism, would raise serious questions about such theological propositions.

Such an interpretation of the development of Western theology can also help us understand why many in the West have refused to accept the Christian religion. Some rejected it on the basis of rationalism, atheistic secularism, the modern concept of progress and evolution which does not recognize the need for religion, or because of a materialistic interpretation of reality, as in Marxism.

What is called secularization is often a rejection by people of elements of religion which they do not find respectful of them, or necessary as an explanation of the meaning of life. This does not necessarily represent the rejection of the divine, as in atheistic secularism, but may be a judgement that a particular interpretation of the divine is not acceptable to them. The process of secularization has, in fact, helped in the purification of religion and religious teachings, for the world has taught the Churches some lessons about some of the less acceptable, or less relevant, aspects of their theology or practice.

Other schools of thinking are also in crisis, since the world is far from experiencing continuing progress; Western civilization is experiencing a moral crisis, and is searching for values on which to rebuild itself. Marxist socialism, too, has failed to resolve problems concerning the ultimate meaning of life, even when it has contributed towards a more just social order. Within this context, Churches are coming together and exploring their identity as disciples of Jesus in a more open dialogue with world religions, which till recently they considered erroneous.

World religions

This critical evaluation of the degrading and dehumanizing of human beings or groups by Christianity is applicable to other religions too. Thus, if any teaching or practice of Hinduism, Buddhism, Islam, Taoism, Shintoism, Judaism, or any other religion, devalues other religions, those which consider themselves as so possessing the truth as to be intolerant of others, or marginalize a section of humanity, such as the poor or women, should to that extent be subject to self-purification. The devaluing of any religion cannot be from God, the Absolute, who cares for and loves all humankind, and it cannot be a principle of genuine enlightenment, that liberates people to fulfilment and genuine lasting happiness.

Evaluating the myths of a religion

Within the framework of this overall principle of critique, I would propose some criteria for evaluating the myths of a religion. A myth is a narrative which seeks to express through symbols an ultimate reality which transcends both the capacity for discursive reasoning, and expression in ordinary human language. Formally, myths are narratives about symbols; functionally, they are vehicles of ultimate meaning.

Since the beginning and end of the universe, and of human life, are beyond our experiential knowledge, the religions claim certain revelations by the Ultimate, beyond or in the universe, and may utilize different myths to interpret these revelations. In this context the word 'myth' is used to signify some primeval event which is considered fundamental to the whole order and regulation of life.

The myths, or conceptual framework, which thus purport to explain human life and its meaning and destiny, cannot be rationally proved, or, for that matter, disproved by empirical evidence, since they are generally placed beyond known and verifiable history. They can be 'truthful' as a good story, which gives feasible explanations, and they may have entered the cultural ethos and collective memory of a people or of whole civilizations.

As Raimundo Panikkar writes:[8]

> Religions deal mainly with the collective ultimate self-understanding of a human group. The truth of religion can be gauged only within the unifying myth that makes the self-understanding possible.

The myths of religions, or of a particular human community, are deep-rooted, collective perceptions that influence thinking and actions at a deep level. They are generally accepted unquestioningly as true and valid. They are part of a strong, emotive subconscious of a people.

Myths generally give an advantage to the dominant group within a community. It may be an ethnic group, a class, a royal family, a priestly caste, or the dominant sex. Myths thus consolidate prevailing inequalities by internalizing them within the mind-set and culture of a people. Myths can even give an aura of sacredness to such convictions, which are therefore to be accepted unquestioningly.

The myths of a religion have to be understood empathetically from within a particular religious tradition, and in relation to the cultural background of their origins and development.

Among myths, the founding myths are of primary importance as the basis of much that follows in belief and life. Such founding myths cannot be evaluated historically, unless they are clearly contrary to proven scientific data and evidence. They cannot be directly verified if they are claimed to represent a divine revelation, as their divine source is not available to us for consultation. They can, however, be evaluated from their consequences.

If the consequences of a myth are opposed to the human fulfilment of one group, then it is natural that such a group would be entitled to reject that myth. Thus, if the creation myth is interpreted so as to discriminate against women from the beginning, there is every justification for rejecting it as unfair to half of humanity. Within an unequal and unjust society it is clear that there must be a hermeneutic of suspicion relating to its myths, especially among those disadvantaged by them.

Another criterion for evaluation can be derived from within a religious tradition itself. If a religion has an understanding of the Divine Absolute as loving and just towards all human beings, it can be assumed that any revelation from such a Divine Absolute cannot be degrading or insulting to any individual or group of people within, or outside, that community. Such an unjust revelation would contradict the very idea of an all-loving and just God or Absolute, for the myth and its development would lack internal coherence.

This criterion is applicable to the original myth or myths, but also to their subsequent developments, even if these are made by the religious bodies constituted within that community to teach the doctrines authoritatively.

The emerging consciousness of humanity can also be a criterion for religious identity. In the past, it may be that slavery, for example, was accepted as legitimate within Christian communities. Today, however, it is seen as clearly opposed to the Christian doctrine of God and the content of divine revelation as understood in the mainstream Christian Churches. The collective conscience of humankind finds slavery a grave denial of human rights.

In a world increasingly unified by communications systems, humanity is more conscious than in the past of the plurality of religions and of their founding myths. In so far as some religions contradict each other or discriminate against others, there would be, at least, some justification for questioning these myths, especially if they are considered universally valid.

The ability of a myth, or traditional mental construct, to respond meaningfully to the new human consciousness regarding gender, feminism, ecology, nature, genetic engineering, astro-physics and the overall development of human personality is also a criterion for evaluating it.

If a myth, or its interpretation, tends to *deflect the attention* of believers from the more important issues and obligations of the core values of a religion, it can be harmful for them and others. Thus, if a myth deflects believers from taking action on the social and ecological causes of diseases, by suggesting that the principal cure for these diseases is to be found in prayers or offerings to a deity, it may be harmful for the human community itself.

A consequent rethinking

In the Asian context, where there are several world religions with different explanations of the origins of human life, of human destiny, and the process of salvation and liberation, it is important to rethink Christology and Mariology at a deeper level than is done in some other contexts. In Europe and North and South America, the need to rethink the key dogmas of the Christian tradition is not always felt so acutely. The other religions are not yet regarded as a major issue for Christian theology and practice, though it is possible to see its beginnings in the book *The Myth of Christian Uniqueness.*[9]

Nonetheless European and Latin American Christology and Mariology do propose a bottom-up approach to the understanding of Jesus and Mary. They are not satisfied with the traditional deductive approach and they contribute very valuable insights from the study of the scriptures, and from their experience of struggling for social liberation. These are most significant contributions to theology.

Latin American liberation theology contributes the concept of human liberation in society, through social analysis and the reading of the scriptures and of tradition. Liberation theologians do not yet, however, question the traditional bases of theology in the Christology of the Councils, which affirm that eternal salvation is only through Jesus Christ. They seem content to highlight the message of societal liberation, and, as it were, to juxtapose it with the traditional theology of salvation through Jesus Christ. For them the concept of mission derived from the tradition is not so problematic, since they do not meet acute questioning by those who practise other religions.

In Asia we are forced to question the basis of a theology that has been damaging our peoples for centuries, and which is still an obstacle for Christians to be fully open to inter-faith dialogue.

In this, it is my contention that a critical rethinking has to be made concerning the basic construct or framework of Christian theology. This will be based on the criteria I have developed earlier and relates to the origin of humanity, our proneness to sin, the nature of salvation, the role of religions and religious foundations in salvation, the identity of

Jesus Christ, Gautama the Buddha, the Prophet Muhammad, and the seers of the other religions.[10]

The limits of religions

In the Asian context with its multi-faith character and the influence of secular and Marxist philosophies, we have carefully to examine the role, function and limits of religions with regard to human liberation and eternal salvation.

Ideologies such as secularism and Marxism do not claim to be agents or agencies leading humans to an eternal other-worldly destiny. Hence, they do not claim to provide alternative or competing paths to eternal beatitude. However, their critique of religions can have a healthy impact for the purification of religions. In a similar manner, the values of the religions can contribute to the humanization of Marxism, social-ism and secularism as they have been expressed in the life of the USSR and Eastern Europe.

A more immediately significant issue is the recognition of the limits of religion in relation to the eternal salvation of humanity. Religions can help in the human search for eternal life through:

- offering a path or teaching a message of personal and societal purification, liberation and fulfilment;
- providing models and examples of people who lead such holy, liberated and liberating lives;
- forming communities of holiness and liberation and fostering the practices of self-purification and worship;
- networking among themselves and providing an undergirding of core values for personal and societal growth and fulfilment.

Beyond these, it may be asked whether religions can mediate the actual transition of a person after this life to the hereafter – in heaven, Moksha, Nirvana. Here it should be noted that religions as commu-nities and organizations are this-worldly realities. Their values may be ethical and spiritual bases for human happiness or otherwise in the next world, but we have no evidence about what happens after death. We may believe in faith, in the help and power of God's grace, but religions, as earthly communities and organizations, cease to have any impact on us beyond death. Our bodies return to dust and ashes, and what happens to the spirit, the soul, the life principle, is a matter of the relationship between that spirit and the transcendent God, Yahweh, Allah, Brahma.

The teaching of the Church is that God's grace is available to every person irrespective of religion and even to those who do not practise a religion. Salvation, Christians believe, is through the redeeming action of Jesus Christ and he has not denied that salvation to any person of goodwill. God's grace, and the merits of Jesus Christ, cannot be controlled or channelled exclusively by any religion or religious authority. Jesus has not left anyone a monopoly over his gifts. Likewise, St Paul in the epistle to the Romans speaks of the just judgement of God (Rom 2.2–16). In this sense the question of the salvation of human beings after death by the religions as organizations is a non-issue.

Discussion about whether religions are salvific in the next life cannot be based on valid evidence. Different religions have faith beliefs concerning the criteria by which salvation takes place, and concerning the agencies enabling such a redemption or liberation. But the earthly religions, as institutions and organizations, do not operate beyond this life.

What is relevant and important is the role of religions in the realization of human fulfilment, salvation and liberation for individuals and communities on this mother earth.

The critique of presuppositions in inter-faith dialogue can, thus, take us to a better understanding of the limits of religious organizations, and of their potential contribution towards ennobling human life and safeguarding nature on this planet.

Notes

1 'Myth' in The *New Dictionary of Theology* (Bangalore: TPI, 1993).
2 Reinhold Niebuhr. *The Nature and Destiny of Man* (New York: Scribner's, 1964).
3 Ibid., p. 194.
4 Ibid., pp. 267–8.
5 J. F. Murphy, 'Holiness of Mary' in *New Catholic Encyclopaedia* (Washington, DC, 1967), vol. IX, p. 348.
6 Ibid., p. 349.
7 George Soares Prabhu, 'Communalism and the role of the theologian' (New Delhi, 1987).
8 Raimundo Panikkar in Leonard Swidler (ed.), *Towards a Universal Theology of Religion* (Maryknoll, NY: Orbis, 1987), p. 129.
9 John Hick and Paul Knitter (eds), *The Myth of Christian Uniqueness* (Maryknoll, NY: Orbis, 1987).
10 Tissa Balasuriya OMI, 'Humanity's fall and Jesus the Saviour', *Voices of Third World Theology* (Dec. 1988), pp. 41–75.

7

❧❧❧❧

The presuppositions of original sin

The evolution of Marian theology in the Catholic Church is a process which has continued for over fifteen centuries, from the early Fathers, through the Council of Ephesus in 431, to the declaration of the doctrine of the bodily Assumption of Mary on 15 August 1950 by Pope Pius XII. Mariology, as I have already suggested, is intimately linked to the development of Christology, which is dependent on the evolution of thinking concerning the role and identity of Jesus Christ in the divine plan of salvation.

Christian theology of salvation has developed on the basis of the human predicament deduced from a reading of the first three chapters of Genesis, and in the light of the apostolic preaching of Jesus as universal saviour, especially the epistles of St Paul and particularly Romans chapter 5.

The Christian tradition concerning the human predicament rests on an acceptance of the Genesis story as historical truth. At least this was so for many centuries, until the development of modern critical studies of scripture. This teaching is based on several assumptions, or pre-suppositions, which are or were unexamined and which resulted in the development of theological understanding in relation to:

1. A state of original justice in relation to humanity.
2. A fall from this state because of original sin.
3. The inability of humanity to redeem itself from this fall, which was regarded as deprivation of the grace of God required for human salvation.
4. The transmission of original sin by human procreation, and its impact on the human intellect and will.
5. The impact of original sin on human life on earth, on nature, work, childbearing, the relationship between the sexes, which might be seen as punishment by God: death as the 'wages of sin'.

6. The need of a redeemer, and the identity of Jesus Christ as a divine-human redeemer.
7. The process of redemption which takes place through Jesus:

- as a teacher, with a message
- as an example, ideal or model
- as one founding a community of salvation
- as bringing about a change in human nature through his death.

8. The role of baptism in relation to original sin and the remission of sins.
9. Exemption from original sin – Mary Immaculate.

- How is it known? – What is its impact on Mary?
- What are its consequences on Marian theology and Catholic spirituality?

10. The role of the Church as:

- dispenser of graces
- related to conversion through baptism
- missionary authority.

All these aspects of Christian theology are affected by traditional understandings of the creation story, and the interpretation given to original sin by biblical texts, presuppositions, ideology and theological development. Once elaborated, teachings acquire the strength of tradition, considered a source of revelation in the Catholic Church.

I should make it clear, however, that I appreciate the Genesis presentation of the origins of the human race as created by God, and of the human condition with its sublime aspirations and inherent weaknesses, and the significance of the natural world in God's creation.

I have no difficulty with original sin in the sense of a human proneness to evil which we all experience, nor with the concept of the collective sinfulness of a society, nor with an environment that has a corrupting influence on people. What I question is the hypothesis of original sin as propounded in traditional theology, according to which human beings are born into a situation of helpless alienation from God, because of the primary original sin of the first parents.

Critical evaluation of the traditional doctrine of original sin

The traditional doctrine of original sin which is generally accepted in Christian theology has several drawbacks, in its sources, in its lack of internal coherence and in its consequences.

In its sources

The Church's teaching on original justice and original sin is not present in the Old Testament in any direct way. The Genesis accounts attribute evil to human freedom, and not to God's intention. God is shown as having good will towards humanity.

The Old Testament does not make any explicit or formal statement regarding the transmission of hereditary guilt from Adam and Eve to the entire human race. It includes texts that refer to the universal tendency towards sin, and relates how sin was present in human history in Genesis. This material is, however, quite different from the subsequent theological definition of original sin made explicit by the Council of Trent.

The concept of a supernatural state, and a fall that cannot be rectified by human repentance, cannot be deduced from the Old Testament. It would seem to be strange that the God of the Bible who spoke to the Jewish people through the prophets and sacred writers did not reveal so important a concept about the human condition. It can be argued, however, that God's ways are not our ways, and that revelation is gradual and progressive.

The Jewish people did not understand the story of Genesis to imply a fallenness from which they could not reach their eternal destiny without a divine redeemer. Nonetheless they had hope in God and expected salvation from God. The Messiah they expected was a redeemer of their race, but the practice of the Torah was regarded as sufficient for them to attain their eternal beautitude.

In addition, Jesus, who taught clearly and powerfully about what constituted holiness and goodness, did not speak of original sin. He did not speak of his mission and ministry as one of redemption, of having to buy back (*emere*) humanity. Such an idea would imply paying a ransom to someone who kept humanity captive. God could not be under obligation to anyone, much less to Satan, as such a theory of redemption would imply. Although Jesus called for belief and trust in him and in his message, this cannot legitimately be used as the basis for such a doctrine of original sin and of redemption from it.

The teaching of Jesus concerning human salvation is that we must love God and love our neighbour as ourselves. The conditions for salvation are stated clearly in his teaching on the last judgement (Matt 25): 'I was hungry and you fed me ... come and possess the Kingdom which was prepared for you.' What makes a person good and holy is honest behaviour and not mere externals.

The teaching of Jesus is one that all human beings can practise, as is indicated in the Sermon on the Mount. Jesus does not say that God's grace is denied to anyone, or is based on the sacraments of the Church.

Likewise, the Gospels do not record Jesus making baptism a condition for being a disciple of his. If baptism were essential for salvation and the spiritual life, he would surely have given it his most serious attention. The conversion that Jesus required was a change of life, witnessed by Zacchaeus who had to repay fourfold his illegal takings. The conversions which characterized Jesus' mission were deep, and did not lead to the rite of baptism.

It is possible, also, to speculate about whether Jesus would have known the future development of doctrine by his disciples in the course of the centuries. If he had seen the disastrous consequences of the doctrine of original sin on the Christian mission, would he not have warned his followers against it?

The apostolic teaching

The teaching of the apostles as revealed in the Acts and in the New Testament epistles clearly presents the message that all human beings are sinners and that salvation is through Jesus Christ. Peter, in his first proclamation after receiving the Holy Spirit, announces the forgiveness of sins and the gift of the Holy Spirit through Jesus Christ (Acts 2.38). Again, in his speech before the members of the Council in Jerusalem, Peter declares:

> 'Salvation is to be found through him alone; in all the world there is no one else whom God has given who can save us.' (Acts 4.12)

In his preaching in Pisidia in Antioch Paul presents a similar message:

> 'We want you to know, my fellow Israelites, that it is through Jesus that the message about forgiveness of sins is preached to you; and that everyone who believes in him is set free from all the sins from which the Law of Moses could not set you free.' (Acts 13.38–39)

The epistles of Paul record similar teaching:

> God offered him, so that by his death he should become the means by which people's sins are forgiven through their faith in him. (Rom 3.25)
> But God has shown us how much he loves us – it was while we were still sinners that Christ died for us. By his death we are now put right with God; how much more, then, will we be saved by him from God's anger! We were God's enemies, but he made us his friends through the death of his son. (Rom 5.8–9)

The first epistle of John states:

We have someone who pleads with the Father on our behalf – Jesus Christ, the righteous one. And Christ himself is the means by which our sins are forgiven, and not our sins only, but also the sins of everyone. (1 John 2.1–2)

There is, thus, a clear apostolic teaching about human sinfulness and forgiveness through Jesus Christ. The only references to original sin being communicated through procreation are in Paul's epistle to the Romans 5.12–21 and in 1 Corinthians 15.21–22. Other references seem to refer to personal sins.

The Apostles' teaching also indicates that God is just, and judges everyone according to their actions. God has no favourites, and divine grace is available to the Gentiles even before baptism, or meeting with the apostles.

The Jewish patriarchs and prophets like Abraham, Moses, Samuel and David were thought of as with God though they had no knowledge of Jesus, and their sayings are invoked as a testimony to the mission of Jesus: Acts 3.13; 3.22–26. The question remains of how the apostles would have conceived of the salvation of these ancient seers, who lived long before the birth of Jesus.

Further light is shed on original sin and the salvation of the Gentiles when Peter and the disciples have a spiritual experience in meeting with Cornelius, to whom the Spirit sent Peter. Acts records that Cornelius, a Gentile captain in the Roman regiment, was addressed by an angel of God who said: 'God is pleased with your prayers and works of charity, and is ready to answer you' (Acts 10.4). Peter began his response to Cornelius thus:

'I now realize that it is true that God treats everyone on the same basis. Whoever worships him and does what is right is acceptable to him, no matter what race he belongs to.' (Acts 10.34–35)

Cornelius was, therefore, pleasing to God before he had heard of Jesus. He received the Holy Spirit in the same way as the apostles had received the Spirit, and consequently Peter baptized him and his household. Here is an account of salvation prior to any contact with Jesus. The words of the voice from heaven to Peter –

'Do not consider anything unclean that God has declared clean.' (Acts 10.15)

– may be inspiring for us, remembering the theology of creation, in which all reality comes from God.

At the meeting of the Council of Jerusalem described in Acts chapter 15 there was a long debate concerning the necessity of circumcision for the Gentiles to be saved:

After a long debate, Peter stood up and said, 'And God, who knows the thoughts of everyone, showed his approval of the Gentiles by giving the Holy Spirit to them just as he had to us. He made no difference between us and them; he forgave their sins because they believed. So then, why do you now want to put God to the test by laying a load on the backs of the believers which neither our ancestors nor we ourselves were able to carry? No! We believe and are saved by the grace of the Lord Jesus, just as they are.' (Acts 15.6–11)

Paul in his address to the city council at Athens refers to their religion which he appreciates positively:

'I found an altar on which is written, "To an Unknown God". That which you worship, then, even though you do not know it, is what I now proclaim to you. God, who made the world and everything in it, is Lord of heaven and earth and does not live in man-made temples.'

Yet God is actually not far from any one of us:

'"In him we live and move and have our being." It is as some of your poets have said, "We too are his children."' (Acts 17.23–28)

Another consideration is that the apostles assert that salvation is through faith in Jesus. How is this salvific faith to be understood? Some of the Reformers thought in terms of a trusting faith as a result of which God redeems humanity irrespective of human actions. The usual Catholic position is that for faith to be salvific it has to express itself in good works. In this sense it is the love of God and love of neighbour that manifest and nourish faith, and lead to holiness and salvation. Since the grace of God is not deficient for anyone, we may presume that anyone who loves God and neighbour would receive the necessary graces for salvation.

Peter, in his first epistle, in which he speaks of the costly sacrifice of Christ that set people free from sin, also says:

You call him Father, when you pray to God, who judges all people by the same standard, according to what each one has done. (1 Pet 1.17–19)

Paul writes to the Corinthians:

For all of us must appear before Christ, to be judged by him. Each one will receive what he deserves, according to everything he has done, good or bad in his bodily life. (2 Cor 5.10)

The Acts of the Apostles also insists on a particular lifestyle that conversion to the discipleship of Jesus meant. It was not a faith of mere belief without a change in life. It was not enough to say 'Lord, Lord' to be saved:

All the believers continued together in close fellowship and shared their belongings with one another. They would sell their property and possessions, and distribute money among all, according to what each needed. (Acts 2.44–45)

There was no one in the group who was in need. (Acts 4.34)

Paul, in the epistle to the Romans, exhorts the disciples:

Share your belongings with your needy fellow Christians, and open your homes to strangers. (Rom 12.13)

The story of Ananias and Sapphira, punished for deception concerning the price for which they had sold a piece of land, indicates that conversion had to include honesty before the community in sharing property (Acts 5.1–11).

James is likewise strong in his insistence on right action as the test of faith:

You will be doing the right thing if you obey the law of the Kingdom, which is found in the scripture. 'Love your neighbour as you love yourself.' (James 2.8)

My brothers, what good is it for someone to say that he has faith if his actions do not prove it? (James 2.14)

You see, then, it is by his actions that a person is put right with God, and not by his faith alone. (James 2.24)

In the New Testament writings, then, there are some texts which stress that salvation is from God through Jesus Christ, and others which make human good will and action the criteria of salvation and the judgement of God. We have to reconcile these two aspects which form part of the mystery of human action and divine inspiration or grace. Both have to be kept in a dynamic relationship in our theological perspective.

These two aspects, however, need not refer to original sin as understood by later theology. The concept of divine grace flowing from Christ need not be a problem for dialogue with people of other theistic religions, provided this grace is regarded as graciously available to all human beings.

The witness of the apostles can be seen in a very different light, however, when emphasis is given to Pauline teaching, and particularly to Romans 5.6–21, in which Paul speaks of reconciliation with God by the death of his son while we were enemies. He writes:

Sin entered the world through one man, and through it death, and thus death has spread through the whole human race because everyone has sinned ...

> As by one man's disobedience many were made sinners, so by one man's
> obedience many will be made righteous ... (Rom 5.12, 19)

These texts in themselves do not promulgate the theological conclusions that were drawn in subsequent centuries by both Catholic and
Protestant theologians and Church leaders. Paul's teachings were elaborated in order to clarify and explain what redemption, reconciliation
and renewal in Jesus Christ meant. The apostle teaches that the death of
Jesus was redeeming for the whole of humanity: 'God has made us
members of Jesus Christ and by God's doing he has become our
wisdom, and our virtue and our holiness, and our freedom' (1 Cor 1.30).
He is 'the lamb of God that takes away the sin of the world' (John 1.29,
Jerusalem Bible).

> He has taken us out of the power of darkness and created a place for us in
> the Kingdom of the son that he loves, and in him we gain our freedom, the
> forgiveness of sins. (Col 1.13–14)

The apostolic preaching and writings contain the idea of a freeing,
redeeming, reconciling, renewing in Jesus Christ through his death.
They do not, however, include explicitly later teachings that were
developed concerning original justice, in which humanity was regarded as immortal. It might even be argued that since Paul says that 'The
results of the gift also outweigh the results of one man's sin' (Rom 5.16),
why should there not also have resulted the removal of human mortality which is said to be a result of Adam's sin?

Paul, like many later Christian teachers, took Adam to be one historical person, as was Jesus of Nazareth. At this stage, the books of the
Bible were not regarded as explaining the origins of human life and its
problems in mythical form. All the same, Paul does not preach the
implications of the fall as they were developed by later generations. On
the contrary, in the same epistle to the Romans, Paul speaks of the just
judgement of God:

> For God judges everyone by the same standard. (Rom 2.11)
> For God will reward every person according to what he has done. (Rom
> 2.6)
> For it is not by hearing the law that people are put right with God, but by
> doing what he commands. (Rom 2.13)
> The Gentiles do not have the law; but whenever they do by instinct what
> the law commands, they are their own law, even though they do not have
> the law. Their conduct shows that what the law commands is written in
> their hearts. Their conscience also shows that this is true, since their
> thoughts sometimes accuse them, and sometimes defend them ... God
> through Jesus Christ will judge the secret judgments of all. (Rom
> 2.15–16)

Paul, then, expresses a doctrine that explains how all people – Jews and Gentiles – can be justified according to their fidelity to their conscience. This is quite different from the future elaborations of Christian thinkers about original sin and the necessity of baptism for the remission of this inherited sin.

Prior to the time of Augustine there was no universal agreement concerning the existence, nature and consequences of original sin. A number of scholars held the view that was to become traditional doctrine, like the Latin writers Hilary and Ambrose. But many others disagreed with this view. Gregory of Nazianzus, for example, taught that unbaptized children were without sin, likewise John Chrysostom.

In the fourth century, Augustine propounded his teaching on original sin as communicated by the first parents through procreation. He opposed Pelagius, who regarded the fall of Adam and Eve as related to them as individuals and not transmitted through them to the whole of humankind. According to Pelagius, humans are free to choose good or evil, and the grace of God is a helpful but unnecessary crutch. Christ's crucifixion did not redeem humankind because humanity did not need redemption. Adam's sin was his personal sin, and no one else's. Jesus' life and teachings simply held up a supreme example of goodness for human beings to emulate.

Augustine developed a position between the two opposites of Manichaeism and Pelagianism. Manichaeism posited the existence of human nature as evil in itself, while Pelagius held that human beings could of their own free will overcome evil. Augustine's position, evolved through these controversies, was that the sin of Adam and Eve is transmitted by procreation to all human beings, principally through the concupiscence connected with sexual relations. Original sin meant for Augustine that human beings are a fallen mass – a *massa damnata* – who would all deserve eternal damnation but for the grace of God, and redemption by Christ. Infants without baptism are therefore destined to eternal damnation, since they are in a state of sin and do not receive the grace of God. Their punishment, however, is most lenient.

Through the concupiscence of the sexual act, original sin is communicated to children by their parents. Hence children are not born children of God, but of the world, even in legitimate marriages.[1]

This teaching became the central Catholic understanding through the Middle Ages, with further developments by Anselm and the thirteenth-century Scholastics.

We can see in the evolution of this doctrine how much the presuppositions and assumptions of a particular group of scholars influenced the development of dogma and provided authority for still other developments. Thus the text of John 3.5, 'unless anyone be born again of water and the Holy Spirit, he cannot enter into the Kingdom of heaven', comes to be interpreted in relation to the later practice of infant baptism. Through a circular argument, infant baptism also sometimes becomes the basis for the traditional understanding of the existence and impact of original sin.

After Augustine the doctrine was further developed, not least in relation to the Immaculate Conception of Mary.

Lack of internal coherence

Such a doctrine of original sin is based on unproved and unprovable assumptions, for instance concerning the conditions in the Garden of Eden. Pope John Paul II, in his recent Encyclical on the Blessed Virgin Mary, cites the Vatican II Constitution on the Church, in turn quoting Irenaeus:

> The knot of Eve's disobedience was untied by Mary's obedience. What the virgin Eve bound through her unbelief, Mary loosened by her faith.

The present Pope and the Second Vatican Council seem to speak of Eve as having been a virgin in the Garden of Eden. This is obviously a presupposition, linked with the idea that the original sin was connected with sexuality. A number of questions must be asked of such a presupposition:

- If original justice were a condition in which their passions were under the control of reason and virtue, how could Adam and Eve have 'fallen' and sinned against God?
- How could the punishment of all humankind for an act of the first parents be reconciled with the justice of God who is love?
- If Jesus atoned for human sin superabundantly, why were not the losses due to the first sin made good?
- In so far as it gives special privilege to the baptized, this doctrine would contradict the teaching of Paul that 'there is no respect of persons with God' (Rom 2.11). If, however, God's grace is available to all people of good will, baptism for salvation from original sin would not be so necessary.

This doctrine is unjust to the rest of humanity, who are unbaptized – they have judgement passed on them without their being responsible for any fault of Adam and Eve. Even a human court of law would not accept such a judgement on the whole of humanity for ever.

The whole doctrine of original sin is built on the assumptions of a particular medieval Western European philosophical understanding of the human person, nature and the supernatural, which is not necessarily valid for all times and places.

In its consequences

Discrimination against females

The interpretation of the Genesis story given by the Fathers of the Church, especially after Augustine, was that woman was the cause of the fall. She was the temptress, the accomplice of Satan and destroyer of the human race. The identification of Eve with evil became so common in Christian thought that the serpent acquired female features, as in Michelangelo's painting of the fall in the Sistine Chapel: Eve takes the fruit from a muscular seductress serpent.[2]

Promoting this same theme, Tertullian wrote viciously against women:

> Do you not realize that Eve is you? The curse God pronounced on your sex weighs still on the world. Guilty, you must bear its hardships. You are the devil's gateway, you desecrated the fatal tree, you first betrayed the law of God, you who softened up with your cajoling words the man against whom the devil could not prevail by force. The image of God, the man Adam, you broke him, it was child's play to you. You deserved death, and it was the son of God who had to die![3]

Male theologians and clergy have been responsible for perpetuating this denigration of women throughout the centuries, sometimes linking it with the praise of Mary.

This simplistic and damaging interpretation of the Genesis story calls into question the origins of the Genesis text, Paul's explanations of the role of Jesus Christ in redemption, and the Church's designation of Mary as the second Eve. How much are these developments the fruit of presuppositions and ideology, and of male superiority and prejudice?

The doctrine of original sin was developed in a manner that was antisexual, for human sexual relations brought into being a person who was a sinner, an enemy of God. Jean Eudes in the seventeenth century thus expressed sympathy with women's plight:

> It is a subject of humiliation to all the mothers of the children of Adam to know that they are with child, they carry with them an infant ... who is the enemy of God, the object of his hatred and malediction, and the shrine of the demon.[4]

Consequently Augustine, Ambrose and Jerome praised celibacy and virginity as a higher and holier state than marriage, as did the Council of Trent in Canon 10 of its 24th session.

> Virginity and celibacy are better and more blessed than the bond of matrimony![5]

This thinking tended to make Catholic moral theology overly conscious of sins associated with sexuality, and correspondingly to neglect other sins, such as those of injustice and the abuse of power. Original sin was *de facto* closely linked with concupiscence and sexuality. Since the female was considered more related to the body, and the male to the spirit and mind, this denigration of sexuality was closely linked with an anti-female attitude. This was particularly so among male clergy who dominated the Church's thinking, its ministry and administration.

Negativity towards nature

This interpretation of the Genesis story of the fall also resulted in attitudes that were opposed to nature and the world, which were, consequently, considered cursed by God. This is quite contrary to our understanding of the goodness of God, and the many passages of scripture which show the earth as fruitful and blessed by God:

> For Yahweh your God is bringing you to a good land ... in which you will
> not lack any thing ...
> You shall eat and be satisfied ...
> You shall bless Yahweh your God in the good land which he has given
> you. (Deut 8.7–10)

But traditional thinking did not contribute to the enjoyment of Christians of the beauty of creation. On the contrary, it could lead to a neglect of the care of the earth and ecology.

Discrimination against people of other religions or of no religion

This doctrine of original sin as developed in Christian theology also taught that humanity was in such a state of sinfulness that only Jesus Christ and his merits could achieve salvation. For many centuries this meant that everyone was called upon to acknowledge Jesus Christ as saviour, and to belong to the Catholic Church. Even today, it is generally understood to imply that salvation is, by some means or other, through Jesus Christ.

Such dogma of original sin implied that Jesus, the universal saviour, conferred the graces merited by him, through the Church which he founded. The Church did so through the sacraments, of which baptism had to be the first. Baptism is said to remove the stain of original sin, not of concupiscence, but of the other consequences of original sin whereby human beings are alienated from God.

This claim of the Church to be the vehicle of eternal salvation has a twofold impact which I would question. First, it claims for a religious institution the power to mediate salvation beyond this life. Even if we maintain that salvation is through Jesus Christ, it does not follow that we can claim that Jesus Christ wanted a Church – say the Catholic Church – to be the mediator of that salvation. In fact both Jesus and Paul speak of a direct relationship between God and human beings. In the ultimate analysis, holiness and salvation lie between a person and one's conscience and God (Rom 2; Matt 25).

This traditional explanation of the doctrine of original sin seems also to reduce the chances of eternal salvation for people of no religion, since human conscience as a guide determining human actions, morality and spirituality was regarded as a less reliable path to salvation.

To me this stance might be regarded as *religionism*, in which one or several religions, as organizations, claim to be able to mediate eternal salvation even after death. This would seem to be an invalid claim because salvation at that stage is a mystery of a person's relationship with the Absolute Transcendent God.

A second aspect of discrimination embodied in this doctrine concerns people of faiths other than Christianity. Though the Churches now affirm the possibility of salvation through other religions, the weight of the Christian tradition has been to explain original sin in such a way that the remedy for it was said to be exclusively in and through the Church, thanks to the merits of Christ.

This understanding of original sin is linked to a concept of God that is not acceptable to the other religions. In Asia, the idea of humanity being born alienated from the creator would seem an abominable concept of the divine. To believe that whole generations of entire continents lived and died with a diminished chance of salvation is repugnant to the notion of a just and loving God.

In fact one of the causes of the excess of missionary zeal against other religions was the theological perspective of 'salvation only in the Church'. Francis Xavier, for example, claimed he was in search of souls to be saved, souls that were otherwise going into hell. People had to be baptized to be saved. Hence, baptisms were carried out even in the womb, when a foetus was in danger of death. That was the impact of the concept of original sin.

A wrong accent on mission

Jesus preached the reign of God and conversion to righteousness. The conversion he required was a personal, internal change of heart and a consequent transformation of human relationships and the structures of society. The conversion he required was from selfishness and hatred to unselfishness and love, as I have already explained.

But, over the centuries, and especially since the Church became a powerful body in the Roman world, the main object of the mission of Christians has been the conversion of individuals and countries to the

Church. Christianity became Church-centred and not Jesus-God, or human-centred.

The theological basis for this movement was such doctrine of original sin and the need for redemption, through Christ, achieved by belonging to the Church. Theologians posited that human nature itself was 'fallen' and needed an ontological redemption (i.e. of human nature itself), through a divine-human person who could redeem humanity and restore friendship with God.

The earliest apostolic teaching contained the idea of conversion to Jesus Christ, baptism and remission of sins (Acts 2.38–40; 3.26). Peter, filled with the Holy Spirit, declared before the princes and the people:

> 'Neither is there salvation in any others. For there is no other name under heaven given to men, whereby we must be saved.' (Acts 4.12)

The Jewish people who accepted this teaching and were baptized then had no understanding of original sin as developed later, nor of the doctrines of justification explored in the Catholic–Protestant debates of the sixteenth century. They understood conversion more in terms of integrity, and salvation was understood more in terms of a radical social transformation:

> And with great power did the apostles give testimony of the resurrection of Jesus Christ; and great grace was in them all. For neither was there anyone needy among them. For as many as were owners of lands or houses, sold them and brought the price of the things they sold. And distribution was made to everyone according as any had need. (Acts 4.33–35)

It was in later centuries that questions were raised concerning the meaning and mode of salvation, and linked with these was the development of ecclesiology based on the assertion that Jesus Christ the redeemer had entrusted to the Church the continuation of his redemptive mission on earth until the end of time.

The Church therefore claimed the right, and felt the obligation, to bring all peoples into its faith community. At the same time it claimed supreme spiritual authority on earth. It considered itself an infallible guide in matters of belief and morality. The clergy of the Church could absolve sins, or even, by refusing to do so, bind people for eternity. This perspective made the Church authoritarian in matters spiritual, and for a long period of history the Church exercised temporal power also.

Original sin, soteriology and missiology were linked together conceptually, something which made the Church historically intolerant of other religions, and even of non-European cultures.

Once again, there is evidence that, though the Church claims to be guided by the Spirit of Truth, it seems also to be influenced by the presuppositions, assumptions and self-interest of theologians, and even by the gift of theological imagination which can be fertile and ingenious in evolving formulations to satisfy the needs of a group of believers who exercise dominant political, cultural and spiritual power in a society.

Here the criteria outlined earlier for evaluating doctrines can be very helpful in questioning the fruits of a theological imagination and reflection which may claim to pass for the inspiration of the Holy Spirit – even where such fruits, in terms of dogma, have prevailed in the Church for centuries.

Usually, the challenge to such dogmas will come from those who are adversely affected by them, and not normally from those who stand to benefit, or do not lose from such teachings. Again, this can be detected in relation to original sin.

Considering the generally baleful effects of this doctrine of original sin, including its missiological implications, we may go further and ask whether this interpretation itself is not the original sin of traditional Christian theology. It is so profound in its impact, even today, throughout the Christian world, that it must be revealed for what it is.

A theology that wishes to meet the challenge of a male-dominated, socially unjust and multi-faith society has seriously to rethink its presuppositions and their consequences in theory and in practical spiritual life.

The Mary of real life, and even of the scriptures, cannot be encountered without a deep questioning of this original sin of Mariology. This is an important challenge for the liberation of Mary to be Mary the mother of Jesus, and hence one concerned with all his concerns.

Notes

1 Augustine, *De peccatorum meritis et remissione* 1.10; 1.57; III, 17: *PL* 44.
2 Marina Warner, *Alone of All Her Sex* (London: Pan, 1985), p. 58 and figure 8.
3 Tertullian, *Disciplinary, Moral and Ascetical Works* (New York, 1959), quoted in Marina Warner, op. cit., p. 58.
4 St Jean Eudes, *The Wondrous Childhood of the Most Holy Mother of God* (New York, 1915), p. 90, quoted in Marina Warner, op. cit., p. 57.
5 *The Canons and Decree of the Council of Trent*, trans. J. Waterworth (London, 1848), quoted in Marina Warner, op. cit., p. 336.

8

❦❦❦❦❦

Reflection on traditional Marian doctrines

A reflection on the traditional Marian doctrines is important because they determine, to a large extent, the presentation of Mary in popular preaching and in the theology and spirituality of Catholics. Vatican II, also, invoked these doctrines in its chapter on Mary in the Constitution on the Church, *Lumen Gentium*. These traditional dogmas frequently highlight the special privileges and graces that Mary received from God, rather than her active role in the life and ministry of Jesus, in their contemporary social situation.

The three foundational dogmas of traditional Mariology are her Immaculate Conception, her divine motherhood and her perpetual virginity. The historic incidents referred to in these dogmas are prior in chronology to the passion, death and resurrection of Jesus. They have, however, evolved in the Church in response to the doctrines of original sin and the consequent need of a divine-human redeemer. In considering these traditional Marian teachings in greater focus, I will note the impact of these presuppositions and ideologies on the evolution and interpretation of Mariology and their consequences for Christian spirituality.

The Immaculate Conception of Mary

The Catholic doctrine of the Immaculate Conception of Mary developed very gradually in the consciousness of the Church. It was finally defined as dogma by Pope Pius IX in 1854. The doctrine is not explicitly present in the scriptures, though scriptural texts are used in its promotion: Genesis 3.15 and Luke 1.28, both partly due to inaccurate translations.

The words ascribed to God in the Vulgate of Genesis read 'I will put enmities between thee and the woman, and thy seed and her seed; she shall crush thy head, and thou shalt lie in wait for her heel'. But it is now generally accepted that a more accurate rendition of the Hebrew is 'And

146

I will put enmity between thee and the woman, and thy seed and her seed; it shall bruise thy head'. It is the seed of the woman, and not the woman, who is to crush the serpent. But the mistranslation stuck as the Council of Trent accepted the Vulgate as the canonical text.[1]

The second text, Luke 1.28, translated 'Hail, full of grace', is more accurately rendered as greatly blessed or highly favoured by God. The same word, *kekharitomene*, is used to describe Stephen in Acts 6.8 where it refers to a close union with God.

These two texts, thus mistranslated, were used for arguing from Genesis 3.15 that Mary would never be under the sway of Satan, and from Luke 1.28 that she would have the plenitude of grace. As the *Encyclopaedia of Biblical Theology* concludes,

> We have to avoid the danger of presupposing as proved what we hope to get from the text. We can, at any rate conclude that Gen. 3.15 refers to Mary not in itself but considered in the light of tradition.[2]

Pope Pius IX had recourse to both these texts in his bull *Ineffabilis Deus* of 1854 defining this dogma.

Tradition

The argument from tradition is based upon the patristic conception of Christ, not least in Justin Martyr and Irenaeus, as the New Adam and Mary as the New Eve. Subsequently, the definition of Mary's divine maternity strengthened the conviction that Mary's holiness was flawless. The feast of Mary's special conception was celebrated in the East from the sixth century.

In the medieval period there were fierce debates concerning the Immaculate Conception of Mary. Bernard of Clairvaux argues against it in his protest to the Canons of Lyons who celebrated the Immaculate Conception: 'Holy Spirit could not have been involved in anything so inherently evil as the conception of a child.'[3] 'Do you mean that the Holy Spirit was a partner to the sin of concupiscence? Or are we to assume that there was no sin where lust was not absent?'[4]

The Dominican Thomas Aquinas held that the Immaculate Conception would detract from Christ's dignity as the universal saviour (*Summa theologica* 3a, 27.2, ad 2). For, immaculately conceived, Mary would not need Christ's redemption. Aquinas taught instead that Mary was sanctified in her mother's womb 'after animation', that is forty to eighty days after conception according to the views of biology of the time. The debate was between those who argued for the Immaculate Conception out of respect for Mary's holiness and those who opposed it because she too needed redemption. It was the Franciscan Duns Scotus who produced the response which became generally accepted, namely that Mary was preserved from original sin from the first instance of her conception by the merits of Jesus.

All the same, the debates were so heated that in 1482 Pope Sixtus IV had to forbid the opposing sides – the Dominicans and the Franciscans – from accusing each other of heresy on this count.

Pius IX's Encyclical of 1854 *Ineffabilis Deus* declared:

> the doctrine, that the Most Blessed Virgin Mary was preserved from all stains of original sin in the first instant of her conception, by a singular grace and privilege of Almighty God, in consideration of the merits of Jesus Christ, saviour of the human race, has been revealed by God.

This doctrine deals with a matter about which again we can have no empirical evidence, and which is not revealed in scripture. It is taught by the Church on the basis of tradition. I have no difficulty in accepting it. My problem is rather with the idea that the rest of humanity is stained or sinful at conception.

This accusation, that all humanity, other than Jesus and Mary, is under the hegemony of Satan at conception, is based on the hypothesis of original sin. I have discussed earlier in some detail my concerns about this. Suffice it to say here that while I appreciate the holiness of Mary, it is not necessary to depreciate the rest of humanity by contrast. When the English hymn sings of 'Mary's unspotted womb', there is an unfair implication that all other wombs are spotted or stained. My criticism, therefore, rests on the outcome of the doctrine of original sin itself, in that it accuses the rest of humanity of such sinfulness.

Some consequences

Catholics who are devoted to Mary find much inspiration and solace in the thought that Mary is immaculate, a powerful intercessor, and loving mother. She is the patroness of many shrines. The clergy and religious men and women find in her a model of dedicated celibacy. Those who live in families see in her a mother who cares for all.

There are some particular responses to the Immaculate Conception from feminist writers that deserve attention. In *Beyond God the Father*, Mary Daly offers the interesting perspective that the Immaculate Conception

> can be understood as the negation of the myth of feminine evil, a rejection of religion's Fall into servitude to patriarchy ... Seen outside its 'normal' context, the symbol of the Immaculate Conception foreshadows the coming Fall into the sacred, in which women are 'conceived' as free from the crippling burden of submission in the role of 'the other' and therefore are able to bring the human psyche beyond the pseudo-sacred of oppressive symbols and values.[5]

For Daly, the slowness of the evolution of this doctrine was a result of male Church theologians who 'dimly glimpsed the unintended threat to male supremacy'.

> Sprung free from its Christolatrous context, it says that, conceived free of 'original sin', the female does not need to be 'saved', by the male. The symbol then can be recognized as having been an infiltrator into sexist territory, an unrecognized harbinger of New Being.[6]

Rosemary Ruether offers a new interpretation too, regarding the Immaculate Conception as exemplifying:

> the primordial potential for good of created existence transformed by sin. In this theology of the male feminine, we sense the hidden and repressed power of femaleness and nature as they exist both beneath and beyond the present male dualisms of nature and spirit. Precisely for this reason we cannot accept this theology on male terms. We must question the male theology of female 'disobedience' and sexuality as the cause of sin, and mortality as the consequence of sin. This very effort to sunder us from our mortal bodies and to scapegoat women as the cause of mortality and sin is the real sin. This sin has alienated us from that fruitful unity of mind and body that we have lost and that we seek in our redemptive quest.[7]

> In the dogma of the Immaculate Conception, Mary is 'pure nature', who affirms the capacity of created beings, to bear the holiness of divine being.[8]

The Greek and Russian Orthodox Churches, and the various Protestant denominations, do not accept the concept of the Immaculate Conception because it removes Mary from the general run of humanity into a separate transhuman category. It robs her of her full humanity and also of the greatness of her achievement. As Marina Warner concludes:

> If on one plane the perfection of Mary is defined as the conquest of the natural laws of child-bearing and death, then the prevailing idea of perfection denies the goodness of the created world, and of the human body, and postulates another perfect destiny where such conditions do not obtain. This is dualism, and the Virgin Mary is a symbol and an instrument of that dualism.

Warner finds that Eve and Mary both create

> the feeling that in its very nature humanity is fatally estranged from goodness, which for a believer is God. Any symbol that exacerbates that pain runs counter to the central Christian doctrine that mankind made and redeemed by God, and more important, it is a continuing enemy of hope and happiness.[9]

From a feminist perspective, the way Mary's special privileges are postulated can reinforce the downgrading of the rest of humanity, especially of women. For those concerned with social transformation, those privileges could be a deflecting of attention from the real issues of society. In the multi-faith and secular contexts of Asian societies, they do not present any hope to people of other religions. On the contrary, the dogma of the Immaculate Conception has its roots in the interpretation of original sin, and requires critical rethinking.

How human is Mary?

If Mary is immaculate, in the sense that she has no stain of sin, or attraction or inclination to sin, how does she merit anything? How can she be virtuous? If this is the case, how far is she a person whom we can imitate or follow? If everything in her is a gift of God, due to the 'foreseen' merits of Jesus, how far is she a human person? Who is this woman who cannot be tempted to sin? Even Jesus was tempted several times. This Mary has no weaknesses, no fallibility. She is, as it were, in a state of original justice.

Is this not the Mary of traditional theology, from which she has to be liberated to be truly human? This is necessary even for us to understand her life, her struggles and her agonies. Otherwise we have a sort of dehydrated Mary, one who cannot feel the attraction of what is less than good. The traditional Mary would not participate in anything in which the body would feel some pleasant sensations, or in which the spirit would be inclined to be selfish or proud. This Mary would not be quite human.

Because within the Church we want to make Mary great, we associate her with these dehumanizing or non-humanizing qualities. She is said to be the perfect mother, because she does not even feel the attraction of sexuality. This is considered a more perfect condition than the present normal condition of human beings, though if life in the Garden of Eden had expressed this view of perfection it may be wondered whether there would have been a human race.

Is it better for Mary to be immaculate, or to be human as other women and men have been and are? Would Jesus have privileged his mother so much that she would not have shared the common condition of humanity? Jesus himself is said to have accepted the condition of a slave while being divine (Phil 2.2–11). The uniqueness of Jesus is in not seeking privileges for himself.

Is it necessarily better to be a virgin mother than an ordinary mother? What is bad about being a mother in the normal way, since this is how the Creator has made human beings? Is not the virgin birth a theological elaboration arising from a framework in which human sexuality, the human body, and women, were considered inferior or not honourable enough for God? Given this perspective, God had to be born without human sexual intercourse. Natural motherhood is devalued by such a stance.

The Protestant Reformers' view of human nature was even more negative than that of Catholics. For them, humanity stood in a purely passive relation to God's grace. Neither the Church, nor Mary as its symbol, can be seen as a co-operator in the drama of salvation. Thus, though the Reformers reaffirmed the goodness of marriage, yet Protestant theology symbolizes the relationship of male and female, as divine headship and creaturely subordination.[10]

The Orthodox Churches accepted the view of Mary as Mother of God – *Theotokos* – and the virginity of Mary, which was already commonly accepted at the time of Chalcedon in 451. They take exception, however, to the dogma of the Immaculate Conception, even though they celebrated Mary's conception as early as the sixth century. They accepted her Assumption but did not welcome its definition in 1950 since it was an affirmation also of papal infallibility. They would place the Assumption at the level of a theological opinion – *theologoumenon*. The Orthodox insist on the mystery of the divine maternity, but, unlike the Latins, do not stress detailed analyses and definition.[11]

Mary ever-virgin

The Church's teaching concerning the virginity of Mary is another example of a doctrine concerning which there is, and can be, no convincing evidence, except that it is traditional belief in the Catholic Church. Again it is a doctrine related to original sin and the ideology of male domination.

Since Jesus is presented as the universal saviour from sin, including original sin, and divinity was attributed to him, he could not at any moment be under the dominion of sin or Satan. However, since it was believed that original sin was communicated by procreation, it was necessary for Jesus to avoid the contamination of original sin. The Immaculate Conception of Mary ensured that Jesus was free from original sin, from his mother's side. The Church's teaching of the virginal conception of Jesus in the womb of Mary was a convenient way of preserving Jesus from original sin from a human male parent. This teaching was consistent with the other Christological doctrines.

The perpetual virginity of Mary – before the birth of Jesus, during his birth and after his birth – also related well to ideologies which tended to devalue human sexuality as undermining the holiness of Mary.

Vivid theological imagination emerged to evolve theories of how the conception of Jesus could take place in the womb of Mary – by the

'overshadowing of the Holy Spirit'. In this, the male function in conception is attributed to the divine. The process of a miraculous birth was
also explained by the Fathers who proposed Mary's virginity while
giving birth, *in partu.*

The scriptural evidence for the virginal conception and perpetual
virginity of Mary has been the subject of theological discussion from the
earliest centuries of Christianity. It became particularly contentious in
Catholic–Protestant debates. Mary, who alone would have known of
such a miraculous divine intervention, is not known to have borne
witness to it. The tradition in the Catholic Church has maintained the
belief in the virginal conception from about the second century, based
on the infancy narratives of Matthew 1 and 2 and Luke 1 and 2.

Raymond E. Brown, the US Catholic biblical scholar, studies the
problem of the virginal conception in his book *The Virginal Conception
and Bodily Resurrection of Jesus.*[12] His conclusion is that while some
writers offer a basis for belief in the virginal conception,

> the general context of the infancy narratives in which the virginal concep-
> tion is preserved, does nothing to increase our confidence in historicity.
> (p. 55)

> If we consider them separately, Matthew's account is redolent of the
> folkloric and imaginative; e.g. angelic appearances in dreams, guiding
> birth star, treasures from the East, the machinations of a wicked king, the
> slaughter of innocent children. Luke's account has less of the folkloric,
> even though it reports several angelic appearances and a miraculous
> punishment of Zechariah. (p. 54)

A collaborative assessment by Protestant and Roman Catholic scholars is made by Raymond E. Brown, Karl P. Donfried, Joseph A.
Fitzmyer and John Reuman in *Mary in the New Testament.*[13] They
conclude:

> The task force agreed that both infancy narratives, and especially the
> Lucan, reflect a Christology which finds its earliest expression in such
> formularies as Rom. 1.3–4. Both narratives have moved Jesus' being
> 'constituted' Son of God back from the resurrection, beyond the baptism,
> to the time of his conception. But such a conclusion does not necessitate a
> virginal conception, and we had to inquire whence that idea was derived.
> Although one member favoured derivation from a putative Hellenistic-
> Jewish tradition about the virginal conception of Isaac, the majority
> found that suggestion unconvincing, as well as other proposed deriva-
> tions from Jewish or pagan sources. Family tradition, coming ultimately
> from Mary, was also deemed an unsatisfactory explanation. It was
> suggested that the 'catalyst' for the notion might have been that Jesus was
> born prematurely (i.e., too early after Joseph and Mary came to live
> together – cf. Matt. 1.18), a 'fact' which was interpreted by his enemies in

terms of his illegitimacy, and by Christians in terms of his having been miraculously conceived. The tenuousness of this hypothesis was acknowledged. The task force agreed that the question of the historicity of the virginal conception could not be settled by historical-critical exegesis, and that one's attitude towards Church tradition on the matter would probably be the decisive force in determining one's view whether the virginal conception is a theologoumenon or a literal fact.

In respect to the Church tradition of the perpetual virginity of Mary, we agreed that the intention of Matt. 1.25 was to exclude sexual relations between Joseph and Mary before the birth of Jesus, so that the verse does not necessarily indicate what took place afterwards in the marital relationship of Joseph and Mary. The fact that the New Testament speaks of the brothers and sisters of Jesus does not constitute an insuperable barrier to the view that Mary remained a virgin, but there is no convincing argument from the NT against the literal meaning of the words 'brother' and 'sister' when they are used of Jesus' relatives. Here again, as in the case of the virginal conception, Church tradition will be the determining factor in the view that one takes, with the important difference that while the tradition of the virginal conception is based on NT evidence, the doctrine of Mary's perpetual virginity goes beyond anything said of her in the Scriptures. (pp. 291, 292)

Throughout the centuries human imagination has been exercised to elucidate the virgin birth. One interesting example is from the nineteenth *Ode of Solomon* (7–9) quoted in *Mary in the New Testament* (p. 277):

So the virgin became a mother with great mercies. And she laboured and gave birth to a son without pain ... She did not require a midwife, since he caused her to give life. She gave birth of her own will as if she were a man [*sic!*].

My point in referring to these discussions is to underline the considerable attention the Church Fathers have given to these aspects of Mariology and their impact on Marian piety and spirituality. While the historicity of the virginity of Mary is an open issue among scholars, it is possible to obscure significant consequences of the Church's emphasis on this teaching.

First of all, this teaching has deflected attention from the ordinary womanhood of Mary. It has presented her life as so extraordinarily grace-filled and miraculous that she has ceased to be a mother in the ordinary way. It has also downplayed the role of Joseph in the life of the holy family, through the assertion of the divine paternity of Jesus, and the perpetual virginity of Mary. Catholic theology, spirituality and popular piety, as I have suggested, neglected the life of Mary which was connected with the redemptive-liberative ministry and death of Jesus. Furthermore, Mary's perpetual virginity fitted in well with a concept of redemption that was effected almost ontologically – through the very essence of the being of Jesus – without much reference to his teaching and impact on society, which were the causes of his death.

The doctrine of Mary's virginity also had the impact of emphasizing celibacy as a higher state. The Council of Trent makes this explicit:

> If anyone says ... that it is not better or holier to remain in virginity or celibacy than to be joined in marriage, let him be anathema. (D.B.S. 1810)

This anti-sexual bias has characterized very much traditional Catholic spirituality and church discipline. Normal sexual expression was bypassed in reflecting on the birth of Jesus. This meant that a normal family or woman could not find much consolation in the holy family, nor in Mary's motherhood, for she was said to be miraculously exempted from the pains of childbirth, something seen as a punishment of Eve and her progeny in the story of original sin.

The virginity of Mary argued on the basis of the divinity, death and resurrection of Jesus is further extended to involve Eve. The reference of Irenaeus to Eve as a virgin is recalled by the Second Vatican Council and repeated by Pope John Paul II in his recent encyclical. This reinforces the interpretation of Jerome: 'We believe that God was born of a virgin because we read it.'[14]

Feminist theologians have expressed differing perspectives on such presentations of Mary. Many would argue that emphasis on her virginity is a downgrading of normal womanhood and motherhood, and is in keeping with a patriarchal, hierarchical ideology which does not recognize the equal personhood of women. Thus Rosemary Ruether argues, in *Sexism and God-Talk*,[15] that Mary is glorified but presented as an impossible model.

Mary Daly, in *Beyond God the Father*, suggests that the dignity of Mary as the Mother of Jesus is a sort of 'compensatory glory', unconsciously or unwittingly offered by Catholicism to women.[16]

Mary has found a place in the inner sanctuaries of a male-dominated Church in which male clergy control the privileges of power and intercession based on the maleness of Jesus. The dignity of Mary, and devotion to her, have given Catholicism a particular human and humane flavour that has been absent in Protestantism. Even if Mary is given a subordinate and derived role in the mystery of redemption, at least she is there in Catholic theology and piety. Her statue, in almost every Catholic place of worship, offers a feminine presence alongside the divine. Popular devotion often gives her a very significant role in prayer life, to the extent that traditional Protestants made accusations of Mariolatry.

Another view of the virginity of Mary is seen in Mary Daly's reflection on the autonomy of woman:

> A woman who is defined as virgin is not defined exclusively by her relationships with men ... When this aspect of the symbol is sifted out of the patriarchal setting, then Virgin Mother can be heard to say something about female autonomy within the context of sexual and parental relationships. This is a message which, I believe, many women throughout the centuries of Christian culture have managed to take from the overtly sexist Marian doctrines.[17]

As I have enquired into Mary's virginity, I have presented the thinking of feminist scholars alongside the Church Magisterium because it is a very sensitive issue, and has been the cause of ecumenical conflict for many centuries.

I do not wish to over-emphasize this issue but to underline how the Church's teaching on her virginity has deflected attention from Mary as a real woman, the woman of the Gospels, and to note the influences of Mary's virginity in giving Catholic spirituality an anti-sexual bias. It has also contributed to the neglect of Mary's message in the Magnificat, and her role as a poor woman engaged in her people's struggle for integral personal and social liberation alongside Jesus.

An analysis of the doctrine of Mary's virginity also reveals the interlocking of Marian and Christological doctrines within the context of a patriarchal theology. In contrast, feminist reconstruction of Marian theology has made explicit her significant place in the biblical tradition of prophetism. As Rosemary Ruether insists, Mary can be a dynamic figure in the overcoming of sexism. Jesus and Mary can be inspiring models of mutuality in liberative redemption, which must include liberation from sexism within a dynamic interconnection of the personal and the social.[18]

Unfortunately, the rather narrow and rigid approaches in the Church towards male–female relations and sexuality were greatly encouraged by the emphasis on Mary as a perpetual virgin.

As Christian women advance in consciousness of their rights, and in the dignity of motherhood, they are likely to claim Mary as an example and model of ordinary human motherhood. With a better understanding of the message of creation spirituality, there will be a more positive approach to human sexuality, the body and the relationships between the sexes.

Mother of God

Another doctrine deduced theologically is that Mary is the mother of God. The direct connection between Christology and Mariology is embodied in her title *Theotokos* proclaimed by the Councils of Ephesus (431) and Chalcedon (451).

The traditional teaching, reaffirmed by Vatican II, is that God sought and obtained Mary's consent to the incarnation of his divine Son. Reflections on the story of the Annunciation emphasize her active collaboration in the divine plan, or her humble, obedient response in her *fiat*, 'behold the handmaid of the Lord', as reported in Luke chapter 1. The interpretations of this text are crucial to an understanding of Mary's virtues and her role.

This is the basis of her greatness. The other privileges of Mary are also deduced from her divine maternity, namely her virginity, her holiness and Immaculate Conception, her participation in the redemptive function of Jesus, and even her Assumption. It is argued that God would have prepared the most perfect person, or receptacle, to be the mother of his son. One argument was *potuit, decuit, fecit* – 'God could, it behoves that God should, and therefore God did it.'

From the motherhood of Jesus was developed the doctrine that Mary is the mother of the Church, since the Church flows from the side of Jesus – his ministry – and is spoken of as his bride. In popular devotion, the love of Mary for all humanity is also derived from her maternal relationship to Jesus – the saviour of all humanity.

The Church's teaching on the divine maternity of Mary is also something which is beyond our human understanding. It is not a doctrine directly revealed in the scriptures, and is consequent on the acceptance of the divinity of Jesus Christ and the nature of the link between the divine and the human in Jesus and in the womb of Mary. It is a doctrine that was contested from the earliest history of the Church and for many centuries. The Docetists maintained in the apostolic times that Jesus had only an apparent body and only *seemed* to suffer and die. Thus, Mary was not really the mother of Jesus. Against this view, the Fathers of the Church defended the humanity of Jesus. In the fifth century, Nestorius, patriarch of Constantinople, held there were two persons in Christ, and that Mary gave birth to the human person, Jesus of Nazareth, in whom the divine person dwelt. Mary, therefore, was the mother of Christ (*Christotokos*), but not the mother of God (*Theotokos*). The argument of Nestorius was that the eternal Word of God could not be born as a baby on Christmas night. This would make Mary a goddess, like those worshipped by the heathens. Patriarch Cyril of Alexandria opposed Nestorius vigorously. The Council of Ephesus (431) condemned the view of Nestorius, and declared Mary the Mother of God – amidst the enthusiastic jubilation of the people of the city of Ephesus.

This debate reveals the role of rational argument and imagination in the evolution of doctrine. It also indicates the role of political power and popular devotion in the decision-making of the Councils of the Church.

In the Asian context, the doctrine of the motherhood of God raises particular questions in relation to our understanding of the divinity of Jesus Christ. For popular religion, the divine maternity is not much of an issue. On the contrary, it accords with the people's concept of various gods and goddesses or deities. In the Hindu–Buddhist context of popular religion people have a concept of several deities and Mary is, or can be, accepted as such. In fact, Catholicism enters more into the people's religious culture, with its festivals and processions of Our Lady and the saints, than does Protestantism, which in our countries is more austere in its celebrations.

The problem, however, is complex at the more philosophical levels of the religions. Hinduism can accept several manifestations of the divine, and there could be an acceptance of Jesus as one of the manifestations or avatars of the Supreme Being. Mary as mother of God would be understood within that framework. But that is not the Christian concept of Jesus as God-man proclaimed by the Councils of Nicaea and Chalcedon. If we insist on the divinity of Jesus as the exclusive and ultimate manifestation of God – and further regard other manifestations as inferior, subordinate or even untrue – the dialogue with Hinduism will be rather difficult. Dialogue with Islam would be even more problematic, considering the Christian doctrine of the incarnation of Jesus, which Islam regards as a dilution of the monotheism to which they hold fast.

In the relationship with Buddhism as a philosophy, contentious issues would focus on the very existence of a God, the Christian view of the origins of the human race, the fall and original sin. Buddhism does not accept the need of an external redeemer – much less of a divine redeemer. Thus the privileges claimed for Mary would be obstacles to an understanding between Christians and Buddhists at the level of intellectual dialogue. Both religions have different interpretations of the human predicament and liberation or Moksha. They begin with different presuppositions and it is at this level that dialogue would need to take place.

The presence of secularists in South Asia can indicate the need to turn our attention in inter-faith dialogue, and in rethinking Christian theology and Mariology, to the presuppositions and theoretical constructs of the religious doctrines.

The presence of other faiths challenges us to think more deeply, not least about the implications of Christology for Mariology. If Jesus was so much God, so divine, that from the beginning he had the fullness of knowledge, including the beatific vision, then what is the relationship between Jesus and Mary? Mary would have had very little to do in the formation of Jesus. Jesus could have known everything from his birth. In this case Mary would have had to learn from the infant prodigy. Again, there is a question about the presence of the divine in Jesus. It is related to the theological concept of the hypostatic union.

Marian doctrines are linked to the teaching of the Church about the divinity of Christ. What is the nature of the divinity of Jesus? It is one thing to say Jesus is divine, another to claim to be able to understand, and even theologically define, the way and extent to which Jesus is divine. Divinity is something which the human mind cannot comprehend or express in language, even though theology often claims to do so.

Traditional theology has defined Jesus as one person having two natures: the divine and the human. This is the teaching of the Council of Chalcedon (451). Yet, who is able to know these things with any degree of acceptable certitude? The Council of Chalcedon would have had its reasons for making this definition and using such language at that time. But today we ask different questions, for example, what is the nature of the divinity linked to the human Jesus? Can we contain the divine in our human formulations?

Along with a rethinking of Christology that sees Jesus as a fully conscious human being, capable of suffering, being angry, and even tempted, we have to rethink Mariology. Mary's full humanity has to be recognized and as it were restored to her in theology and spirituality.

The Assumption of Mary

There is no reference to the birth or death of Mary in the scriptures. The Assumption of Mary was defined in 1950 by Pope Pius XII principally on the basis of tradition in the Apostolic Constitution *Munificentissimus Deus:*

> At the end of her earthly life, Mary ever Virgin, the Immaculate Mother of God, was assumed body and soul into heavenly glory.

The Assumption implies a connection in Catholic thinking between sin, sex and death following the fall of Adam and Eve. Since Mary was immaculately conceived she was sinless; as a virgin her body was considered intact, and because of this, both her death and her conception were said to have no sway over her. Pope Pius XII left open the question of whether Mary died.

Once again Mary's privilege is linked with original sin and Christology. There are also innumerable legends and apocryphal stories concerning her death or Assumption to heaven. The tradition in the

Church is itself not unrelated to these stories which popular religion gave rise to and handed down from generation to generation.

As in the case of the Immaculate Conception, there are comments by feminist theologians about the implications of the Assumption for sexism. Mary's Assumption is due to God's grace and due to her son's merits and is, therefore, said to be dependent on a male. On the other hand, it is also argued that in the Assumption a woman enters bodily the heavenly company of the Trinity, something to be regarded as an affirmation of the goodness of woman, including her body. Mary Daly comments:

> The extreme dichotomy between quasi-prophetic symbolic exaltation and social degradation of women by the Roman Catholic Church can of course be analysed in terms of compensation mechanisms – compensation for the women being held down and compensation for a celibate all-male clergy seeking 'the spiritual essence' of their undiscovered other halves. However, I think the most important aspect of the phenomenon has to do with the harnessing of women's power by this quintessentially hierarchical and sexist institution.[19]

The Assumption of Mary is said to foreshadow the ultimate resurrection of the body of all human beings, something which is an article of Christian belief, and an act of faith in the revelation. Again, the other Asian religions have different perceptions, for example the Buddhist view of the flux of matter and life, linked to rebirth until the end of the *samsaric* process of life, death, and life. This represents a different world-view, but neither one, nor the other, can be proved intellectually by humans whose experience is limited to one life.

Mary as co-redemptrix and mediatrix

These two functions of Mary are somewhat distinct from, but closely related to, each other. They both depend on the doctrine of redemption by Jesus Christ, which itself depends on the doctrine of original sin.

If the doctrine of original sin and its consequences are questioned, then the concept of redemption is also questioned. If we do not understand human nature as essentially fallen then there is no need of an ontological redemption by Jesus Christ, in which case Mary is not co-redemptrix, in an ontological sense of participating with Jesus in atoning to the Father and restoring human nature to a position of friendship with God.

If co-redemptrix means a sharing with Jesus in his mission of revealing the path of salvation – liberation, in being a model of witness to his teaching and the values of the Kingdom of God, and in founding the

Christian community of his disciples – it is a dogma which has relevance to our Asian context.

The traditional understanding of redemption, in which Jesus Christ is
considered the unique, universal and necessary redeemer in an ontological sense which transforms fallen human nature, is one which it is
not possible to use in our multi-faith context as well as among secular
people. Again, this is an issue which is of great significance in our
context, but which is hardly raised in European and North American
theology or in Latin American liberation theology.

Within an Asian context, therefore, it is necessary to reflect more
deeply on Mary's mediation. Mediation may be understood in the sense
of atoning and reconciling humanity and individuals with God, or as a
channel of divine grace as in mediatrix of graces. Here too, popular
religion will readily accept Mary as such a mediator and channel of
divine favours. But if this is linked to the view that Jesus Christ is the
unique reconciler and mediator, dialogue with other religions becomes
difficult if not impossible.

Clearly, we should not dilute doctrine for the sake of dialogue; but it
is possible to regard this doctrine itself as the result of a previous
adjustment to another context, and not necessarily from Jesus Christ or
God, or even directly and clearly from the Bible. Our having to dialogue
with other religions, and other world-views, can be a positive occasion
for reassessing our own traditional theological assumptions and their
conclusions.

These are not direct issues for Mariology, but consequences of the
Christology which is so crucial for the development of Marian dogma.
Mary, as presented in the Gospels, is a loving and lovable personality
who is acceptable in an Asian context as one of the mediators between
humanity and God. Her example is also eloquent, in its silent but
courageous participation in the life witness of her extraordinary son. It
is this Mary who must be known, loved and invoked in our context as
well as in the universal Church.

Similar comments can be made about the other attributes or privileges of Mary, like queen of heaven, mother of humanity, queen of the
universe. it is understandable that popular Catholic devotion, and even
Popes in their doctrinal teachings, lavish such honours and responsibilities on Mary. But once again, in our context, they cannot be presented
in an exclusive sense, as if there were no other such persons in human
history or in eternal life. This is a claim to a uniqueness concerning
which we have no evidence except in terms of our presuppositions,
ideology and theological elaborations. While we cannot grudge Catholics such convictions, we can ask what objective validity they possess.
How much are they obstacles to harmony and understanding among

religions and people of different persuasions? Such presentations of Mary would provide only obstacles to her acceptance as a universal mother.

In so far as she is a mother of all, Mary would understand other religions and cultures. She would not, then, want to be the mother goddess merely of the European tradition, which excludes people of other religions and contexts. She would also be a mother who is concerned about a chance of life for all her children, a 'mirror of justice' who requires a fair sharing of the world's resources for everyone.

Some consequences of traditional Mariology

Marian theology and spirituality have had an enormous impact on the lives of Catholic and Orthodox Christians throughout the centuries. Some Protestant Christians, too, are now developing a Mariology and Marian devotions. Mary, as understood in tradition, has brought to Catholicism the warmth and affectivity that the veneration of a woman, and mother, very close to divinity, can engender. Her devotion has given a popular and populist flavour to Catholic piety. This has helped Catholics to relate to pre-Christian cults which include mother goddesses or various female deities in different countries. In Sri Lanka, the Marian shrines are popular places to which people of many different religions come in large numbers.

Marian spirituality has inspired millions of people to seek holiness in a faithful response to God as they understand it. Mary is a model for very many women, especially women religious. She is a source of solace and consolation to Catholics in their times of anxiety and difficulty.

The acknowledgement of Mary as the mother of each one, and of the Church, brings a certain family spirit and togetherness which can be experienced powerfully in places of pilgrimage. This shared love of the common mother may also explain the world-wide solidarity of Catholics which has persisted for many centuries.

While recognizing these innumerable positive contributions of traditional Mariology, I have also to note some of its less desirable influences. The presentation of Mary as the obedient, docile, faithful, virgin mother has also had the impact of rendering Marian spirituality pietistic, somewhat passive, and even individualistic. This does not accord with the gospel presentation of Mary, but is present in the Mariology of the later tradition.

Marian spirituality, associated closely with the consequences of the fall and original sin, has encouraged a certain sense of weakness, dependency and powerlessness among human beings, particularly among women. Mary is presented as the refuge, consoler, mediatrix who intercedes for us with God. While it is true that human beings are finite, fallible and mortal, it is also important that our own strengths and potentialities be recognized, encouraged and developed. As innumerable prayers and hymns indicate, these human capabilities are not so much encouraged in Marian devotions as is the attitude of dependence based on a helplessness.

This aspect of Marian devotion has been significant in contributing to the feudal society which prevailed in Europe during much of the Christian era. It echoed feudal concepts of stratified social relations, helping to legitimize the class and status distinctions between lord and serf, lady and ordinary woman. This Marian spirituality did not foster the transforming social consciousness that can be discerned in the Magnificat and in the teaching of Jesus.

The presentation of Mary as docile and obedient to God was rather conveniently interpreted as the path of holiness for Christians. They were to obey the clergy as representatives of God: this was the sure path of holiness. There was thus a mutually supporting correlation between obedience to the feudal lord of the manor, and the leaders, or lords, of the Church. This connection was especially effective in subordinating women to male clergy, who claimed to represent God for them. Much traditional spirituality was based on the view that obedience was the most important virtue for holiness, as well as for social harmony. The rules of religious institutes were built on the foundation of an unquestioning, almost unthinking, obedience to the will of God expressed through the superiors. Mary's *Ecce ancilla Domini*, 'Behold the handmaid of the Lord', served well to buttress this thinking.

In capitalist and colonial situations, Marian devotions can also have a domesticating influence, by inducing Christians to accept hard realities as the will of God. Throughout the centuries of European colonialism, Catholic missionaries had no concerns that propagating their cult of Mary might have a revolutionary impact on the working classes or colonized peoples.

Mariology and male domination

Thought of in this way, Mary fitted well the traditional domination of women by men, prevalent in Jewish society, where the Jewish male thanked God for not being a female. The holiness of Mary was shown to be one of complete obedience and filial loyalty towards God, understood as a male, a Father.

In addition to this, the particular privileges of Mary are warranted because of the special relationship between her and her more important son, Jesus. She is born immaculate because of the foreseen merits of

Jesus. This is the traditional argument that was given, following Duns Scotus, of a preservative redemption of Mary from original sin. All her glories are due to her being the mother of Jesus. She is mediatrix of grace, because of her relationship to the life and passion of Jesus. God and Jesus are the active agents in her graced and privileged existence.

The relationship of Mary to Jesus has met with a variety of different reactions. Generally, Protestant response has been that Catholics do her too much honour and are guilty of Mariolatry – giving to Mary the worship due only to God.

Other responses include the argument that the conception of Mary as an Immaculate Virgin Mother downgraded ordinary women, who are the children of Eve, and who cannot be virgin mothers.

Catholic Mariology was proposing Mary as a model to be emulated, whereas ordinarily women were more akin to the image of Eve after her fall. It should be noted that, according to the hypothesis of original justice, Eve was also born immaculate – even if from the side of Adam. Eve had no original sin until she herself contributed to originating it. Mary Daly takes up this point:

> Total identification of women with evil would be dysfunctional. Catholicism has offered women compensatory and reflected glory through identification with Mary. The inimitability of the Virgin-Mother model (literally understood) has left all women essentially identified with Eve. At the same time, it has served to separate the 'feminine' ideal of good from the active role attributed to Jesus.[20]

Mary Daly nonetheless detects a positive aspect in Catholic Mariology – one unintended by its male originators. Though Daly is far from sympathetic to traditional Catholic theology, she suggests that Mary has been able to contribute to the emergence of some strong independent women within Catholicism.

> Aided by such screening mechanisms, some women have managed to absorb from the Mary image a vision of the free and independent woman who stands alone.

She sees in the Immaculate Conception the possibility of the 'negation of the myth of feminine evil, a rejection of religion's fall into servitude to patriarchy'.[21]

The doctrine of the Assumption, as I have indicated earlier, could also have the effect of locating a woman in heaven alongside the divine and thus helping overcome a traditional tendency in which 'symbolically and socially, women have been identified with matter, sex and evil'.[22]

In Marian theology, there is a strong sense of Mary's openness and receptivity to God's grace and her auxiliary role in Christ's redemptive mission. If receptivity implies a lack of an autonomous existence and fulfilment for women, then it is subordinating woman to the other, male, humanity in general or a male concept of the divine. Rosemary Ruether speaks of the need for Mariology to be freed from these connotations:

> Mariology becomes a liberating symbol for women only when it is seen as a radical symbol of a new humanity freed from hierarchical power relations; and not when 'femininity' is seen as the complementary underside of masculine domination.[23]

Mary can thus be a symbol either of women's subordination and submission, or of a new humanity in which woman is not subordinate to subjugation by patriarchy and hierarchy. She is freed from the curse which is said to be on Eve and her progeny. She is able to bring the qualities of love, mercy and forgiveness to the understanding of God and Christ, presented as judge and justice. The fully human lies in a combination of all these aspects.

Neglect of the social dimension

In the evolution of doctrine, what is not said and not done is sometimes as important as what is actually proposed within theology or spirituality. Since Marian devotion is vitally important to the Catholic Church and to a country like Sri Lanka, what is omitted can have serious consequences for the lives of believers.

In Mariology, throughout the centuries there has been an emphasis on Mary as a help of Christians, and a refuge of all those in need. This has been understood in terms of individual personal needs, of eternal salvation, and sometimes of community needs like overcoming enemies in a war, for example of Christians against the Turks at Lepanto (in 1470).

But Mariology has traditionally lacked a clear and systematic relationship with the social transformation which would bring about justice within communities and nations and internationally. There is hardly any shrine of Mary, or any popular prayer or hymn addressed to her, that stresses the sharing of material goods 'so that no one is in need'. There is no analysis in traditional Marian theology of the conditions in society which prevent the realization of effective social justice, love and peace.

On the contrary, the effect of Marian devotions, at least indirectly, seems to be to bring about a greater conformity to the prevailing social system. The virtues emphasized in Marian spirituality, of faith, love of

God, obedience, docility, humility, contemplation, are *de facto* interpreted without bringing out their social implications of justice and
sharing.

The devotions that have evolved around traditional Mariology do
not adequately focus the attention of Christians on issues of justice. On
the contrary, Christians are among the world's worst exploiters, and
traditional Marian devotion may even deflect them from considering
their responsibilities towards the poor, the needy and the oppressed. In
that sense, traditional Mariology, with all its popular flavour, can be
harmful for a genuine holiness, which must include justice and effective
love.

These harmful aspects are not inevitable, for Mary is regarded as the
mother of humanity. A genuine mother's concern would ensure that all
her children are cared for and provided for. She would grieve if some of
her children exploited the others, and deprived them of the means of
subsistence. She would struggle with all her might to change situations
in which millions of her children die of starvation while others take too
much from the common stock. A universal mother would want peace
among her children. She would regret the building up of armaments by
different groups of her children to destroy each other. She would
oppose the local and international corruption that leads to the resources
of poor people being deposited in banks by the people and companies
who exploit and rob them.

These would be the implications of the Magnificat of Mary. But
throughout the centuries Marian spirituality has hardly ever been
developed significantly to oppose the evils and injustices of feudal
societies, of capitalism, of imperialist colonialism and male domination.
Despite this, Marian shrines have been places where oppressed peoples
met and prayed for their liberation, as in Sri Lanka during the Dutch
persecution of Catholics in the seventeenth and eighteenth centuries, in
Ireland under the British, and in Eastern Europe under communist
rule.

This dimension of Mariology as socially liberating has emerged only
in recent times, with the growth of overall consciousness of the relationship between social justice and Christian holiness. Holiness in
traditional Marian spirituality has missed this dimension, as witnessed
by its absence from almost all religious congregations which have had
a Marian spirituality during the past few centuries. They have often
exercised social service and charity toward their neighbour as one of
their objectives. But social justice that critically analyses social relations
and wants a radical transformation of consciousness and social structures has not been part of their Marian spirituality.

Why this neglect?

Why has this been so? Clearly, it can be argued that this has been a result of the emphases given in Marian spirituality. The accent has been on the special privileges of Mary that have been proposed in dogmatic teachings and their interpretation in an individualistic and other-worldly sense. The Immaculate Conception, perpetual virginity, the divine motherhood and the Assumption into heaven have been high-lighted in writings and sermons, and related to Mary's intercessory power with God for the personal sanctification and eternal salvation of souls. But they have not been regarded and promoted as having a dimension of social transformation.

Even in the Vatican II statement on Mary in chapter 8 of the Constitution on the Church, the social dimension of Mariology is not brought out. In the fifty-page, one hundred-column articles on Mary in the *New Catholic Encyclopaedia*, edited by the Catholic University of America (Washington, DC, 1967), this dimension is not dealt with because it has not been important in Mariology.

The emphasis on the themes of the dogmatic proclamations, combined with the priority given to Christological dogmas, made for a neglect of the material that is available concerning Jesus and Mary in the Gospels.

Why have theology and spirituality accentuated these Christological and Mariological dogmas? It is, perhaps, because they were important for the claims of the Church, which considered itself the unique means, or vehicle, of salvation for all humanity. Further, the dogmas helped to establish and legitimize the authority of the clergy and theologians, and did not question the ruling social and political establishment of the day.

The influence of tradition on Catholic theology and spiritual life also explains the long-continued, and almost exclusive, centrality of these dogmas. The promotion of dependence and passivity was both the consequence of the interpretations of dogmas and, in turn, a cause of their continuingly dominant influence on Catholic life and thought.

Tradition is particularly powerful in relation to Mariology, as Catholics have had to defend it against denial or minimization by Protestants throughout the centuries. In the fourth and fifth centuries Mariology was significant at the Council of Ephesus (431) against Nestorius, and by implication at Chalcedon in 451, where the divine-human nature of Jesus Christ was defined. Catholics are particularly sensitive about the privileges and role of Mary and this makes theological discussion even more problematic. Reactions to such issues are often of an emotional nature which do not encourage quiet, rational inquiry.

Notes

1 E. D. O'Connor, 'Immaculate Conception' in *New Catholic Encyclopaedia* (Washington, DC, 1967).

2 Marina Warner, *Alone of All Her Sex* (London: Pan, 1985), p. 245.

3 *New Catholic Encyclopaedia*, p. 380.

4 Marina Warner, op. cit., p. 240.

5 Mary Daly, *Beyond God the Father* (Boston: Beacon, 1973), p. 86.

6 Ibid., p. 87.

7 Rosemary Ruether, *Sexism and God-Talk* (Boston: Beacon Press, 1983), pp. 151–2.

8 Rosemary Ruether, *Mary the Feminine Face of the Church* (London: SCM, 1979), p. 61.

9 Marina Warner, op. cit., p. 254.

10 Rosemary Ruether, *Mary*, pp. 60–2.

11 René Laurentin, *Mary's Place in the Church* (London: Burms & Oates, 1964), pp. 127–34.

12 Raymond E. Brown, *The Virginal Conception and Bodily Resurrection of Jesus* (New York: Paulist Press, 1973), p. 39.

13 Raymond Brown (ed.) *Mary in the New Testament* (Philadelphia: Fortress Press, 1978).

14 Jerome, *Adv. Helvidium* 19 (PL 23, 213A), quoted in Raymond E. Brown, *Virginal Conception*, p. 37.

15 Rosemary Ruether, *Sexism and God-Talk*, p. 145.

16 Mary Daly, op. cit., p. 81.

17 Ibid., pp. 84–5.

18 Rosemary Ruether, *Mary*, pp. 20–6.

19 Mary Daly, op. cit., pp. 90–1.

20 Ibid., p. 81.

21 Ibid., p. 86.

22 Ibid., p. 87.

23 Rosemary Ruether, *New Woman New Earth* (New York: Seabury, 1975), p. 58.

9

❧❧❧❧❧

A Marian Way of the Cross

The 'Way of the Cross' is an important exercise of piety among Catholics, and especially in Catholic families. It is one of the principal devotions during the six weeks of Lent each year, prior to Holy Week and Easter. The theology and the spirituality that animate the 'Way of the Cross' are also means of Christian instruction, and of the spiritual nurture of children in families and schools. They also form the substance of much of the preaching during this period. Often the popular traditional passion plays reflect such a theology. The *pasan* that were recited or sung in homes from the times of the Oratorians also echo this spirituality.

Now, in small groups, and in some parishes, there is a different presentation of the passion and death of Jesus based on a renewed theology and spirituality. According to this thinking, Jesus pays the price of his non-violent opposition to the wrongs of the Jewish social and religious leaders and the Roman colonial rulers. Some groups may combine this new approach with a more traditional interpretation. Inevitably, there are reflections on Mary, and her role in the passion and death of Jesus, and in human redemption.

Two different spiritualities

Christian theologies and spiritualities are dependent on the interpretations given to the basic data of revelation and history that are available concerning Jesus Christ, his message and mission. Two different positions can be discerned which are based on two different interpretations of the human situation, of the understanding of God and of the significance of Jesus' death for the redemption of humanity. These approaches are evoked if the question is asked: did Jesus die for our sins, or was he killed because of opposition to his radical life and message? The different approaches influence the manner of performing or conducting the 'Way of the Cross'. They reveal and express two different ways of being the Church. The role of the Christian community in human society would be understood and practised differently according to these two differing interpretations.

Traditional interpretation

The first, more traditional, interpretation begins with a theological position, assumption, or revelation concerning life in the pre-historical Garden of Eden. It understands original sin as alienating the whole human race from God and requiring a divine-human redeemer to appease the anger of God the Father. Jesus has to pay the price for the sins of humanity as expiation to the Father. Such a theology of original sin, based on certain texts of Paul (such as Rom 5:9, 12), was evolved especially by Augustine, and the need for atonement to the Father was further developed later in the Middle Ages by Anselm. These are extra-historical interpretations of the fundamental human condition and of the life and death of Jesus.

The concept of God of this perspective is one of an angry God who judges and punishes the whole of humanity for the sins of the first parents. This God is one who wants sacrifice and appeasement. According to this, while love flows from the sacrifice paid by Jesus, the superabundance of God's love is not often portrayed as an integral part of life. It is as if creation has faltered with the fall and only redemption by Jesus restores divine grace and goodwill to humanity.

Redemption by Jesus is through his taking on the sins of humanity and atoning for them. He bears all our sins and we participate in crucifying him. It is a theology of a 'top-down Christology', that is, one derived more from dogmatic affirmations than from the life story narrated in the Gospels. It is interpreted in a largely individualistic sense: Jesus is paying the price for my or our sins.

Hence this 'Way of the Cross' emphasizes the personal sins of the group performing it. The duty of avoiding such sins is stressed, as they cause the suffering and death of Jesus. The path to salvation is individualistic, without much concern for social and communitarian relationships and realities. While this has good aspects, it also gives the one performing the exercise a sense of guilt for the death of Jesus. This spirituality does not question the social and structural causes of many of the evils of our time. It generally encourages social passivity and conformism. It leaves the downtrodden and marginalized to fend for themselves, except for what charity offers them.

Such a traditional spirituality of the 'Way of the Cross' can be seen in the booklets used by pilgrims at the national basilica of Our Lady of Lanka at Tewatte. At the different stations, Jesus is said to pay the price to God the Father for our sins. Jesus is said to have seen all the sins of humanity at the agony in the garden and offered himself as a sacrificial victim for their reparation.

From this perspective, the gospel story of the death of Jesus is neglected in its contextual, socio-economic, religious and political implications. The heinous act of the crucifiers is not given much significance in this 'Way of the Cross'. The suffering of Jesus and Mary at the hands of religious leaders, and the Roman imperialists, is not reflected on seriously. Jesus is said to have gladly accepted the cross for the redemption of humankind. His mother Mary is also said to accept this suffering because she was aware of the mystery of human redemption by the death of Jesus. From this theological perspective, the greatness and honour of Mary is in the privileges with which she is endowed from her conception. The accent is not on her participation in the teaching, life and passion of Jesus. She has more a glory that is imputed to her, than a merit due to her active bearing of the cross and suffering of her son Jesus in that society.

Likewise, the socio-political significance of the passion of Jesus is not stressed. It is not clear that Jesus was killed because of his commitment to a cause that had political implications also. There is hardly any mention of the radical message of justice and truth that led to the High Priests, Pharisees and Sadducees opposing Jesus, and deciding that it is better that he dies than that the Romans move against the Jews. Right through the Middle Ages, there was much devotion to the passion of Jesus which reflected this thinking. It went hand in hand with a Christian sense of superiority over, and intolerance of, others. Christians considered themselves the direct and privileged beneficiaries of the merits of the sacrificial death of Jesus. The Church, as an institution, was said to be the dispenser of these merits or graces. The teaching that 'outside the Church there is no salvation' was related to this view of the human condition and of the passion and death of Jesus.

A Church living such a 'Way of the Cross' would be socially and politically neutral. But, in effect, it would be socially conservative, and *de facto* in favour of the *status quo*. The dominant powers would not only tolerate it but also encourage it. It would have a tranquillizing effect, contributing to the continuance of social evils, and not opposing them. Imperialism and global exploitation would not be challenged by such a spirituality. Would this not be a travesty of the way of the cross that Jesus underwent in his opposition to the unjust local social and religious élites and the imperial exploiters of his day?

A socially liberative perspective

The second spirituality takes the Gospel stories literally, and seriously applies their direct message to our situation today, both in a personal context and in a larger social context. According to this position, Jesus is seen as part of real life. He opted for the liberation of the oppressed, as he announced in his mission statement in Luke 4.18. He, therefore, took up a stance against the oppressors of the poor and the weak; against the hypocrites like those who wanted the woman taken in adultery stoned to death. His whole life and message contested the falsehood of the dominant religious and social order of his day.

The Gospel stories recall him being killed because the Romans, and the Jewish leaders, opposed his views and wanted him destroyed. His arrest and death follow soon after his cleansing of the temple of Jerusalem, chasing away those who had made it a 'den of thieves'. Those who came to seize him were 'the chief priests, the officers of the temple police, and the elders'. 'When day broke, the elders of the nation, chief priests, and doctors of the law assembled and he was brought before their Council' (Luke 22.52, 66). 'The troops and their commander, and the Jewish police, now arrested Jesus and secured him' (John 18.12). Thereafter, he was accused before Pilate of subverting the nation. 'If you let this man go you are no friend to Caesar, any man who claims to be a king is defying Caesar' (John 19.12). Yet he did not accept the absolute sovereignty of Caesar over human lives; he said 'give to God what belongs to God'. All those who were against the genuine liberation of the marginalized joined hands to exterminate him.

From this perspective God is Love, as Jesus proclaimed. God's plan for humanity, revealed in Jesus, is the Kingdom of God built on earth through human effort and continued in eternal life. 'Thy kingdom come on earth . . . ' The incarnation of the second person of the Blessed Trinity represents the continuing divinization of human beings, as the Fathers of the Eastern Church stressed, and not in order to pay a price to God for redeeming humanity from captivity under Satan. We are adopted children of God called to be increasingly godlike, while being creatures.

Sin, including original sin, is understood by those who promote this stance as both personal and collective, individual and social. Original sin is not denied, but interpreted as human proneness to sin, the attraction to self-love in each human being from birth, and the social sin in the world, the sin of the world, and sin in the structures of society.

The redemptive function of Jesus is seen as including both the conversion of individuals to unselfish love, and the changing of social relationships and structures so that they become bearers of the values of the Kingdom of love, truth, justice and peace. Jesus suffered in this process and accepted the way of the cross as a consequence of his mission, given the sinfulness of the people and structures of his time. Jesus was not neutral towards the social evils of his time in both society and religion. Salvation is communitarian. It includes the care of nature, which nurtures all life on earth, and it promotes, therefore, ecological and environmental concerns.

The redemptive value of the death of Jesus would not be understood as an expiation to the Father as such, but rather as a way of showing the way to salvation from sin, in paying the price of his life for truth, justice, love and human dignity and equality in a given social environment, and founding a movement of loving service to others, even unto death at the hands of opponents. This movement from the cross vibrates throughout history, especially through the impact of the life witness of Christians. The enemies of Jesus could kill his body, but not his soul and his message, and its impact on history. This stance indicates that redemption has to include a human effort to transform the people and structures of society, to be more in accordance with values of the Kingdom of God witnessed to, and presented by, Jesus.

The Gospel narratives record how the religious leaders and the imperial rulers are seen in a very real way to bring about the death of one who opts for the rights of the people. His crucifixion is a political assassination. If he is not killed Pilate would not be a friend of Caesar. 'The wording of the placard, "The King of the Jews", reveals that the crime for which Jesus was condemned was not the Sanhedrin's charge of blasphemy, but the political crime of high treason, generated by messianic claims, which to Roman ears sounded like a threat to Caesar's sovereignty' (J. M. Bassler, 'Cross' in *Harper's Bible Dictionary*).

Jesus' way of the cross then had immediate social and political relevance in the concrete situation of the life of the Jews of his day. Christianity, likewise, is not asocial and apolitical, but deeply committed to the integral liberation of human beings. In that process ordinary women and men are with Jesus, as against the High Priests and the agents of imperial law and order who condemn and kill him.

This form of discipleship includes participation in, and contribution to, the continuing effort to build the Kingdom of God on earth. We too can join in the redemptive action through history, by living according to Kingdom values, in spite of the mammonic opposition of the civil and religious societies. Spirituality, then, includes a reflection on the sin of people and of the relationships and structures of society. Today it would require, especially, reflection and action concerning the global aspects of these relationships, and the structures of world sin and global exploitation.

The Way of the Cross is a spirituality not merely for Good Friday, nor only for the period of Lent. It is a way of life. It is not a mere plea for suffering with the weak, and bearing up in life's troubles. It is a call to strength, to courage, to stand up and be counted in the building of a world of truth and justice. It is a speaking out against falsehood and the abuse of power, against torture and the violation of human rights.

The crucified Jesus is a leader teaching the path of love, of moral strength, of unflinching resistance to all the Caesars, Pilates, Caiaphases and Pharisees of our times. He was killed, yet he lives, risen, and calls us to follow him. That is the ever present call of the cross.

A Way of the Cross experienced from this perspective would involve a personal and collective exploration of two levels of sin and grace. Such a Way of the Cross would not be a value-free, socially neutral and politically uncommitted spiritual exercise. It would not be neutral before the ongoing violation of human rights in our country by different power groups. It would be a dangerous and challenging experience, like the reading in public of the prophets of the Old Testament, as the South Korean Catholics did during their struggles for human rights against the dictators. As Cardinal Jean Daniélou once said at a public lecture in Paris in the 1960s, 'prayer is political'. The 'Our Father', with its 'give us this day our daily bread' and 'forgive us as we forgive others', is a political agenda. Politics, here, does not necessarily mean party politics. It indicates rather that issues cannot be resolved outside the framework of the *polis* or civil society and its agencies and struggles.

Mary participates in the redemptive action of Jesus, by sharing his life and his risks and eventual arrest, torture and death. She, too, is not neutral in relation to social injustice and discrimination, as the Magnificat indicates. She, more than anyone else, would have understood the liberating message of Jesus. Her whole life with Jesus from Bethlehem to Calvary was as one of the marginalized. Her own way of the cross could be understood in relation to the suffering of the poor, and especially of the women of today. She is co-redemptrix of humanity in intimately sharing with Jesus in his life mission and message and in the life of the early Church.

My reflections here are based on the inspiration of the stations of the cross which are depicted at the national basilica and shrine at Tewatte. The fourteen stations are in ascending order on the hill. Each station has three figures, one of whom is Jesus.

The more commonly understood individual and personal dimension can be added to the societal and structural approach presented here.

Some personalities in these stations

Mary is present at a number of the stations, as the gospel narratives record. It is likely, therefore, that she followed Jesus on the way from Pilate to the cruxifixion and burial. She offered the first, and ultimate, sacrifice with Jesus on this first and actual way of the cross.

Women are present in many stations. They console Jesus. Jesus speaks to them and tells them of their sufferings and those of their children. These women are witnesses to his death and later to his resurrection. They are not frightened of the Roman soldiers nor of the High Priests.

The *Roman soldier* is present in several of the stations. From the perspective of the artist, the Roman soldier is the principal inflicter of punishment on Jesus. Jesus and Mary would have known who it is who is killing Jesus. A strong anti-imperialist feeling must have welled up in them. They would have known the reason why the Romans, along with the High Priests, were killing him.

Simon the Cyrenian is present in several stations – a stranger, probably a Jew from Cyrene in North Africa, who was compelled to help Jesus carry the cross. He could symbolize the contribution of many others to the redemption of the world.

The *apostles* are not there, except John at the foot of the cross. The substantial absence of the predecessors of the future male clergy from the offering of the first and primordial sacrifice of the New Testament is significant.

The Gospels bear witness that the *chief priests*, whose hypocrisy Jesus had castigated, were among the principal agents of his murder. The 'chief priests and the elders of the nation met in the palace of the high priest, Caiaphas; and they conferred together on a scheme to have Jesus arrested by some trick and put to death' (Matt 26.3–4).

There is also *Joseph of Arimathea*, an honourable and good man who comes forward to ask for the body of Jesus and to offer his own tomb for the burial of the condemned Jesus.

1st Station: Jesus is condemned to death

Jesus, crowned with thorns, is condemned to death. 'Behold the Man', *Ecce Homo*. The accusation of the Jewish leaders against Jesus was 'We found this man subverting our nation, opposing the payment of taxes to Caesar, and claiming to be Messiah, a King ... His teaching is causing disaffection among the people all through Judaea. It started in Galilee and has spread as far as this city' (Luke 23.2–5). Pontius Pilate, the Roman Governor, is apparently worried that he has had to make this decision as a concession to the Jewish leaders, and the mob, which wanted the crucifixion of Jesus, rather than of Barabbas, the bandit or insurgent. Pilate knows that he himself is not innocent, but pretends that he is, or tries to absolve himself of this crime: he washes his hands.

Mary, who was with Jesus, would have been profoundly sad when the crowd shouted 'Crucify him, crucify him'. She would have seen the gravely unjust nature of the whole trial and condemnation of Jesus by the High Priests, out of opposition to his stance, and by Pilate, out of fear of the High Priests and Caesar. She would have liked to plead his cause, and may have actually done so. But it was of no avail. She would have, thus, been conscious of the political implications of the killing of her son.

This scene has become symbolic of authority that colludes in the oppression of the innocent. Pilate does not have the courage of his convictions. He is afraid of his position before Caesar. If he does not punish and kill Jesus, Caesar will be against him. He wants to safeguard his power. Therefore, he acquiesces in the killing of the innocent Jesus, the troublesome prophet who said power is for service. There is thus a political, even imperial, significance in the killing of Jesus. It is the result of the network of power linking the local élites, Jewish religious leaders, and the Roman imperial rulers. Today, too, do we seek to wash our hands of any responsibility for the injustices of our society, because we are afraid of the political or even religious authorities? Do we, like the Jewish mob, share in creating a public opinion which asks for the punishment or death of innocent ones? Do we contribute to mob violence by spreading rumours?

2nd Station: Jesus takes the cross

Jesus is given the cross to be carried up to Calvary for his own crucifixion. Jesus accepts the cross, knowing that he has no way out of the situation, except in renouncing his teachings and his judgement on the religious interpretations of the High Priests, the exploitation of the Scribes and Pharisees, and the unjust colonial rule of the Romans. His option is to suffer the death that was due to his teaching. He gives us the example of an alternative way of life. His is a non-violent protest unto death which Mahatma Gandhi, perhaps better than anyone else prior to him, understood clearly as a political protest and powerful strategy involving self-sacrifice for the freedom of his people.

Mary had to suffer the immense pain and shame of her son being condemned to a public execution by crucifixion – a punishment imposed on criminals and rebels. This was part of her cross. She saw clearly how the innocent suffer at the hands of powerful, wicked rulers.

For us, too, following Jesus is a call to live according to the values he has taught us. This is not an easy task. It implies accepting our cross and carrying it to the end. This traditionally came to mean humbly and patiently bearing troubles and sufferings, but it also involves bearing the cross of transforming ourselves, our values, relationships and social structures. This, too, involves suffering, and even danger to oneself. It may require contesting the evils of society and religion, as Jesus had to do. This is particularly difficult when the whole social establishment is controlled by people and forces that are for the maintenance of injustice, and even the increase of inequalities. This is so today, not only in our country, but globally. It means that the disciple of Jesus has to be prepared to suffer for justice, truth, peace, love and sharing. Martyrdom was common in the early Church and many in our times have had to sacrifice their lives for this cause. What are we called to do in this regard and what is the cross we have to bear?

3rd Station: Jesus falls the first time

Jesus falls with the weight of the cross on him. A Roman soldier looks on. Perhaps he is mocking Jesus, telling him to get up, as the carter tells the bull that falls down fatigued under the weight of his burden. Jesus is bleeding. What would Jesus be thinking at this time? He perhaps asks himself whether he has to go through this process until the end. He perseveres, he does not give up under the weight of the cross on his body, though he is thoroughly wounded because of the crown of thorns and the merciless scourging of the previous night.

Mary would have felt the pain of this fall of Jesus. She would have been aware of how much Jesus was sensitive to human pain and to the evil that brought it about. The very innocence and purity of heart and mind of Jesus, and the cruelty of the political and religious oppressors, would make her own pain more intense. It also strengthens her resolve to resist the evil of the self-righteous rulers of these times. Mary sees, today, the pain of those who fall under the burden of their sufferings. She empathizes with them. She strengthens them. She leads them in the struggle for true liberation.

How much suffering the poor people of our country undergo at the present time because of economic difficulties! How many suffer in the factories because of harsh working conditions? How many suffer on the plantations, and in foreign lands as migrant workers? How many fall down because of heavy work to be done under semi-starving or semi-slave conditions? How much pain there is in the way to and from work in the terribly overcrowded buses and trains!

We do not quite see how all this can be ended, and more just relationships be brought about. We fail, yet we must persevere in carrying our cross in union with Jesus and Mary.

4th Station: Jesus meets his mother

The Roman soldier, insofar as he had a heart, would have been embarrassed by the presence of the mother of Jesus on this journey. Like many officials he would have had to execute this cruel assignment. He had to participate in the torture of the innocent Jesus. He had been trained to carry out orders even when they were unjust.

Mary is conscious of why her son Jesus is suffering. She is conscious of the Roman soldier and the cruel power signified by, and effected through, him. She can do nothing to save her son, whom she had to safeguard from the time of his birth from the cruel political power of Herod, and for whose sake she lived a political exile in Egypt. She perhaps thinks: is there no way of saving my son's life? What mother would not do that? Sorrowfully, and perhaps angrily, she had followed Jesus from the previous night, when he was tortured by the soldiers.

When the eyes of Jesus and Mary met, Mary would have felt the bitter pain of the stark reality of the abuse of power by the political and religious leaders of the day. At this stage, there was no concept of Jesus paying the price for the sins of past and future humanity, for the sin of Adam and Eve and their progeny, as traditional spirituality usually portrays.

Torture is part of the cruelty that is imposed on many people today. How many mothers have to wait outside police stations, and the torture chambers of armed factions? How much mothers suffer because of the insecurity of human life today – sometimes far from home, in order to earn their living.

How many people today work in jobs in which the rich exploit the poor, the powerful lord it over the weak? This system is accepted, perhaps because there is no other way of living. How many live on the sale of arms, or drugs, on the suppression of truth and the transfer of resources from the poor to the rich?

It is also sad to reflect that the community which took its origin from the wounded hearts of Jesus and Mary has, not infrequently in history, been a cause of violence to others, and of the violation of human rights among its own people.

5th Station: Simon the Cyrenian helps Jesus

Perhaps because Jesus was scourged before being led to Calvary, he was too weak to carry the cross. Simon, a bystander, was pressed into helping him by the Roman soldiers. This Gospel story of Simon from Cyrene, in North Africa, shows the international dimension of the killing of Jesus. The temple of Jerusalem was a trading centre of the region. The life of the Jewish people from the East was invaded by the Roman imperialists of the West. They coerced the services of a North African to carry the cross.

Mary would have been intensely grieved to see that Jesus was exhausted. She would have appreciated the help of Simon, a foreigner, even though he was at first compelled to it, and though this help did not prevent Jesus from being killed. She would have noticed how the Romans used a North African to help them in their crucifixion of Jesus, a Galilean Jew.

We have many opportunities to be of help to others in loneliness, in trouble, often, because of injustice, in involuntary poverty, in conditions of war. We can ask ourselves whether we fulfil our civic and social obligations in these circumstances. Or are we content to stand by and let the victims bear the pain? Even if we cannot fully resolve someone's problem, we can at least be helpful in some way, as Simon the Cyrenian was. We can participate in the people's struggle for human rights and justice in society. We can reflect on our social responsibility, and on the global aspects of our problems, characterized by trade liberalization, the arms trade and the impact of the mass media. This shows concern for others in their difficulties.

Every day as we go through life, we are called to share the pain of another, of others who may not be known to us, or towards whom we may not have an obvious obligation. A road accident, a bomb blast, the experience of refugees, the homeless, those arrested unjustly or on suspicion. We are called to bear the cross of others on their way of the cross. This is at the heart of Christian, Marian, spirituality. In bearing another's cross we are in communion with Jesus and Mary, perhaps unexpectedly.

6th Station: Veronica wipes the face of Jesus

Veronica, who wiped the bleeding and battered face of Jesus, was a brave person. She was prepared to face the anger of the Roman soldiers, and of the high priests, and of the Jewish mob which wanted Jesus crucified. When a man is being punished by the authorities for being a traitor to the rulers, or an enemy of the people's religion, it is a dangerous thing to show him any support or even sympathy. Veronica was a strong woman, with a true sense of values and priorities.

Mary and the women who were with Jesus followed him and showed him, and the soldiers, their sympathy for him. Luke 23.27 says 'A large crowd of people followed him: among them were some women who were weeping and wailing for him'.

Wiping the face of Jesus is not something to be done only on Good Friday. Veronica most probably had a life commitment to the solace of the suffering, the unjustly punished. Mary would have seen in her the values of courage and Gospel priorities. She was not thinking of adorning herself. She did not want to attract attention to herself.

We see this very often in situations of internal conflict, when human rights are easily disregarded and people are first tortured even before they are tried. One can perhaps understand that the men, especially the apostles, were in greater danger from the authorities, and a woman was safer in showing such kindness. The way of the cross of Jesus was an occasion in which women played a more active role than the men who were with him. Veronica is said to have been favoured with an imprint of the battered face of Jesus on the veil with which she wiped his bleeding face. Can we try to see his face in every suffering person? As he said in Matthew 25.40, 'Whenever you did this to the least of my brethren you did it to me'. Even when we cannot prevent some cruelty and injustice among individuals and in society, we can at least empathize with the victims, listen to them in their difficulties, and thus share their burden.

Within families, reflection on the values of Mary and Veronica can show us the way to use our time, our resources and our talents, conscious of the needs of others, especially those suffering because of poverty and the cruelty of the powerful.

7th Station: Jesus falls a second time

Jesus falls again; he is physically weak. But he is morally, spiritually, strong. He does not flinch under persecution, even when he falls with the cross. He does not compromise his mission and his message.

Mary's heart would have been torn at seeing Jesus fall under the weight of the cross. She may have wanted to help him, or even save him, as any mother would. She would have felt intensely how hard and cruel the system of Roman law and the Jewish religion were on her innocent son.

This happens often nowadays, in the inhuman treatment ordered by governments and militant groups. The agents of big companies, too, make boardroom decisions that adversely affect the lives of the poor. Today, big corporations and the world powers impose burdens on the poor everywhere – for the sake of their profits. Increases in the price of essential goods, and the implementation of plans that deprive people of their jobs, lands, and sometimes homes, may be forced by officials of the state and corporations. These policies cause the poor to become poorer, their real incomes falling with each major decision of the rich and powerful. How do we react to such measures?

Mary would have seen the unbending determination of her son, his faithfulness to the end. Perhaps this is what she taught him in his younger days 'as he grew in age and wisdom'. Both Jesus and Mary knew the price of human liberation.

Christian discipleship, the following of Mary, is a call to determination, courage, endurance, through difficulties of all sorts. As believers, we are called to strive together to transform the evil system that makes so many fall under the weight of their daily cross.

8th Station: Jesus meets the women of Jerusalem

Once again it is the women of Jerusalem, and those who had followed him from Galilee, who come forward to console Jesus. He tells them: 'Women of Jerusalem! do not cry for me, but for yourselves and your children . . . For if such things as these are done when the wood is green, what will happen when it is dry?' (Luke 23.27–31).

Mary may have recalled, then, the words of Simeon the prophet, three decades earlier, in Jerusalem: 'and sorrow, like a sharp sword, will break your own heart' (Luke 2.35). She would have tried to understand, within this deep sorrow, why Jesus, in being faithful to his mission, had to undergo this passion.

Today, the women of Sri Lanka have much to weep about. The process of development that is enforced on the country and the people is leading to the subjection of women to many hardships. The harsh conditions in the Free Trade Zones, where over 50,000 young women work, are such that they are exploited in the short term and often physically ill in the long term.

Women, mothers of families, often feel obliged to go abroad as domestic workers because the earnings of their husbands are not enough to supply food, housing and education for their children. They are subjected to many hardships in these foreign countries, especially in the Middle East, without any effective support from the Sri Lankan state, which benefits from their foreign exchange earnings. Prostitution, even of children, is increasing with tourism, and the growing impoverishment of the poor. The civil war also makes many women widows or lose their sons, the hope of their future. They suffer the trauma of such killings, and become refugees in their own country. All this makes the conditions of women now much worse than a few decades ago. With present social trends, and the influence of the mass media, the quality of life for children of the coming generation is likely to be worse in many ways than that of the children of the previous generation.

What can we do to prevent the break-up of our social fabric, of family life and of the sense of community? How do we direct the influence of television on children, and on family life? In these situations the words of Jesus, and the example of Mary supporting Jesus, can be a source of strength to the mothers and daughters of Lanka.

9th Station: Jesus falls the third time

Jesus falls to the ground; he is in a pitiful situation. But a Roman soldier looks on as the one with power and authority over life and death.

Mary would have felt the oppression of the foreign ruler who was leading Jesus to his crucifixion in such a brutal manner. The political implications of the passion and death of Jesus are poignantly revealed in this scene. There is no question here of Jesus paying the price for the sins of humankind. The story is one of the brutal use of imperial power, allied with a local élite, to kill a prophetic leader of the Jewish people. Mary has known and sees the plight of the oppressed and lonely.

Today, in spite of the agonizing poverty of the poor, especially in impoverished countries, their ruling élites and foreign companies and governments continue to press them further and further. More debts are imposed on them. Subsidies are cut. Services are reduced. Almost everything is commercialized. The weak go to the wall. Entire countries suffer from exhaustion and internal conflict results. The poor and marginalized experience deeper and deeper troubles: poverty, unemployment, insecurity, loneliness, drugs, divorce, broken families, neglected children, depression, trauma, suicides. Sri Lanka is said to have one of the world's highest rates of suicide. To free ourselves from all these troubles at personal and societal levels, we need to seek the values of unselfish love, justice and peace, for which Jesus died.

Here, too, we are called not merely to grieve at the suffering of Jesus, but to see his strength. He is a strong leader. He does not give up under the weight of the cross. He falls physically, but he continues his struggle, his resistance to the abuse of power and the falsification of religion. He witnessed to true religion. He cleansed the temple of the merchants, those who made money in and from the temple. 'He came to make the human heart a temple, and the soul an altar, and the mind a priest' (Kahlil Gibran, *The Crucified*).

10th Station: Jesus is stripped of his garments

First the soldiers mocked him, dressing him in a purple cloak and insulting him: 'Save yourself if you are the king of the Jews' (Luke

23.36). Now they shame him, through his nakedness on the cross, in the last few hours of his life. The shameless soldiers cast lots for his stolen garment.

Mary has to bear this insult. She would have felt his shame and pain as his garments were ripped off his bleeding skin. She witnessed the abuse of a human body in this cruel way.

Today, the human body is abused in different ways: in the media, in the tourist trade, in harassment at work, in torture, in prisons, and even in hospitals where little attention is given to poorer patients. Do we, also, sometimes strip others of their human dignity through prejudice, racism, sexism, casteism and other forms of discrimination? Do we add to the sorrow and shame of others through gossip and slander?

Another way of stripping Jesus is to take away the core of the message for which he died, and to distort it so it becomes a means of intolerance and injustice to others. Pope John Paul II in his 1994 apostolic letter *Tertio Millennio Adveniente*, preparing for the Jubilee of the Year 2000, calls Christians to repentance for 'acquiescence given, especially in certain centuries, to intolerance and even the use of violence in the service of truth . . . Many factors frequently converged to create assumptions which justified intolerance and fostered an emotional climate from which only great spirits, truly free and filled with God, were in some way able to break free' (35).

We too, in our history, have been responsible for so interpreting the life, message and death of Jesus as to be intolerant of others. How can we repent of this stripping of the Jesus message?

11th Station: Jesus is nailed to the cross

Mary would have witnessed this cruel deed with profound sadness. She would have realized how far the religion of the day had become an engine of oppression to such a good person as her son. The Roman procurator, Pilate, alone had the authority to impose this death sentence.

The cross is a symbol of Christianity, of the love of God for humanity, and of the price of fidelity to Gospel values. Unfortunately, the cross became in later times a symbol of the domination of those who were not Christians. It was carried by Christians in religious wars like the Crusades, and even in wars of colonial conquest. Conversely, Jesus says that if we are his disciples, we shall have to bear a cross similar to his. Where do we meet the cross in our lives and how do we bear it? When we try to be faithful to the teaching of Jesus, and to contribute to his mission on earth, we too shall be nailed to the cross in different ways – sometimes by social, political and religious leaders, sometimes by our companions or public opinion. We can follow Jesus and Mary in refusing to give up our call and mission in spite of such pain and crucifixion.

The cross of Jesus is the triumph of unconquerable love which has inspired billions of humans – Christians and others. 'Jesus never lived a life of fear, nor did He die suffering or complaining ... He lived a leader; He was crucified as a Crusader, He died with a heroism that frightened His killers and tormentors. He feared not His persecutors nor His enemies. He suffered not before His killers. Free and brave and daring He was. He defied all despots and oppressors. He muted Evil and He crushed Falsehood and He choked Treachery' (Kahlil Gibran, *The Crucified*).

He is a redeemer who has inspired countless martyrs throughout the centuries.

12th Station: Jesus is raised on the cross and dies

Jesus entrusts the apostle John to his mother: 'Behold your son', and his mother to John: 'Behold your mother'. This is the only appearance of an apostle in the tradition of the Way of the Cross. Nor is there Gospel evidence that the apostles followed Jesus to Calvary. It would most probably have been too risky for them. But John, 'the disciple Jesus loved' (John 19.25), was there at the foot of the cross with Mary and the other women.

Mark testifies that the 'inscription giving the charge against him read "The King of the Jews" ' (Mark 15.18). Once again we can reflect on the suffering and sorrow of Mary when the moment of his death came. This is something she would have feared for a long time, given the manner of his life and his teaching, which went against the social and religious establishment. Her sadness would have been intense when he said 'I thirst', and the soldiers gave him some sour wine on a sponge. The soldiers further saddened her by piercing his side, and blood and water flowed from his pierced heart. All the same, she stood, sad, but firm, at the foot of the cross. *Stabat Mater dolorosa*. She was with him to the end. It would have seemed as if his whole enterprise was ending in utter failure and shame, as he hung naked, dead, on the cross.

Jesus was killed because he bore witness to the truth, the love of God: 'My commandment is this: love one another, just as I have loved you. The greatest love a person can have for his friends is to give his life for them. And you are my friends if you do what I command you ... If the world hates you, just remember that it has hated me first. If you belonged to the world, then the world would love you as its own. If they persecuted me, they will persecute you too' (John 15.12–14, 18, 20).

Genuine discipleship of Jesus will mean that we too have to suffer much at the hands of those whose values are those of the 'world' and not of God. As Jesus said, we lose our lives to gain them.

Pope John Paul II calls Christians to repentance and reminds us to 'express profound regret for the weaknesses of so many of her sons and daughters who sullied her [the Church's] face, preventing her from fully mirroring the image of her crucified Lord, the supreme witness of patient love and of humble meekness' (*Tertio Millennio Adveniente* 35).

Our preparation for the Jubilee of 2000 should include a renewal of our theology and spirituality.

13th Station: Jesus is in the arms of Mary

This moment, drawn by many artists and called the *Pietà*, was a most harrowing experience for Mary. Jesus was dead. She knew he was not only innocent, but doing God's will in his witness to the Kingdom of God and its demands. Yet the traditional religious leaders, and the imperial rulers, wanted him killed. She would have seen the cruelty of the alliance between that religion and the social power of the day. In this situation, the whole life mission of her wonderful and radical son seemed lost. The forces ranged against him had triumphed. The apostles seemed dispersed, except for John. Mary his mother, the sad but strong woman, persevered in her belief in the cause that Jesus died for. Her faith was a trust beyond death – in the truth and justice of his message. Having accepted the disciple, John, as her son, she stood firm in her conviction and gathered together the shattered group of the followers of Jesus, and awaited the better day that he had foretold.

South Korean artists have depicted this scene, linking it with the weeping of mothers after the killing by the state forces in Kwanju in 1982. How many such scenes we have in Sri Lanka, with the continuing killings of the civil war and the underworld operations of gangs, often linked with political leaders.

Mary teaches us to have confidence in the values of the Kingdom of God which Jesus announced and was killed for, even when the odds are strongly against those values, when the enemies of the poor and the marginalized triumph. Like her, we have to go through the dark night of the soul, when all seems lost and even God seems distant. We can learn from Mary steadfastness in adversity, both in our personal lives and in struggling in society for a better humanity.

The dying Jesus forgave his enemies, 'for they do not know what they do'. In his supreme wisdom he saw their ignorance. We may not always acknowledge that others, who do evil to us, 'do not know what they do'.

But even then, discipleship of Jesus calls us to forgiveness, admitting our limited insights into the minds and hearts of others.

Jesus killed is our hope, our example, our redemption, our conviction in the ultimate triumph of good over evil. 'And if Humanity were wise, she would stand today and sing in strength the song of conquest and the hymn of triumph' (Kahlil Gibran, *The Crucified*).

14th Station: Jesus is buried

Joseph of Arimathea, 'a respected member of the Council, a man who was eagerly awaiting the Kingdom of God, bravely went to Pilate and asked for the body of Jesus' (Mark 15.43). He had, himself, been a disciple of Jesus. It was dangerous, even after his death, to identify with the crucified Jesus. Yet Joseph of Arimathea sympathized with the suffering of the followers of Jesus, and offered his own unused tomb, cut out of the rock, for Jesus' burial.

Mary would have been present on this sad occasion. It must have been a funeral which took place in fear, for a disgraced religious leader had been crucified as a criminal. Mary had to bear the cross of living without him. She gave support to the small community of faithful and threatened disciples in their fidelity to Jesus and his message.

Joseph of Arimathea and Nicodemus were both men who came secretly, or by night, to Jesus because they were afraid of the Jewish authorities (John 19.38–40). Joseph of Arimathea was an honourable and good man. He was a respected member of the Jewish Council, who had not agreed with their decision and action (Luke 23.50–53).

While rich families did not offer Mary and Joseph a place for the birth of Jesus, Joseph, a rich man, offered, for the burial of Jesus, his own tomb.

It is noteworthy that the women who followed Jesus from Galilee, the women of Jerusalem, Simon of Cyrene, Joseph of Arimathea and Nicodemus were all lay people, to use contemporary language. At the moment of crisis, lay people seem to have responsibilities which the official apostles found unsafe to undertake. When people are made to suffer in many ways at personal, family, social and national levels, and the religious leadership is unable or slow to correct such sufferings, the laity could have a special duty and privilege to come forward, to bear witness to the values for which Jesus gave his life.

As we prepare for the third millennium, we can reflect on how we Christians lived the second millennium, 1000–1997: 'On the threshold of the new millennium Christians need to place themselves humbly before the Lord and examine themselves on the responsibility which they too have for the evils of our day' (Pope John Paul II, *Tertio Millennio Adveniente* 35).

The Way of the Cross can be a very meaningful preparation for Jubilee 2000.

The Sri Lankan national basilica at Tewatte, fostering such an integral redemptive message implicit in the stations of the Way of the Cross, could really be a national shrine of the Kingdom of God, of human values and human rights.

There could be feasts, not only for healing the sickness of personal illnesses, and the exorcizing of people possessed by demons, but also for the healing of social relationships and structures, and exorcizing the mammonic presence in them. Then the basilica would have a social significance. Myongdong Cathedral in Seoul, where Cardinal Stephan Kim resides, is a symbol of Korean democracy, where people struggling for human rights under dictatorial regimes found sanctuary. The Marian shrines in Poland were sanctuaries for human rights and freedom when Poland was under Communist dictatorship. Our Lady of Guadalupe in Mexico has been, and is, an inspiration for the liberation of the native peoples of the Americas.

Every Marian shrine in the world can bear witness to Mary as a liberator of humankind, as Pope Paul VI does:

> The modern woman will note with pleasant surprise that Mary of Nazareth, while completely devoted to the will of God, *was far from being a timidly submissive woman* or one whose piety was repellent to others; on the contrary, she was a woman who did not hesitate to proclaim that God vindicates *the humble and the oppressed*, and removes the powerful people of this world from their privileged positions (cf. Lk. 1:51–53). The modern woman will recognize in Mary, who 'stands out among the poor and humble of the Lord', *a woman of strength*, who experienced poverty and suffering, flight and exile (cf. Mt. 2:13–23) ... These are but examples, which show clearly that the figure of the Blessed Virgin does not disillusion any of the profound expectations of the men and women of our time but offers them the perfect model of the disciple of the Lord: the disciple who builds up the earthly and temporal city while being a diligent pilgrim towards the heavenly and eternal city, the disciple who *works for that justice which sets free the oppressed and for that charity which assists the needy*; but above all, the disciple who is the active witness of that love which builds up Christ in people's hearts.

Public statement of the Catholic Bishops' Conference of Sri Lanka

(Catholic Messenger, 5 June 1994)

Mary and Human Liberation

For the past twenty centuries, Christians the world over have witnessed to the uniqueness of Jesus Christ by attempting to interpret Him as One who gave meaning to their lives and fulfilled their deepest yearnings. Thus, for example, in an age of religious controversy, His divinity was emphasized; in the more recent context of market social inequality, He is presented as the great Liberator who will free people from oppression and misery.

A similar process of presenting a sacred figure as an icon of the times has gone on regarding the Blessed Virgin Mary, the Mother of Jesus. In the middle ages, she was the Madonna that inspired greatness and piety. In times closer to us, She has a different significance. Considering the closeness of Mary to Jesus and the immense veneration that Catholics of all ages have had towards her, this loving attachment was to be expected.

Trying to present Jesus and Mary in categories that are considered relevant to time and place is in itself a laudable exercise. We know from history that these efforts have met with varying degrees of success or failure.

The Church on her part, has been like a vigilant shepherd, ever anxious to lead the flock to safe pastures. She has been like a loving mother, finding the best of spiritual nourishment for her children. Throughout the centuries, she has jealously guarded the deposit of faith, and perfected her catechesis. She has fulfilled this task, entrusted to her by her Divine Founder, through the instrumentality of her Pastors, the Bishops in communion with one another and with the Supreme Pastor, the Pope.

In this regard our attention has been drawn to a publication entitled *Mary and Human Liberation* by one of our priests, Rev. Fr Tissa Balasuriya OMI. In it the author has made an attempt to give a fresh interpretation to Jesus and Mary. It is obvious that he had cherished the hope of making these sublime figures more acceptable in our milieu – a milieu that is multi-religious in character, and scarred by social injustices.

As responsible Pastors, we have sadly to state that this presentation is not compatible with the Faith of the Church. The book as we have it today, contains serious deficiencies which can cause positive harm to the faith of our people.

Without going into all the details we wish, in this statement, to point out some of the more glaring errors.

1. The author downplays the validity of Sacred Tradition, which in the Church's teaching, is on par with the Sacred Scriptures themselves as a source of Revelation. He, rather portrays it as some sort of unwarranted creation of some self-interested churchmen.

2. The author minimises the validity of Faith, which is a free gift of God, with his view that doctrine or elaborations of theology become objectively valid only to the extent that they are:

(a) Rationally convincing and
(b) in keeping with the core-values of other religous persuasions.

3. His presentation of original sin brings up serious questions on the basic teachings of the Church regarding Jesus Christ and His Mother Mary and casts serious doubts with regard to the:–

(a) Divinity of Christ,
(b) Role of Christ as the Redeemer,
(c) Privileged position of Mary in the history of Salvation.

4. The author often gives the impression, directly or indirectly that the role of religion is basically to ensure humanistic and social liberation of mankind and help it to reach that goal.

Looking at it globally, the book questions the veracity of traditional dogma, and the Church's understanding of it. This questioning coupled with the inference that dogmas have been manipulated by fallible human agencies to suit their own interests, can cause doubts to enter the minds and hearts of our faithful.

Considering the above, we the Catholic Bishops of Sri Lanka admonish our faithful to refrain from reading this book as it could be detrimental to their faith.

BISHOP OSWALD GOMIS
Secretary General
on behalf of the Catholic Bishops' Conference in Sri Lanka

❀❀❀❀❀

Some Observations on the Book Mary and Human Liberation
SCDF, 27 July 1994

Good intentions can certainly be found in this work of Fr Tissa Balasuriya: the desire to favor the dialogue between Christianity and oriental religions; the desire to contribute to the moral and social advancement of his people; the desire to link Mariology to Christology; the desire to offer a view of the figure of the Blessed Virgin that illuminates her values of mature and responsible womanhood; the desire to emphasize the centrality of the doctrine of love; the desire to criticize aberrations in certain expressions of Marian piety. Nevertheless, it is necessary to underscore that these objectives can be pursued, in whole or in part, without undermining essential points of Christian faith.

1 Methodological deficiencies

1.1 From the theological point of view, the book by Fr Balasuriya is very deficient. In fact, truths of faith, theological formulations, opinion of preachers are all put on the same level to the point that the author seems to ignore the distinctions between them. He even substitutes subjective criteria for ecclesial criteria in evaluating Revelation. In addition, the volume in question lacks that which is characteristic of genuine theological method (the careful evaluation of sources, the well-pondered exegesis of Scripture, the respectful consideration of the perennial Tradition of the Church, the *sensus fidei* that is manifested in the liturgy, the sober and docile reflection on the most solemn interventions of the Magisterium).

1.2 The author practically seems to equate the oriental religions and Christianity, denying to the latter its revelatory character.[1] Religion is reduced to 'myth' and, in our case, to the initial myth of original sin, interpreted by ecclesiastical authorities without any authority.[2] A further element that arises in the view of Fr Balasuriya is the reduction of religion to ideology;[3] both, in fact, have the same criteria of individuation and interpretation.[4]

189

1.3 The author finds it necessary on several occasions to distinguish what Jesus really said from that which thereafter was formulated by the Church.[5] The only expressions that are accepted as belonging to Jesus are his messages of love, justice, and liberation.[6] All that which follows does not appertain to him but to the Church and, therefore, is only theology. All Church teaching can be modified in order to construct a theology that is capable of serving the inter-religious dialogue and woman's liberation.

2 Statements regarding the Revelation and its sources

Nowhere in the work does one find a concept of divine Revelation corresponding to that expounded in the Dogmatic Constitution *Dei Verbum* (cf. nos. 1–13) of Vatican Council II. The author has a view of Revelation very much different from the thought of the Church.

2.1 Hermeneutic Principle Proposed by Fr Balasuriya

In order to judge the various theologies and their sources, the Bible and Tradition, the author proposes two criteria, one negative and one positive, centered on the commandment of love. According to the negative criterion, every element of theology and its sources that dehumanizes or discriminates cannot come from God via Christ; according to the positive criterion, everything that in a religion human-izes and ennobles is, in the final analysis, of divine origin.[7] The author then inevitably inclines toward relativism. According to him, not a few elements of the Bible are contrary to love and therefore do not come from God; many elements in the sacred books of other religions speak of love and justice and thus come from God.

2.2 Sacred Scripture

The explicit statement of the Second Vatican Council that 'Holy Mother Church relying on the faith of the apostolic age, accepts as sacred and canonical the books of the Old and the New Testaments, whole and entire, with all their parts, on the grounds that, written under the inspiration of the Holy Spirit (cf. Jn 20:31; 2 Tim 3:16; 2 Pt 1:19–21; 3:15–16), they have God as their author, and have been handed on as such to the Church herself (*DV* 11)' is in effect set aside by the author. According to him not a few pages in Scripture have to be removed because they are incompatible with human rights.[8] In 'reading' the Bible, the author disregards the rules of Christian hermeneutics (cf. *DV* 13) he does not take account of the fact of the 'condescension of divine Wisdom' (ibid.), of the patient pedagogy of God, of the gradualness of

Revelation and of its incarnation in history, of the literary genres used in the Old and the New Testaments, of the Semitic way of expression. Vatican II teaches that 'all that has been said about the manner of interpreting Scripture is ultimately subject to the judgement of the Church which exercises the divinely conferred commission and ministry of watching over and interpreting the Word of God' (*DV* 12). The author on the other hand holds that the Bible and Tradition must be submitted to the scrutiny of criticism, an activity in which the Church has no right to intervene because her teachings have been intolerant or harmful toward third parties, for example, to other religions and women.[9]

2.3 Tradition

The author shows that he does not have a clear view of the nature of Tradition, as a way of knowledge of divine Revelation (cf. *DV* 8–10) such that in the words of the Second Vatican Council: 'Sacred Tradition and Sacred Scripture make up a single sacred deposit of the Word of God, which is entrusted to the Church' (*DV* 10). He ignores the concept of divine-apostolic Tradition reducing it to mere human, and frequently, deleterious tradition. This human tradition, he says, has led to simple myths becoming dogmas of faith in the Catholic Church.[10] In the entire volume, but especially in chapters 5 and 6, the author supposes that the single criterion of truth are the Gospels and not Tradition which culminates in the formulation of dogma, denying in this way the normative value of Tradition itself as a source of revelation.[11]

2.4 The Magisterium

The exact nature of the Magisterium, its function of safeguarding the faith and of fathoming the revealed Word, the diversity of forms with which it expresses itself, are not recognized by the author. The doctrine of papal infallibility, in the terms defined by Vatican Council I, is reduced to a simple point of division between the Churches.[12] According to the author, the Magisterium of the Church, whether conciliar or papal, even in its most binding pronouncements from a formal point of view, has been the cause of simple myths or doctrines, products of the imagination becoming dogmas of faith. This is said to be the case with the doctrines of original sin defined by the Council of Trent,[13] of the Immaculate Conception,[14] and of the Assumption of Mary into heaven.[15]

With respect to the uniform development of a doctrine by means of a deeper understanding on the part of the Church under the direction of the Holy Spirit, the author deems it necessary to adopt as a parameter of judgment the 'hermeneutics of suspicion'.[16] The asserted assistance of the Holy Spirit in the Magisterial activities of the Church is, according to the author, simply a claim which is uncontrollable and unverifiable that does not restrain theologians and pastors from indulging their theological imagination. Such claimed assistance often becomes a means to satisfy the needs of one group of believers especially when they exert dominant political power or cultural or spiritual influence in the society.[17]

3 Christological problems

3.1 The divinity of Jesus

What Fr Balasuriya affirms of the identity of Jesus is extremely little. This is all the more true since the context demands a clear response to the question who Jesus is.[18] The author, no doubt because of his own presuppositions concerning the protocol of the interreligious dialogue, fails to make explicit mention of the divinity of Jesus. Christ is described merely as someone who had a particular experience of the divine and a union with God.[19] The author neglects the most important symbols of the faith (the Nicene-Constantinopolitan Creed) and the solemn dogmatic definitions of the Councils of Nicea, Constantinople, Ephesus, and Chalcedon. In the entire work it is never said that Jesus is God, the eternal and consubstantial Son of the Father. Naturally, the author knows the teaching of the Church on the divinity of Jesus but shows himself hesitant or reluctant to express this fully.[20] He is not inclined to profess that Jesus is really God, but says only that he is considered like God: divinity was attributed to Jesus.[21]

3.2 The salvific mission of Jesus

From the point of view of the Catholic faith it is quite surprising to see Jesus aligned with Buddha, Mohammed and the seers of other religions,[22] as if the question of Christ's identity were not already radically clarified by the Gospels and by the great Ecumenical Councils.

According to the author, in Asia it would be necessary to revise all the elements of Christian faith which impinge on the sensitivities of Asian countries and oriental religions, particularly the conception of salvation. Salvation is held to be a personal problem which is resolved in the direct relationship between God and the creature.[23] Man is said to reach salvation through dedication to the moral obligation both in his personal and social life. The author does not see the need for a salvific intervention realized by a divine-human Redeemer. Christ was a master who taught us how to take up the moral obligation, both personal and social. The work of Christ is not properly soteriological but didactic, transmitting a teaching. Jesus was a promoter of interpersonal relations against any kind of discrimination among peoples, races, sexes; a liberator and purifier from oppressive structures of religion; a champion of social and political liberation.[24] The necessity of objective redemption of the human race is a simplistic presupposition of theologians.[25]

4 The doctrine of original sin

4.1 Negation of the reality of original sin

In chapter four entitled 'The Basic Presupposition of Original Sin',[26] a key chapter of the volume, the author denies resolutely the dogma of original sin defined as by the Council of Trent. The author does not attempt a new interpretation of the dogma, inculturating it in the Asian context (an undertaking which could be quite legitimate), but rather resolutely refutes the doctrine of the Church, attacking its essential contents. In fact, for Fr Balasuriya the doctrine of original sin is founded on various presuppositions acritically acquired.[27] This doctrine is seen to be a simple hypothesis which he believes it is necessary to contest.[28] According to the author the traditional doctrine of original sin: (1) is discriminatory and unjust with respect to women and is the cause of the anti-sexual attitude dominant in the Church;[29] (2) is responsible for the negative attitude in the Church with regard to nature ('anti-nature') and to the world ('anti-world') as well as contrary to the goodness of God;[30] (3) is discriminatory of members of other religions and non-believers in God and therefore unworthy of God himself;[31] (4) has led the Church to emphasize in an erroneous way the mission 'ad gentes'.[32]

4.2 Connection with other points of Christian faith

The author expounds lucidly the connection between the doctrine of original sin and other important pillars of Christian doctrine.[33] The 'theological imagination,' which is at the origin of the doctrine of original sin and which has determined its development, has exercised its influence also on many other doctrinal points. Among these: the situation of 'original justice' in which the first parents of the human race were created, the loss of original justice as a result of original sin, the question of the transmission of original sin, the consequences of original sin in the order of nature and in the order of grace, the relationship 'original sin/death,' the necessity of a redeemer and consequently of a divine-human redeemer, the way in which redemption occurred by means of Christ, the necessity of Baptism for salvation, the Baptism of infants, the Immaculate Conception of Mary, the role of the Church as community of salvation. All these questions and others have been influenced by the doctrine and therefore must be radically revised.

4.3 The dogma of redemption

Fr Balasuriya attributes the development of doctrine regarding the dogma of redemption to the acritical reception of presuppositions concerning original sin.[34] Typical of the mind of the author is his statement that there is no ontological need for the redemption accomplished by Christ.[35]

In conclusion, the opinions of the author on original sin are incompatible with the faith of the Church.

5 Ecclesiology

Fr Balasuriya's notion of Church also appears very deficient. In fact, according to him the current teaching on the nature of the Church does not seem to correspond to the thought of Jesus, since it is founded on the assumption that Jesus is the redeemer of mankind and has entrusted to the Church the mission of continuing his redemptive work in all places and in all times.[36] In addition, the doctrine of the Church as community of salvation would be the result of the abnormal development of the dogma of redemption which in turn was determined by the presuppositions regarding original sin.[37] The claim of the Church to be the vehicle of eternal salvation or mediatrix of salvation is completely unfounded. Various claims of the Church herself derive from having assumed that Christ entrusted to her the task of continuing his salvific work: to have the right/duty to draw all peoples into her own community of faith; to be the supreme spiritual guide in the whole world; to have the power to absolve sins or to deny absolution with eternal consequences.[38] Finally, the author denies in fact the dogmas of primacy and infallibility.[39]

6 Marian doctrine

In chapter five the author reflects on traditional Marian doctrine. He shows himself prejudiced from the outset against the Marian doctrine of the Church. Not even chapter VIII of *Lumen Gentium* receives a positive judgement from him because it emphasizes more the privileges and graces granted by God to Mary than her active role in the life and ministry of Jesus in the social context of the time.[40]

6.1 The Immaculate Conception

The dogmatic definition of the Immaculate Conception is, according to Fr Balasuriya, an example of the extent to which the theological imagination can reach.[41]

Consistent with his denial of original sin, the author has no difficulty in accepting that Mary was conceived without original sin,[42] precisely because original sin does not exist. But he does object to limiting the immaculate conception only to Jesus and Mary.[43] The author holds that the doctrine of the Immaculate Conception is in opposition to the true humanity of Mary and includes in the concept of 'immaculate conception' elements absolutely foreign to the dogma defined by Pope Pius IX, for example, that it was impossible for Mary to be tempted.[44]

6.2 Mary's virginity

The doctrine of the virginity of Mary is said to result from presuppositions regarding original sin, the ideology of the dominance of men, and the recourse to theological imagination.[45] The author asks furthermore whether it is not better to be a normal mother than a virgin-mother.[46] From the text it can be deduced that for Fr Balasuriya the virginal conception of Christ is not a fact, a way chosen by God for the incarnation of the Word, but is a theological notion that originated from some dominant assumptions according to which all that concerns human sexual activity is unworthy of God. In this ideological structure God was forced by theology to be born apart from human sexual relations.

The doctrine of original sin has also determined the rise and confirmation of the doctrine of the virginal conception of Christ. If Jesus is to be without sin, he would have to be born virginally.[47] From the first centuries, the biblical testimony of Matthew and Luke of the virginal conception of Christ was the object of theological discussions and is still a question of controversy between Catholics and Protestants.[48] For the author, the historicity of the virginity of Mary is an 'open question' for scholars.[49]

Finally, the author, in an effort to enhance the figure of Mary, presents her as the first priest of the New Testament insofar as she participated in a particular way at the sacrifice of the cross. On the basis of this Marian reality it cannot be understood why the Church does not permit the ordination of women.[50]

Notes

[The Observations (and following documents) refer to and quote the original edition of *Mary and Human Liberation*. In the notes below, the quotations are from that edition; page numbers for this edition may be added in square brackets.]

1 'A first consideration would be that the presuppositions of one religion are not necessarily more valid than the presuppositions of another religion' [pp. 113–14].

2 'In Christian theology we have the situation in which the original mythical presentation of the beginnings of the universe and of human life have been the subject of interpretation in later centuries by the ecclesiastical authorities. These in turn have claimed divine authority to do so on the basis of divine inspiration and the power given to them by Jesus Christ. These interpreters have also been at the same time male clergy, feudal lords and later medieval political rulers as in the Holy Roman Empire' [cf. p. 117]. Cf. more of the same on pp. [115; 124–5].

3 'The Catholic Church which has exercised both spiritual and political power for centuries over whole civilizations can therefore be particlarly susceptible to making its theology an ideology, i.e, making its religious teachings suit the interests of the powerholders in the Church' [cf. p. 115]. Cf. also pp. [116–23].

4 Cf. p. [116].

5 'We must distinguish between the faith due in Christianity to what Jesus teaches and to what the Churches (*sic*) have subsequently developed as interpretations of his teaching. The direct teachings of Jesus can be considered the communication of his primordial spiritual experience' [cf. p. 111].

6 Cf. pp. [121–3].

7 Cf. pp. [122–3].

8 'However there are many elements in the Bible which are less praiseworthy or are even undefendable specially as they impinge on the rights of human beings. Thus the Book of Deuteronomy calls for the total extermination of the seven nations that will be inhabiting Canaan when Israel occupies it. (Deut 7.1–5, 20, 16–18). The Israelites are to "utterly destroy them" (Deut 7.2; and to "save nothing" that breathes (Deut 20.16). Before the interest of Israel, the chosen people of God, the lives of these others do not count' [cf. p. 121].

9 Cf. p. [121].

10 'In Christian theology we have the situation in which the original mythical presentation of the beginnings of the universe and of human life have been the subject of interpretation in later centuries by the ecclesiastical authorities. These in turn have claimed divine authority to do so on the basis of divine inspiration and the power given to them by Jesus Christ. These interpreters have also been at the same time male clergy, feudal lords and later medieval political rulers as the holy Roman Empire. It is therefore necessary to exercise a critical judgment on the evolution of the myth (or from the myth)

into religious teaching and later even defined dogma of the Catholic Church'
[cf. p. 117].

11 'This Mary of the New Testament does not have much in common with the
Mary of theological elaborations, which are derived from a particlar interpretation of one sentence or other of the scriptures. It is from such types of
elaborations that Mary has to be liberated; a presentation which has made
her a woman who is not female; a woman who does not know what it is to
be human, who does not go through the birth pangs of bringing forth Jesus,
who does not know sin, who does not feel the trials of human existence' [cf.
p. 77]. Cf. also pp. [150, 153].

12 'Thus the teaching concerning the infallibility of the Roman Pontiff is a point
of division of the Churches' [cf. p. 113].

13 Cf. pp. [118–19].

14 Cf. pp. [146–7].

15 Cf. p. [158].

16 Cf. p. [120].

17 'The claim of the Church to be guided by the spirit of Truth does not prevent
the theologians and pastors of the Church leaving room for their theological
imagination. This is particularly likely in matters concerning which there is
no empirical evidence or criteria of positive verification, and no clear biblical
statement. But problems arise when conclusions of such theological evolution are harmful to others or the the whole of humanity. Then we are entitled
to ask how is one sure that the teachings are from the Holy Spirit? Could
they be influenced by the presuppositions and assumptions of the theologians, by the self interest of the group theologizing and even by the "gift"
of theological imagination which can be quite fertile and ingenious in
evolving formulations to satisfy the needs of a group of believers especially
when they exercise dominant political, cultural and spiritual power in a
society?' [cf. p. 145].

18 [The Observations cite nine references here.]

19 Fr Balasuriya states that that 'he (Jesus) is intimately united to God is also a
matter of faith' (p. [112]) but 'in what way is Jesus united to God' ([ibid.]) is
a question which has been elaborated later on in the history of Christianity.
'Church definitions concerning these can claim only a faith that is due to the
Church in her teaching power. They are not necessarily directly from Jesus'
[cf. ibid.].

20 [p. 158 is] significant in this regard. Fr Balasuriya, formulating some question on issues already 'resolved' by the Councils, shows both his reluctance
to accept that Jesus has the identical divine nature of the Father and his
skepticism of the faith defined at Chalcedon: 'The Marian doctrines are
linked to the concepts of the divinity of Christ. What is the nature of the
divinity of Jesus? It is one thing to say Jesus is divine; another to claim to be
able to understand, clarify and even theologically define the way and extent
to which Jesus is divine. Divinity is something which the human mind
cannot comprehend or express in language, even though theology often
claims to do so.

'The traditional theology has defined Jesus as one person having two natures: the divine and the human: This is the teaching of the Council of Chalcedon 451. Who is able to know these things with any degree of acceptable certitude? The Council of Chalcedon would have had its reasons for making this definition and using such language at the time. But today we ask questions such as, what is the nature of the divinity linked to the human Jesus? Can we contain the divine in our human formulations?'

21 'Since Jesus is presented as the universal saviour from sin including original sin, and divinity was attributed to him [. . .]' [cf. p. 151].

22 'In this it is our suggestion that the critical rethinking has to be concerning the basic construct or framework of Christian theology. This is based on the responses given to the issues raised by us elsewhere concerning the origin of humanity, our proneness to sin, and the nature of salvation, the role of religions and religious foundations in salvation, the identity of Jesus Christ, Gautama the Buddha, the Prophet Mohammed and the seers of the other religions' [cf. pp. 128–9].

23 Cf. [pp. 142–3].

24 Cf. [pp. 93–5].

25 'Theologians posited that human nature itself was "fallen" and needed an "ontological" redemption, i.e. of human nature itself. It was argued this could be done only by a divine-human person who could redeem humanity and restore the friendship with God' [cf. p. 144].

26 Cf. pp. [131–45; now Chapter 7].

27 'This teaching is based on several assumptions or presuppositions which are or were taken for granted' [cf. p. 131].

28 'We appreciate the Genesis presentation of the origins of the human race due to creation by God, and of the human condition of sublime aspirations and inherent weaknesses, and the relationship to nature.

'We have no difficulty with original sin in the sense of a human proneness to evil, that we all experience; nor with the concept of the collective sinfulness of a society or an environment that has a corrupting influence on persons. What we question is the hypothesis of original sin as propounded in traditional theology according to which human beings are born in a situation of helpless alienation from God due to the originating original sin of the first parents' [cf. p. 132].

29 Cf. pp. [141–2].

30 Cf. p. [142].

31 'The traditional perspective of original sin is linked to a concept of God that is not acceptable to the other religions in our Asian countries. In our countries this idea of humanity being born alienated from the creator would seem an abominable concept of the divine. To believe that whole generations of entire Continents lived and died with a lesser chance of salvation is repugnant to the notion of a just and loving God' [cf. p. 143].

32 Cf. pp. [143–4].

33 Cf. pp. [132–4].

34 'The dogma concerning redemption was developed from the presupposi-

tions concerning original sin. Jesus the universal saviour was said to confer the graces merited by him through the Church founded by him. The Church did so through the sacraments of which baptism had to be the first. Baptism is said to remove the stain of original sin, not concupiscence but the other consequence of original sin whereby humans are alienated from God' [cf. p. 142].

35 'If the doctrine of original sin and its consequences are questioned, then the concept of redemption is also questioned. If we do not understand human nature as essentially fallen and incapable of doing good on its own as God is not alienated from the whole of humanity by original sin, (i.e. God's grace is avilable to all insofar as it is necessary) then there is no need of an ontological redemption by Jesus Christ' [cf. p. 159].

36 Cf. p. [144].

37 Cf. above, note 34.

38 'The Church therefore claimed the right and felt the obligation to bring all peoples to her faith community. At the same time it claimed supreme spiritual authority on earth. She considered herself the infallible guide in matters of belief and morality. The ministers of the Church could absolve sins or even by refusing to do so bind persons for eternity' [cf. p. 144].

39 'There is no reason: biological, psychological, pastoral, theological or spiritual, why we cannot have a yellow, brown, black or white woman Pope.

The Papacy is a function in which sexuality is not significant. The functions of the Pope are similar to those of a head of State or of a spiritual community. There is nothing that the Pope has to do which an Indira Gandhi, a Margaret Thatcher, a Cory Aquino, or Benazir Bhutto could not do' [cf. p. 91 – and p. 219 below].

40 Cf. p. [146].

41 'This doctrine deals with a matter about which we can have no empirical evidence, and is not revealed in Scripture. It is taught by the Church on the basis of tradition. It shows the extent to which the theological imagination can be operative. We have no difficulty in accepting it. Our problem is rather with the concept that the rest of humanity is stained or sinful at conception' [cf. p. 148].

42 Cf. p. [148].

43 'Our problem is rather with the concept that the rest of humanity is stained or sinful at conception.

This accusation that all of humanity other than Jesus and Mary are under the hegemony of Satan at conception is based on the hypothesis of original sin; and this is what we find unproved and unprovable' [cf. p. 148].

44 Cf. p. [150].

45 'The teaching concerning the virginity of Mary is another example of the evolution and widespread internalization within the Catholic Church of a doctrine concerning which there is and can be no convincing evidence, except, again, that it is traditional belief in the Church. It is a doctrine related to the presuppositions concerning original sin, the ideology of male domination and a generous recourse to theological imagination' [cf. p. 151].

46 'Is it necessarily better to be a virgin mother than an ordinary mother? What is bad about being a mother in the normal way, as this is how the Creator has made human nature? Why have we to imagine such manner of divine intervention in the conception and birth of Jesus? Is this theological elaboration not part of a situation in which human sexuality, the human body and woman were considered not so good or honourable for God? In this framework, God had to be born outside of human sexual intercourse. Natural motherhood was downgraded in such a theological perspective' [cf. pp. 150–1].

47 'Since Jesus is presented as the universal saviour from sin including original sin, and divinity was attributed to him, he could not at any moment, be under the dominion of sin and Satan. But as it was held that original sin was communicated by procreation it was necessary that Jesus should be not thus contaminated by original sin. The immaculate conception, posited of Mary, ensured his prevention from original sin, from the mother's side. The teaching on the virginal conception of Jesus in the womb of Mary was a convenient way of preserving Jesus from original sin from a human male parent. Thus the teaching on the virginal conception by Mary fitted in well into the other Christological doctrines' [cf. p. 151].

48 Cf. p. [152].

49 Cf. p. [153].

50 Cf. pp. [90–2].

On the Observations of the SCDF on my book Mary and Human Liberation

On 27th July 1994 Joseph Cardinal Ratzinger, Prefect of the SCDF, sent me through the Superior General of the Oblates, the SCDF Observations on my book *Mary and Human Liberation*. The Superior General wrote to me:

> This supreme Church body discussed the question of your book in their meeting of 22nd June and decided to initiate the procedures foreseen in such cases, that is, the author be requested to withdraw the opinions which are erroneous and contrary to the faith expressed therein ...

I am grateful for the acknowledgement of good intentions in my writing this book. I have written here very brief comments on the 11-page document of the SCDF. The SCDF text is in italics. I have noted 58 shortcomings in it: Some are distortions and even falsifications. A more detailed explanation of my position is in the fuller note sent herewith.

Where there are two columns the left-hand column is from the SCDF Observations, and the right-hand column is from the text of my book; sometimes these are quoted as footnotes by the SCDF as proof of their charges. My comments are written across the whole page.

SCDF Observation   From *Mary and Human Liberation*

Chapter 1 – Methodological Deficiencies

1. Ignoring distinctions in theology

From the point of view of theology, the book of Fr Balasuriya is very deficient. In fact, truths of faith, theological formulations, and opinions of preachers are placed on the same footing, to the extent that the author seems to ignore the distinctions among them. (1.1)

All the teachings of a religion do not merit the same type of faith – some of them are directly from the founder, others are elaborations by successive generations who are members of the religious community ... (p. [111])
We must distinguish between the faith due in Christianity to what Jesus teaches and to what the Churches have subsequently developed as interpreters of his teaching. (Cf. p. 111])

My book on the contrary makes several distinctions. The entire exercise on presuppositions and the analysis of the dogmas is an attempt to 'distinguish what is the essential teaching of Jesus and what are later elaborations?' [p. 112].

2. Equalizing Religions (1.2)

The author practically seems to equate the oriental religions and Christianity denying to the latter its revelatory character.

A first consideration would be that the presuppositions of one religion are not necessarily more valid than the presuppositions of another religion. ([pp. 113–14])

It is one thing to ask whether one set of presuppositions is more valid than another and another to equate them. I am not dealing here with the equality of the religions but of their presuppositions especially when some have tended to dominate others.

3. Denying the revealed character of Christianity (1.2)

We can thus accept the Gospels, the New Testament and the Bible as a divine revelation. ([Cf. p. 112])

Can the SCDF prove this from my text? The footnote quoted does not support this charge of the SCDF. It is one thing to say that we must be careful about the interpretation of Christian revelation and another to deny the revealed character of Christianity.

4. *'denying its revealed character'*

This statement of the SCDF seems to imply that the other Oriental religions do not have a *revealed* character. This is contrary to the teaching of Vatican II even in its Constitution on Divine Revelation, which recognizes revelation by God from creation and the beginnings of the human race.

5. Reduces Religion to Myth (1.2)

Religion is reduced to 'myth', and in our case, to the initial myth of original sin, interpreted by ecclesiastical authorities without any authority.

In Christian theology we have the situation in which the original mythical presentation of the beginnings of the universe and of human life have been the subject of interpretation in latter centuries by the ecclesiastical authorities. These in turn have claimed divine authority to do so on the basis of divine inspiration and the power given to them by Jesus Christ. These interpreters have also been at the same time male clergy, feudal lords and later medieval political rulers as in the Holy Roman Empire [cf. p. 117]. Cf. in the same sense pp. [114, 124–5].

My text does not warrant this conclusion:

First I am dealing here with Christian theology and not with 'religion' as such. Does not the SCDF wrongly equate religion with theology?

6. Secondly, the statement (1.2) that I *reduce* religion to myth is false. I do not reduce even theology to myth.

7. Thirdly, the SCDF statement says that myth has been interpreted by the ecclesiastical authorities without any authority (1.2). This is not what I say as my text quoted in the SCDF footnote shows. In any case is not the right of the ecclesiastical authority to interpret the faith subject to some limits, as according to the Vatican II Constitution on Divine Revelation 'the teaching office is not above the word of God, but serves it . . . ' (art. 10).

8. That I reduce religion to ideology (1.2)

A further element that arises in the view of Fr Balasuriya is the reduction of religion to ideology, both, in fact, have the same criteria of individuation and interpretation.

The Catholic Church which has exercised both spiritual and political power for centuries over whole civilizations can therefore be particularly susceptible to making its theology an ideology, i.e. making its religious teachings suit the interests of the power holders in the Church [cf. p. 115]; cf. also pp. [116ff.].

What I have written concerning ideology is that it influences, is a tendency that affects (p. [115]), is a 'conscious or unconscious influence' ... 'tainted with an ideological taint' [ibid.]. My text does not warrant this charge of 'reduction of religion to ideology'.

9. 'reduce religion to ideology'

Here I am not dealing with religion, but with theology. Theology is not the whole of religion. The footnote quoted speaks of 'religious teachings', this is not the same thing as religion.

10. Jesus' Teachings and Subsequent Church Formulations

1.3 The author finds it necessary on several occasions to distinguish what Jesus really said from that which thereafter was formulated by the Church.

We must distinguish between the faith due in Christianity to what Jesus teaches and to what the Churches [*sic!*] have subsequently developed as interpretations of his teaching. The direct teachings of Jesus can be considered the communication of his primordial spiritual experience. [p. 111]

What is incorrect with this distinction?

11. Jesus' message of Love
The only expressions that are accepted as belonging to Jesus are his messages of love, justice and liberation. All that which follows does not appertain to him, but to the Church and, therefore, is only theology. All Church teaching can be modified in order to construct a theology that is

capable of serving the inter-religious
dialogue and woman's liberation.
(1.3)

I do not say the *only expressions* that come from Jesus are his message of love, justice and liberation. What I say throughout the work is that the core teaching of Jesus is love.

12. I have not written: 'All that which follows does not appertain to him, but to the Church and, therefore, is only theology.'

13. *All Church teaching can be mod-*
ified in order to construct a theology
that is capable of serving the inter-
religious dialogue and woman's
liberation (1.3)

Where do I say this? What I say in the book is that the core message of Jesus can be the motivation of inter-religious dialogue and liberation of women as well as of social justice and care of nature. Thus this message of love is against male domination and patriarchy which are based on the use of power to discriminate against women.

Whether all the rest *can be modified* depends on what is meant by this term. What I say is that all the rest can be evaluated by the love-criterion of Jesus.

Chapter 2 – Statements Regarding Revelation and its Sources

2.1 The hermeneutical principle proposed by me

14. *He even substitutes subjective cri-*
teria for ecclesial criteria in
evaluating revelation. (1.1)

The SCDF author has to prove this. The *twofold criterion* that I propose is not '*subjective*'. It is based on the core teaching of Jesus that God is love. Is this not a/the criterion that Jesus himself gave? 'By this will they know that you are my disciples that you love one another'. Love wants the good of all the loved ones. Hence God, who is love, would not want the dehumanization, oppression and humiliation of any section of humanity. This criterion is implicitly used by many others: e.g. feminist theologians.

15. Relativism
The author then inevitably inclines
towards relativism. According to

*him, not a few elements of the Bible
are contrary to love and therefore do
not come from God; many elements in
the sacred books of other religions
speak of love and of justice and thus
come from God. (2.1)*

(a) This charge of *relativism* must be explained and proved by the SCDF.

16. (b) *The author then inevitably
inclines towards relativism.*

What is the inevitable causal or chronological link between my criterion for evaluation and the movement towards relativism?

17. Comparison of religions
*According to him, not a few elements
of the Bible are contrary to love and
therefore do not come from God; many
elements in the sacred books of other
religions speak of love and of justice
and thus come from God. (2.1)*

The Second Vatican Council acknowledges that there are spiritual values in the other religions, in its document on *The Relationship of the Church to Non-Christian Religions*: 'The Catholic Church rejects nothing which is true and holy in these religions ... ' (art. 2).

2.2 Sacred scripture

The explicit statement of the Second Vatican Council that 'Holy Mother Church, relying on the faith of the apostolic age, accepts as sacred and canonical the books of the Old and New Testaments, whole and entire, with all their parts, on the ground that, written under the inspiration of the Holy Spirit (cf. Jo. 20:31; 2 Tim 3:16; 2 Pet. 1:19–21; 3:15–16) they have God as their author and have been handed on as such to the Church herself' (Dei verbum 11 [DV]), is in effect set aside by the author. According to him, not a few pages in

However there are many elements in the Bible which are less praiseworthy or are even undefendable specially as they impinge on the rights of human beings. Thus the Book of Deuteronomy calls for the total extermination of the seven nations that will be inhabiting Canaan when Israel occupies it. (Deut 7.1–5; 20.16–18). The Israelites are to 'utterly destroy them' (Deut 7.2) and to 'save nothing' that breathes (Deut. 20.16). Before the interests of Israel the chosen people of God, the lives of these

Scripture have to be removed because   others do not count. [Cf. p. 121]
they are incompatible with human
rights.

18. (a) According to the Vatican II *Dogmatic Constitution on Divine Revelation* God is not the sole author of the Bible. The Vatican II document *Dei Verbum* (*DV*) speaks of *both a divine and a human authorship* (Chapter III).

(b) Given human authorship also can one not expect some undefendable elements in the Bible? Indeed, at one point the document of Vatican II admits

> although they also contain *imperfect and provisional elements,* these books nevertheless describe the true divine pedagogy. (art. 15)

19. Removing passages of the Bible
According to him, not a few pages in
Scripture have to be removed because
they are incompatible with human
rights.

Firstly I am not asking that these passages be *'removed'* from the Bible. What I am saying is that such passages are less praiseworthy and are undefendable. Elsewhere I have said that such dehumanizing elements in a theology 'should be exorcized from the body of acceptable Christian theology' (p. [121]). This is quite different from removing them from the Bible.

20. Secondly, any fair evaluation of my position would show that I accept the Bible, despite such drawbacks, as a valid, valuable and substantial source of Christian theology and inspiration for Christian spirituality. Just prior to the word 'however' in the passage quoted by the SCDF author I write:

> While appreciating the innumerable and unfathomable benefits Christian theology has brought to many millions of human beings during nearly two millennia, we need to evaluate it in relation to some of its drawbacks both for the sake of believers, the Church and of inter-religious relations specially in Asian countries. ([Cf. p. 120])

The Bible has a core teaching of love and unselfish service which are truly meaningful, redeeming for all humanity.

21. How can these passages referred to, from Deuteronomy 7.1–6, be reconciled with the universal love of God, that is the core message of God in Jesus? Thus Deuteronomy 16:

> So devour all the peoples whom Yahweh your God puts at your mercy, show them no pity, do not serve their gods, or you will be ensnared.

2.3 Tradition

The author shows that he does not have a clear idea of the nature of Tradition, as a way of knowledge of divine revelation, (cf. V 8–10), such that in the words of the Second Vatican Council: 'Sacred Tradition and Sacred Scripture make up a single sacred deposit of the word of God, which is entrusted to the Church' (DV 10). He ignores the concept of divine-apostolic Tradition reducing it to mere human, and frequently, deleterious tradition. This human tradition, he says, has led to simple myths becoming dogmas of faith in the Catholic Church.

In Christian theology we have the situation in which the original mythical presentation of the beginnings of the universe and of human life have been the subject of interpretation in later centuries by the ecclesiastical authorities. These in turn have claimed divine authority to do so on the basis of divine inspiration and the power given to them by Jesus Christ. These interpreters have also been at the same time male clergy, feudal lords and later medieval political rulers as in the Holy Roman Empire. It is therefore necessary to exercise a critical judgment on the evolution of the myth (or from the myth) into religious teaching and later even defined dogma of the Catholic Church [cf. p. 117]. What I am saying is:

it is necessary to exercise a critical judgment on the evolution of the myth (or from the myth) into religious teaching and later even defined dogma of the Catholic Church.

22. I do not *reduce Tradition to mere human tradition . . . nor do I state that simple myths have become dogmas of faith (2.3)*

23. That I deny the normative value of tradition as a source of revelation (2.3)

I am not denying that tradition can have a normative value. On the contrary I am asking the question how we can have valid criteria for evaluating tradition. There are traditions that have been dehumanizing and have hurt us for many centuries.

Is my discussion on original sin not based on the issue of tradition? In fact I am affirming that the early tradition of the Church did not teach the doctrine of original sin as developed later by St Augustine and defined by the Council of Trent. In that sense I am conserving the early tradition.

24. Inter-relation of Scripture, Tradition, Magisterium and Truth

In the entire volume, but especially in chapters 5 and 6, the author supposes that the single criterion of truth are the Gospels and not Tradition, which culminates in the formulation of dogma, denying in this manner the normative value of Tradition itself as a source of revelation. (2.3)

This Mary of the New Testament does not have much in common with the Mary of the theological elaborations, which are derived from a particular interpretation of one sentence or other of the scriptures. It is from such types of elaborations that Mary has to be liberated: a presentation which has made her a woman who is not female; a woman who does not know what it is to be human, who does not go through the birth pangs of bringing forth Jesus, who does not know sin, who does not feel the trials of human existence. [Cf. pp. 77; 150ff.]

This is a very general charge concerning the whole book. The question of the interrelation of the concepts and realities of revelation, scripture, tradition, Magisterium and *sensus fidei* or *sensus fidelium* are not easy to determine, and reconcile. It is not so simple, straightforward and the same always throughout history. Christian communities have been grappling with these issues over the centuries in many different circumstances.

25. Infallibility and divisions of Churches

The doctrine of papal infallibility, in the terms defined by Vatican Council I, is reduced to simple point of division between the churches. (2.4)

The reference given in the footnote from my text reads in context thus:

Even within the same religious tradition such as Christianity there are certain presuppositions that are acceptable by all – e.g. that Jesus is the supreme teacher and that he gave his life in fidelity to his teaching. There are other

> claims of some churches that are
> not accepted by others. Thus the
> teaching concerning the *infallibil-*
> *ity of the Roman Pontiff is a point of*
> *division of the Churches* ... ([Cf. p.
> 113])

This quotation is from the pages on the 'Validity of Presuppositions'. In it I am not dealing with papal infallibility as such, but merely giving an example of issues on which some churches are divided. I make no mention whatsoever of the definition of Vatican I as such.

B. Theological methodology

In addition, the volume in question
lacks that which is characteristic of
genuine theological method (the care-
ful evaluation of sources, the
well-pondered exegesis of Scripture,
respectful consideration of the per-
ennial Tradition of the Church, the
sensus fidei *– that is manifested in*
the liturgy, the sober and docile reflec-
tion on the most solemn interventions
of the Magisterium) (1.1)

26. This charge is an exaggeration. Do I not begin by an analysis of the hymns often used in the liturgy, and Marian prayers and feasts? Is not my whole section on presuppositions, an evaluation of the 'perennial' tradition of the Church, especially as it impinges on the victims of Christian intolerance?

The SCDF comments on my methodology can lead to a good discussion on methodology in theology. Yet those doing Christian theology, i.e. the subjects of theology, are not only the scholars who are learned in Hebrew and Greek, but also persons and groups reflecting in real-life situations on the message of Christ. Does not the concept of the *sensus fidei* or *sensus ecclesiae* imply this? Revelation is not closed. Is not contemporary experience also a source of God's revelation to humankind?

27–9. On the patient divine pedagogy and gradualness of revelation.

Magisterium

The exact nature of the Magisterium,   (12) Thus the teaching concerning
its function of safeguarding the faith   the infallibility of the Roman Pon-

and of fathoming the revealed Word,
the diversity of forms with which it
expresses itself, are not recognized by
the author. The doctrine of papal
infallibility, in the terms defined by
Vatican Council I, is reduced to a
simple point of division between the
Churches. (2.4)

tiff is a point of division of the
Churches. [Cf. p. 113]

My book does not discuss at length theology concerning the Magisterium of the Church. It was not meant to do so. What does the Magisterium being under the word of God mean? At least that it is subject to the supreme law of the Gospel: namely love of God and of one another, including enemies. Hence anything that the Magisterium teaches, which is against this law of love, would not be from the Holy Spirit in Jesus. This is what I called the principle or criterion for evaluating Scripture and Tradition.

Imagination and myth, and doctrines and dogmas

According to the author, the Magis-
terium of the Church, whether
conciliar or papal, even in its most
binding pronouncements from a for-
mal point of view, has been the cause
of simple myths or doctrines, prod-
ucts of the imagination becoming
dogmas of faith. This is said to be the
case with the doctrines of original sin
defined by the Council of Trent, of the
Immaculate Conception, and of the
Assumption of Mary to heaven.
(2.4)

Imagination and theology

These two statements of the SCDF are very general covering several issues. First of all the meaning of the statements is not quite clear. What does the SCDF phrase *'products of the imagination'* refer to: to simple myths, or doctrines or both? My analysis of myth and imagination is more nuanced than the SCDF credits me with.

That myths and human imagination have had some influence on dogmas does not mean that the contents of these dogmas are entirely reducible to the mythical envelope and the imaginative fantasy. To recognize the presence and use of myth is not equivalent to myths and fruits of the imagination 'becoming dogmas of faith'.

Ideology and theology

Likewise, the influence of power need not be the whole explanation of a doctrine or dogma, or the sole cause of its evolution. A task of theology is to discern the core of faith in the admixture of these elements.

I would invite the SCDF to prove from my text their charges:

30. That for me the doctrines of the Church are 'the products of imagination'.

31. That 'The Magisterium of the Church has been the cause of simple myths or doctrines, products of the imagination becoming dogmas of faith.'

That this is what I have said concerning:

32. the doctrines of original sin defined by the Council of Trent.

33. doctrine of the Immaculate Conception,

34. and of the Assumption of Mary to heaven. (2.4)

I have not said that the doctrine of the Immaculate Conception is a myth become dogma. The pages [pp. 146–7] referred to in the footnotes do not entitle such a deduction by the SCDF.

The Hermeneutics of Suspicion

With respect to the uniform development of a doctrine by means (of) a deeper understanding on the part of the Church under the direction of the Holy Spirit, the author deems it necessary to adopt a parameter of judgment the 'hermeneutics of suspicion' [footnote 16 cf. p. [120]]. (2.4)

These considerations show that it is important that we adopt a hermeneutic of suspicion *in order to try to evaluate the importance of myth, ideology, imagination and prejudice in the evolution of dogmas.* This is particularly necessary in situations in which dogmas have a divisive impact in a pluralist society or deflect the attention of Christians from the more important issues of human community living and the core message of the Gospels.

35. The text of my book referred to in the footnote gives quite a different use of the 'hermeneutic of suspicion' and does not warrant such a

conclusion. How did the SCDF conclude that my view is that the hermeneutic of suspicion is to be applied

> to the uniform development of a doctrine by means (of) a deeper understanding on the part of the Church under the direction of the Holy Spirit

Assistance of the Holy Spirit

The asserted assistance of the Holy Spirit in the Magisterial activities of the Church is, according to the author, simply a claim which is uncontrollable and unverifiable that does not restrain theologians and pastors from indulging their theological imagination. Such claimed assistance often becomes a means to satisfy the needs of one group of believers especially when they exert dominant political power or cultural or spiritual influence in the society. (2.4)

The claim of the Church to be guided by the Spirit of Truth does not prevent the theologians and pastors of the Church leaving room for their theological imagination. This is particularly likely in matters concerning which there is no empirical evidence or criteria of positive verification, and no clear biblical statement. But problems arise when conclusions of such theological evolution are harmful to others or to the whole of humanity. Then we are entitled to ask: how is one sure that the teachings are from the Holy Spirit? Could they be influenced by the presuppositions and assumptions of the theologians, by the self-interest of the group theologizing and even by the 'gift' of theological imagination which can be quite fertile and ingenious in evolving formulations to satisfy the needs of a group of believers especially when they exercise dominant political, cultural and spiritual power in a society? [Cf. p. 145]

36. The SCDF again presents a simplistic view of my position.

Where do I say 'The asserted assistance of the Holy Spirit in the Magisterial activities of the Church is ... *simply a claim which is uncontrollable and unverifiable*'? The twofold criteria proposed by me are precisely to have a means of critically evaluating any theological development. As I have mentioned in this chapter these two criteria are in keeping with the core teaching of Jesus that God is love. In my text quoted in the SCDF footnote I mention criteria such as 'empirical evidence, criteria of positive verification and ... clear biblical statement'.

37. *Such claimed assistance (of the Holy Spirit) often becomes **a means** to satisfy the needs of one group of believers especially when they exert dominant political power or cultural or spiritual influence in the society.* (2.4)	Where have I said this? What I have asked is: Could they be influenced by the presuppositions and assumptions of the theologians, by the self-interest of the group theologizing and even by the 'gift' of theological imagination which can be quite fertile and ingenious in evolving formulations to satisfy the needs of a group of believers especially when they exercise dominant political, cultural and spiritual power in a society?

I am not speaking here of the assistance of the Holy Spirit to the Magisterium of the Church. The simplistic SCDF interpretation of my position is an unfair reduction of a whole chapter to two sentences that are not my thought.

38. The SCDF document *takes this paragraph out of context* and applies it to the whole of theology. The immediately preceding paragraphs are concerning the excesses of the Church in the understanding and practice of the Church, particularly during its authoritarian past. I am dealing here with theological positions that have been positively harmful to others and which have now been implicitly given up by most of the Church, especially after Vatican II.

Chapter 3 – Christological Problems

3.1 The Divinity of Jesus

The document says that in the whole book I do not say that *Jesus is God* the son eternal and consubstantial with the Father. (3.1)	It is one thing to say Jesus is divine: another to claim to be able to understand, clarify and even theologically define the way and extent to which Jesus is divine. Divinity is something which the human mind cannot comprehend

or express in language, even
though theology often claims to
do so. ([Cf. p. 158])

When I write 'what is of the nature of the divinity of Jesus' ([p. 158]) I
am implying the divinity of Jesus, not denying it.

3.2 The Salvific Mission of Jesus: Soteriology

*From the point of view of the Catholic
faith it is quite surprising to see Jesus
aligned on the basis of an equal dignity with Buddha, Mohammed and
the seers of other religions …*

39. I have not raised any question in my text about the equality or
inequality in dignity of these religious founders and seers.

*The work of Christ is **not properly
soteriological but didactic,** transmitting a teaching. Jesus was a
promoter of interpersonal relations
against any kind of discrimination
among peoples, races, sexes: liberator
and purifier from oppressive structures of religion, a champion of social
and political liberation.*

40. I have not said 'the work of Christ Jesus is not properly soteriological'. On the contrary in the pages referred to [cf. p. 83] I have
stressed the soteriology of Jesus that is in Matt. 25.31–46 concerning the
final judgment, regarding Zacchaeus, Dives and Lazarus, and Matt.
23.1–36.

Objective redemption

*The necessity of objective redemption
of the human race is **a simplistic**
presupposition of theologians. (3.2)*

Theologians posited that human
nature itself was 'fallen' and needed an 'ontological' redemption
i.e. of human nature itself. It was
argued this could be done only by
a divine-human person who
could redeem humanity and
restore the friendship with God.
[Cf. p. 144]

41. I am not dealing here with *'objective'* redemption. My text quoted in

the footnote is about the need 'of an "*ontological*" redemption i.e. of human nature itself'. These two are quite different things.

42. Why does the SCDF say that I say this 'is a mere *simplistic* presupposition'? First of all I am not dealing with objective redemption. Secondly in relation to 'ontological' redemption my chapter explains how the theologians of that school came to that conclusion from their teaching on original sin. Hence it is not a question of a mere simplistic presupposition.

Salvation and Moral Righteousness

Man [sic] is said to reach salvation through dedication to the moral obligation both in his personal and social life. The author does not see the need for a salvific intervention realized by a divine-human redeemer. (3.2)

The SCDF document makes a distinction between what humans have to do in moral righteousness and salvation, which is regarded as something else: 'objective redemption'. The SCDF has to show what else this 'objective redemption' consists in. The Gospels present salvation in Jesus as right living. This is not without the grace of God; and the grace of God does not save without moral righteousness.

The Dogma of Redemption

*Typical of the mind of the author is his statement that there is **no ontological need for the redemption** accomplished by Christ. (4.3)*

If the doctrine of original sin and its consequences are questioned, then the concept of redemption is also questioned. If we do not understand human nature as essentially fallen and incapable of doing good on its own as God is not alienated from the whole of humanity by original sin (i.e. God's grace is available to all in so far as it is necessary), then there is no need of an ontological redemption by Jesus Christ. [Cf. p. 159]

43. *The SCDF document alters the meaning of my sentence by changing it from 'there is no need of an ontological redemption' to 'there is no ontological need for the redemption accomplished by Christ'.*

The first is about whether individual human beings as such need *some* form of redemption, while the second is about the need for redemption *of human nature* itself. This subtle change of my text by the SCDF distorts the entire issue concerning the understanding of redemption.

44. My text quoted in the footnote says 'If . . . then there is no need of *an* ontological redemption by Jesus Christ.' The SCDF interpretation of my text says 'Typical of the mind of the author is his statement that there is no ontological need for *the* redemption accomplished by Christ.' This is a further distortion of my text which makes me deny *the* actual redemption accomplished in history by Jesus Christ (whatever be its content). Whereas my text is that '*then* there is no need of *an* ontological redemption by Jesus Christ', and that in a conditional sentence. The SCDF in changing an indefinite article 'an' to a definite article 'the' wrongly attributes to me a denial of the redemption by Jesus Christ. I have not done so.

45.

Chapter 4 – The Doctrine of Original Sin

The document emphasizes the centrality of the teaching on original sin in classical theology after Augustine. This issue is crucial for our mission and ecclesiology.

The SCDF document elaborates my position thus:

*In fact, for Fr Balasuriya the doctrine of original sin is founded on various presuppositions acritically acquired. This doctrine is seen to be a **simple hypothesis** which, he believes it is necessary to contest.*

This teaching is based on several assumptions or presuppositions which are or were taken for granted. [Cf. p. 131]

We appreciate the Genesis presentation of the origins of the human race due to creation by God, and of the human condition of sublime aspirations and inherent weaknesses, and the relationship to nature.

We have no difficulty with original sin in the sense of a human proneness to evil, that we all experience; nor with the concept of the collective sinfulness of a society or an environment that has a corrupting influence on persons. What we question is the hypo-

> thesis of original sin as propoun-
> ded in traditional theology
> according to which human beings
> are born in a situation of helpless
> alienation from God due to the
> originating original sin of the first
> parents. [Cf. p. 132]

'Negation of the reality of original sin' is the misleading subtitle given by the SCDF to its section 4.1. I do not deny original sin(fulness) as understood by many modern theologians, and as implicit in Vatican II (*LG* no. 2: *GS* nos. 10, 13 and 22).

It is wrong to say that for me this doctrine is merely a 'simple hypothesis'. The very footnote following this shows that I appreciate the biblical foundations of the Christian understanding of sin as from the beginnings of the human race. The issue is concerning the nature of the fall attributed to humanity in interpreting the Genesis story. *The consequences* of this position have been disastrous for many aspects of Church life, thought and mission.

Connection with other points of Christian faith *(4.2)*

> *The author expounds lucidly the con-
> nection between the doctrine of
> original sin and other important pil-
> lars of Christian doctrine.*

The subsequent sentences of this paragraph have to be distinguished when they refer to my view of original sin.

> 46. *The 'theological imagination'
> which is at the **origin** of the doctrine
> of original sin and which has **deter-
> mined** its development, has exercised
> its influence also on many other doc-
> trine points. (4.2)*

Theological imagination implied in the Genesis narrative has an impor-
tant role in the evolution of these doctrines. Within the story there is a recognition of basic human sinfulness, a situation of sin in the world, and structures of sin that contribute to the development of Christian theology on the human condition. This doctrine is not mere subjective imagination. There are other more objective elements that contribute to its elaboration. Hence it is not correct to say that my view is that only theological imagination is at the origin of this theology. I do not say that

theological imagination *'determined'* the development of the doctrine on original sin.

48. The conclusion of the SCDF on the important issue of original sin is:

In conclusion, the opinions of the author on original sin are incompatible with the faith of the Church. (4.3)

On the other hand, *the conclusion of Fr Dalston Forbes* in his Note to the OMI Superior General is:

> The author has no difficulty with Original Sin in the sense of proneness to evil that we all experience nor with the concept of the collective sinfulness of society nor an environment that has a corrupting influence on persons (p. [132]). He will find that the rich interpretation of today's theology is not far from the position he holds, goes beyond it and is much better based on biblical and theological foundations. (p. 5)

Chapter 5 – Ecclesiology

Fr Balasuriya's notion of the Church also appears very deficient . . .

49. This is a loose statement concerning a serious issue.

50. The SCDF document *is unfair to me* in not taking note of many other statements in my book concerning the nature of the Church and of the mission of Jesus, and of the Church, as the conversion of persons and relationships to those of love and sharing as in the early Church: for example pp. [79–83; 133–4; 143]. Such *selective use of the author's texts for evaluation* is an unjustifiable feature in the SCDF methodology.

51. It is not correct to say that I am dealing here with the *current teaching on the nature of the Church*. This quotation is from Chapter 4 'On the Basic Presuppositions of Original Sin', and its subsection 'IV – Led to a wrong accent on mission.'

The SCDF document has pieced together sentences from different sections of the book to present them as my ecclesiology.

Most of what the SCDF attributes to me in its section 5 on ecclesiology is regarding the consequences for ecclesiology of the classical interpretation of the doctrine of original sin as a fall of human nature as such. It is such an ecclesiology that I say discriminates against females, is negative towards nature, discriminates against persons of other religions and of no religion, and led to a wrong accent on mission (pp. [141–5]).

52. *Founded on the assumption that*
Jesus is the redeemer of mankind.

The SCDF document interprets my position unfairly in not distinguishing different understandings of redemption, based on different interpretations of the Genesis story of the 'fall' and other Bible texts in different contexts. In what does redemption consist? In what sense is Jesus the redeemer of humankind, and is he the unique redeemer? The different interpretations of the nature, role and mission of the Church that have prevailed in the Church need to be discussed. Have there not been grievous faults committed by Christians over the centuries due to their intolerance of others, even in Asia?

53. *The claim of the Church to be the*
vehicle of eternal salvation or media-
trix of salvation is completely
unfounded.

I do not say so. The Church has a function in mediating eternal salvation. Our difficult task especially in our pluri-religious context, is to discern issues such as:
– what is this salvific function;
– given human freedom and the widespread ignorance concerning Jesus Christ, what is the relationship between evangelization, announcing the good news in Jesus, and eternal salvation?

Mission of the Church

54. *on the nature of the Church does*
not seem to correspond to the thought
of Jesus, since it is founded on the
assumption that Jesus ... has entrus-
ted to the Church the mission of
continuing his redemptive work in all
places and in all times.

I do not deny that the Church has a universal mission. The question is, what is that mission? How has it been understood historically in its message, means of universal spread? Has there not been a close connection between the classical doctrine of original sin and the theology and practice of mission?

Fr Dalston Forbes in his Note says that

> the great theses (God's universal will to save all men [*sic*], universal abundance of Grace, and that no one is condemned except for his/her own voluntary fault) may have been soft pedalled in the periods of European mission expansion (16th–19th centuries) but they were always known and held. They have taken their proper place in today's mission theology.

55. Primacy and infallibility

Finally the author denies in fact the dogmas of primacy and infallibility.

There is no reason: biological, psychological, pastoral, theological or spiritual, why we cannot have a yellow, brown, black or white woman Pope.

The Papacy is a function in which sexuality is not significant. The functions of the Pope are similar to those of a head of State or of a spiritual community. There is nothing that the Pope has to do which an Indira Gandhi, a Margaret Thatcher [*sic*], a Cory Aquino, or Benazir Bhutto could not do. [Cf. p. 91]

I fail to see how the sentence quoted in this footnote 'in fact denies the primacy and infallibility'. I am not dealing here with the functions of the papacy, as such, to affirm or deny them. What I am saying is that gender is not necessarily relevant to them.

Chapter 6 – Marian Doctrine

He shows himself prejudiced from the outset against the Marian doctrine of the Church. Not even chapter VIII of Lumen Gentium *receives a positive judgment from him because it emphasizes more the privileges and graces granted by God to Mary than her active role in the life and ministry of Jesus in the social context of the time.*

Vatican II also invoked these doctrines in its chapter on Mary in the Constitution on the Church *Lumen Gentium*. These dogmas highlight the special privileges and graces that Mary received from God rather than her active role in the life and ministry of Jesus in the contemporary social situation.

56. This is not a correct interpretation of my text. What I say is that Mary

is presented in *Lumen Gentium* in the traditional way. This is not a negative criticism of *Lumen Gentium* which was the result of much debate at the Vatican Council. Vatican II (1962–65) had not yet come to the presentation of Jesus and Mary in relation to the anthropology of modern woman and social liberation in the preferential option for the poor as has been developed by Popes Paul VI and John Paul II.

57. Virginity and Motherhood

The author asks furthermore whether it is not better to be a normal mother than a virgin-mother. From the text it can be deduced that for Fr Balasuriya the virginal conception of Christ is not a fact ... (6.2)	is it necessarily better to be a virgin mother than an ordinary mother? What is bad about being a mother in the normal way, as this is how the Creator has made human nature? [Cf. p. 150]

58. The subtle change in the questions posed by me changes the accent, distorts the sense of my question and imputes to me a view that is not in my book.

For thus after changing the wording of my question the SCDF says: 'from this text it is deduced that for Fr Balasuriya the virginal conception of Christ is not a fact ... ' (6.2). *I have not said* that the virginal conception of Jesus is not a fact. *Is not the SCDF falsifying my position on this?* I am not denying the virginity of Mary. I have no evidence to deny it, even though many aspects of this issue have been debated among theologians throughout the centuries.

In fact, the SCDF document itself refers in its footnote 49 to my position that the 'historicity of the virginity of Mary is an open issue among scholars'. I have given the differing views of some scholars including feminist theologians.

SDCF Methodology?

The methodology of the SDCF document can also be enquired into. Too easily it makes tendentious statements on specious arguments, e.g. in 1.2 that I seem to equalize the oriental religions to Christianity. There are several such insinuations or conclusions that do not necessarily correspond to what I say in the book.

The SDCF document sometimes manipulates my text to find a theological error that seems wanted: cutting sentences, removing commas, fullstops: e.g. concerning the Bible (2.2); regarding the primacy and infallibility: virginal birth of Jesus 6.2. This type of argumentation is not only intellectually untenable but tendentious and potentially misleading if one does not very carefully discern it with the whole text and context in mind.

What redress do I have against 58 such unproved generalizations, misrepresentations, distortions and even falsifications by some (unnamed) officers of the SCDF?

Tissa Balasuriya OMI
Director
Centre for Society and Religion
14 March 1995

Profession of Faith
20 November 1995

1. With firm faith I believe everything contained in the Word of God, whether written or handed down in Tradition, which the Church, either in solemn judgment or by its ordinary and universal Magisterium, sets forth as divinely revealed and calling for faith.[1]

In particular:

2. I believe that by Divine Revelation God wished to manifest and communicate both Himself and the eternal decrees of His will concerning the salvation of mankind.[2]

3. I believe in Jesus Christ, the only-begotten Son of God, generated from the Father before all ages, Light from Light, true God from true God, begotten not made, one in being with the Father.[3] 4. I confess one and the same Son, Our Lord Jesus Christ, the same perfect in divinity and perfect in humanity: two natures, without confusion or change, without division or separation. 5. The distinction between the natures was never abolished by their union but rather the character proper to each of the two natures was preserved as they came together in one person.[4] 6. For us men and for our salvation He came down from Heaven: by the power of the Holy Spirit He was born of the Virgin Mary and was made man. 7. For our sake He was crucified under Pontius Pilate, suffered, died, and was buried. 8. On the third day He rose again in fulfillment of the Scriptures; He ascended into Heaven and is seated at the right hand of the Father. 9. He will come again in glory to judge the living and the dead, and His Kingdom will have no end.[5]

10. I believe in one, Holy, Catholic and apostolic Church, built by Jesus Christ on that rock which is Peter. 11. She is the Mystical Body of Christ, at once a visible society hierarchically structured as well as a spiritual community.[6] 12. I believe that the Church, a pilgrim now on earth, is necessary for salvation: the one Christ is the mediator and the way of salvation; He is present to us in His Body which is the Church. 13. Hence they cannot be saved who, knowing that the Catholic Church

was founded as necessary by God through Christ, refuse either to enter it, or remain in it.[7]

14. I believe as divinely revealed that Mary, ever Virgin,[8] is truly Mother of God,[9] 15. I also believe that from the first moment of her conception, by a singular grace and privilege of Almighty God and in view of the merits of Christ Jesus the savior of human race, she was preserved immune from all stain of original sin,[10] 16. and that when the course of her earthly life was finished, she was taken up body and soul into the glory of heaven.[11]

17. I believe that the Bishops have by divine institution taken the place of the apostles.[12] St Peter and the rest of the apostles, in accordance with the Lord's decree, constitute a unique apostolic college.[13] I believe that the successor of Peter with the assistance of the Holy Spirit jealously guards and faithfully explains the Revelation or deposit of faith that was handed down through the apostles.[14] I believe, therefore, that the Roman Pontiff, when he speaks *ex cathedra*, that is, when acting in the office of shepherd and teacher of all Christians, and defines, by virtue of His supreme authority, a doctrine concerning faith or morals to be held by the universal Church, he possesses through the divine assistance promised to him in the person of Blessed Peter, the infallibility with which the divine Redeemer willed His Church to be endowed in defining doctrine concerning faith or morals. 20. I believe that such definitions of the Roman Pontiff are therefore irreformable of themselves, and not because of the consent of the Church.[15]

21. I believe that what was handed on by the apostles is the Gospel which Christ commanded them to preach to all men as the source of all saving truth and moral discipline.[16] 22 That comprises everything which serves to make the People of God live their lives in holiness and increase their faith.[17]

23 I believe that the divinely revealed realities, which are contained and presented in the text of Sacred Scripture, have been written down under the inspiration of the Holy Spirit. 24 All the books of the Old and the New Testament, whole and entire, with all their parts, have God as their author, and have been handed on as such to the Church herself. 25 I, therefore, acknowledge that the books of Scripture, firmly, faithfully and without error, teach that truth which God, for the sake of our salvation, wished to see confided to the Sacred Scriptures.[18]

26 I believe as divinely revealed that in Adam all have sinned, which means that the original offense committed by him caused the human race, common to all, to fall to a state in which it bears the consequences of that offense. 27 And so, it is human nature so fallen, deprived from the gift of grace with which it had been first adorned, injured in its own natural powers and subjected to the dominion of death, that is commu-

nicated to all men; it is in this sense that every man is born in sin. 28 Therefore I hold that original sin is transmitted with human nature by propagation, not by imitation, and that it is in all men, proper to each; it cannot be taken away by the powers of human nature. 29 I believe that our Lord Jesus Christ by the sacrifice of the Cross redeemed us from original sin and all the personal sins committed by each one of us. 30 I believe in and confess one baptism instituted by our Lord Jesus Christ for the forgiveness of sins. 31 Baptism should be administered even to little children who themselves cannot have yet committed any sin.[19]

32 I also firmly accept and hold each and everything that is proposed by that same Church definitively with regard to the doctrine concerning faith and morals.[20]

In particular:

33 I acknowledge that Christ, in calling only men as His Apostles, He did not proceed from sociological or cultural motives peculiar to His time but rather He acted in a completely free and sovereign manner.[21] 34 Therefore, I firmly accept and hold that the Church has no authority whatsoever to confer priestly ordination on women.[22]

35 What is more, I adhere with religious submission of will and intellect to the teachings which either the Roman pontiff or the college of bishops enunciate when they exercise the authentic Magisterium even if they proclaim those teachings in an act that is not definitive.[23]

Notes

1 Cf. CDF *Professio fidei*

2 Cf. *Dei Verbum* 6

3 Cf. *Symbolum Constantinopolitanum*, DS 150

4 Cf. *Symbolum Chalcedonense*, DS 301–302

5 Cf. *Symbolum Constantinopolitanum*, DS 150

6 Cf. Paulus VI, *Sollemnis professio fidei*, n. 19

7 Cf. *Lumen Gentium* 14

8 Cf. *Symbolum Apostolicum*, DS 10: *Simbolum Toletanum*, DS 189; *Concilium Constantinopolitanum II*, DS 422; *Concilium Lateranense IV*, DS 801

9 Cf. *Concilium Ephesinum*, DS 252

10 Cf. Pius IX, *Ineffabilis Deus*, DS 2803

11 Cf. Pius XII, *Munificentissimus Deus*, DS 3903

12 Cf. *Lumen Gentium* 20

13 Cf. *Lumen Gentium* 22

14 Cf. *Pastor Aeternus*, DS 3070

15 Cf. *Pastor Aeternus*, DS 3074

16 Cf. *Dei Verbum* 7

17 Cf. *Dei Verbum* 8

18 Cf. *Dei Verbum* 11

19 Cf. Paulus VI, *Sollemnis professio fidei*, AAS 60 (1968), n. 16–18. Cf. *Concilium Tridentinum, Decretum de peccato originali*, DS 1511–1514
20 Cf. CDF *Professio fidei.*
21 Cf. Johannes Paulus II, *Ordinatio Sacerdotalis* 2
22 Cf. Johannes Paulus II, *Ordinatio Sacerdotalis* 4
23 Cf. CDF *Professio fidei.*

Letters to Fr Tissa Balasuriya from the Oblates of Mary Immaculate in Rome

Dear Father Balasuriya,

As you are already aware, the General Administration has been following your case closely and with concern. Father General, who is at present absent from Rome, has passed on your documents to the Cardinal Prefect of the Congregation for the Doctrine of the Faith and has, on a number of occasions, contacted the authorities of the Congregation. On June 5 a meeting of the Cardinal members of the Congregation was held and two days later, June 7, the Cardinal Prefect submitted their proposals for approval to the Holy Father. The situation is as follows:

a. As a gesture of goodwill, the Congregation for the Doctrine of the Faith has granted an extension of three weeks as requested by you for the definitive signing of the Profession of Faith composed by the aforementioned Congregation and communicated to you in November of last year. It must be signed without conditions and be given your assent of faith. In fact this Profession of Faith is composed of texts from the Magisterium. The document must reach the abovementioned Congregation before the stated date.

b. The Congregation for the Doctrine of the Faith holds that your recourse to a civil instance is a grave act against the Bishops. The Bishops, in fact, have the right and the duty to protect the faithful from confusion and error in matters of faith. This is part of their ordinary magisterium. The Holy See will consequently take measures to protect the Bishops and to preserve ecclesial communion.

I believe that we have now reached the final stage of your case. It seems to me that the Congregation for the Doctrine of the Faith has shown all the goodwill possible. I trust that you will take the necessary decisions which are substantially:

1. that you refrain from summoning the Bishops before a civil instance. I believe you have nothing positive to hope for from this

recourse. The Bishops' method of procedure cannot be separated from the content of your book because they have the obligation to protect the integrity of the Church's faith.

2. that you accept the Profession of Faith by putting your signature to it as required. By doing so you are accepting the living Magisterium of the Church, to which every Catholic theologian is obliged to submit.

Should you refuse to do so you must expect a *suspension* (Canon 1333) which means that you will not be permitted to exercise some or all of the priestly functions, and a declaration that you cannot be considered to be a *Catholic theologian*.

I shall conclude this letter by expressing the wish that no more energy be spent on this case. I wish that it may be so both for you and for us of the General Administration. Would it not be becoming for you to spend the latter years of your life in interior peace and constructive cooperation with the local Church?

The Superior General hopes that your next letter will bring good news for yourself and for the Congregation. That, of course, depends on you.

Daniel Corijn OMI
Vicar General
June 11, 1996

Dear Father Balasuriya,
I acknowledge your letter of 1st July 1996 in answer to the letter addressed to you by Fr Daniel Corijn on my behalf on June 11.

This morning I met with His Eminence Cardinal Ratzinger, Prefect of the Congregation for the Doctrine of the Faith. In that conversation His Eminence expressed three decisions which have been taken by the CDF:

1. *There will not be any further delay* for your acceptance of the profession of faith. In fact, at your request, and as a gesture of goodwill, the Congregation for the Doctrine of the Faith granted you a further delay of three weeks at the beginning of June to sign the Profession of faith they had submitted to you. This was a decision of the Congregation of Cardinals, members of the CDF, a decision which was later approved by the Holy Father.

2. The Congregation for the Doctrine of the Faith is preparing a Note about your theological dissent with the Church's faith and the Magisterium. This Note will be submitted for the approval of the Cardinal Members of the Congregation and duly promulgated.

3. The Congregation for the Doctrine of the Faith will also further define the juridical consequences of its Statement.

Should you, however, finally decide to sign the Profession of faith before the publication of the CDF's statement, the situation would become less mortifying for you.

You also mention in your letter that you have not pursued your petition against the Sri Lankan Bishops with the State Mediation Board. I hope that 'not pursued' means 'dropped'.

Several times in your correspondence you have stated that the request of the CDF is a punitive measure. This is not so. It is a means to dissipate doubts concerning your theological positions which seem to be not clearly enough in conformity with the Church's Magisterium. The text of the Profession was drafted to clarify explicitly some of the points dealt with in your book.

You must also consider that the articles of the Profession of faith are taken from the Church's Magisterium, for which the proper references are provided in the text. A religious assent is due to these articles. You have not been requested to do a critical analysis of the Church's doctrine and thus postpone indefinitely your submission.

While I earnestly invite you to take decisions that will restore communion and peace in the Church and in your heart, I wish to assure you of my fervent prayers in Christ and Mary Immaculate.

MARCELLO ZAGO OMI
Superior General
23 July 1996

Resolution of the Ecumenical Association of Third World Theologians (EATWOT)
Manila, 16 December 1996

We, the members and friends of the Ecumenical Association of the Third World Theologians, who have come from the three continents, Asia, Africa and Latin America, representatives of US minorities, and Fiji (Pacific), meeting in Manila for the Fourth Assembly of EATWOT, heard with a sense of shock and great concern that one of the founding members of EATWOT, Fr Tissa Balasuriya, OMI has been served with an administrative declaration threatening his excommunication from the Roman Catholic Church.

We appeal to the Pope and the Superior General of the Oblates of Mary Immaculate to give Fr Balasuriya, the benefit of due process and fair hearing; and to respect the sentiments of the churches in the Third World which will continue to accept and respect Tissa as a Christian, Catholic brother, priest and theologian. We believe that any decision that does not consider this body and similar bodies of theologians who are committed to the Church is unfair and arbitrary. Leaders of the Church should not disregard the norms of natural justice when they deal with the people who serve the Gospel of Christ. We Christians all over the world are seeking unity based on mutual understanding, justice and solidarity. It is significant that the major confessions no longer resort to the practice of excommunication as a way of safeguarding the truth of the Gospel. The ecumenical vocation of all Christian churches requires a more profound dialogue between different voices of Christians.

Moreover, the Church has to interpret the message of Christ in every context taking into account the new challenges it faces in that particular context. The writings of Tissa Balasuriya, we believe, help the Church to rediscover the message of Christ in our contemporary situation.

We stand in solidarity with Tissa Balasuriya and appeal to His Holiness the Pope and the authorities to cease all harassment of Fr

Balasuriya and to stop all proceedings for excommunicating him from the Church.

K. C. Abraham
President
Ecumenical Association of Third World Theologians
Carmelo Alvarez
General Secretary

Notification concerning the text
Mary and Human Liberation
SCDF, 2 January 1997

Introduction

On 5 June 1994, the Bishops' Conference of Sri Lanka publicly declared that the publication entitled *Mary and Human Liberation*[1] by Father Tissa Balasuriya OMI contained statements incompatible with the faith of the Church regarding the doctrine of revelation and its transmission, Christology, soteriology and mariology. The Bishops concluded by admonishing the faithful to refrain from reading the book. The author, on his part, reacted negatively, contending that his text had been interpreted erroneously and demanding that the truth of the accusations be demonstrated to him.

In spite of the declaration by the Bishops' Conference of Sri Lanka, the erroneous ideas continued to be disseminated among the faithful, even beyond the borders of Sri Lanka. It was for this reason that the Congregation for the Doctrine of the Faith, in keeping with its responsibility for safeguarding the faith throughout the Catholic world, decided to intervene. At the end of July 1994, the Dicastery sent the Superior General of the Oblates of Mary Immaculate some observations on the text, confirming that it contained statements manifestly incompatible with the faith of the Church. In addition, the Superior General was invited to take the measures appropriate in such a case, including a request for a public retraction.

Response

In his response of 14 March 1995, Father Balasuriya once again stated his positions and maintained that the observations of the Congregation had misunderstood and falsified his doctrinal positions.

To assist the author to demonstrate his full and unconditional adherence to the Magisterium, in November 1995, the Congregation forwarded a text of a *profession of faith* to the Superior General of the

Oblates of Mary Immaculate centred on magisterial definitions relative to those truths of the faith which the author had denied or had interpreted erroneously. Moreover, it was stated that if Father Balasuriya would agree to sign the *profession*, it would then be decided how most adequately to repair the harm done to the faithful: should he not agree, in addition to the disciplinary measures which would follow (can. 1364), the possibility of a public *Notification* would be taken into consideration by the Congregation.

In May 1996, Father Balasuriya responded by sending a different text, the 'Solemn Profession of Paul VI' which had been signed by him with the addition of the following clause: 'I, Father Tissa Balasuriya OMI make and sign this Profession of Faith of Pope Paul VI in the context of theological development and Church practice since Vatican II and the freedom and responsibility of Christians and theological searchers, under Canon Law'. Prescinding from the fact that the author had responded with a text different from the one requested, the addition of such a clause rendered the declaration defective, since it diminished the universal and permanent value of the definitions of the Magisterium.

Invitation to sign Profession of Faith

In June 1996, the Congregation again asked the Superior General of the Oblates of Mary Immaculate to invite Father Balasuriya to sign the text of the *profession of faith* already given to him, within a period of three weeks and without any conditioning clause.

In the meantime, the Secretary of the Bishops' Conference of Sri Lanka had communicated that Father Balasuriya had made recourse to the State Mediation Board against the Episcopal Conference, as well as against the Archbishop of Colombo and the editors and manager of the Colombo Catholic Press, in response to the declaration regarding *Mary and Human Liberation* and its subsequent publication in Catholic newspapers.

On 16 July 1996, the Procurator General of the Oblates of Mary Immaculate transmitted the response of Father Balasuriya, dated 1 July 1996, in which he stated that he had suspended the civil proceedings against the Bishops, giving as the reason for this his hope that there would be a re-examination of his case within the Church. He was, in all probability, referring to his appeal against the Bishops of Sri Lanka, dated 13 June 1996, to the Supreme Tribunal of the Apostolic Signatura, in which he maintained that the procedures that led to the declaration regarding his text had been marred by serious irregularities. The Tribunal responded, however, that the question did not fall within its competence. In a similar way, the Congregation for the Evangelization of Peoples, having received an appeal by Father Balasuriya dated 17 July 1996, recognized its lack of competence in this case and forwarded the author's letter to the Congregation for the Doctrine of the Faith.

Father Balasuriya also asked the Congregation for the Doctrine of the Faith to allow him some time to reflect further on its request that he sign the *profession of faith* without any conditioning clause and promised a response before the end of September; such a response, however, never arrived.

Given the clear refusal of Father Balasuriya to publicly and unequivocally profess his adherence to the faith of the Church, on 22 July 1996, the Congregation, at a meeting with the Superior General and Procurator General of the Oblates of Mary Immaculate, communicated that such a situation could not be allowed to continue, and that, therefore a *Notification* would be published in his regard.

Offer to demonstrate faith

Father Balasuriya was offered a further opportunity to demonstrate his unconditioned adherence to the faith of the Church when, on 7 December 1996, he was called, together with his Provincial Superior, to the Apostolic Nunciature in Sri Lanka. At that time, the Apostolic Nuncio read to Father Balasuriya the text of a proposed *Notification* which would be published should he not sign the *profession of faith* mentioned above. Father Balasuriya once again refused and appealed to the Holy Father, asking that a letter he had prepared be delivered directly to the Pope. In this letter, Father Balasuriya continued to maintain that everything he had written in his text *Mary and Human Liberation* was within the limits of orthodoxy.

Pope's approval

On 27 December 1996, in the name of the Holy Father, His Eminence Angelo Cardinal Sodano, Secretary of State, responded with a letter to Father Balasuriya, assuring him that the Pope had personally followed the various phases of the procedure used by the Congregation for the Doctrine of the Faith in its examination of his writing and that the Holy Father had expressly approved the *Notification* of the Congregation.

Therefore, given the failure of this latest attempt to obtain from Father Balasuriya an expression of adherence to the faith of the Church, the Congregation is compelled, for the good of the faithful, to publish the present *Notification*, in which the essential elements of the above-mentioned observations are made public.

Evaluation of the text Mary and Human Liberation

The aim of Father Balasuriya's publication is, in his own words, 'the critique and evaluation of theological propositions and presuppositions' (p. [18]) of the Church's mariological teaching. In pursuing this intention, the author arrives at the formulation of principles and theological explanations which contain a series of grave errors and which, to different degrees, are distortions of the truths of dogma and are, therefore, incompatible with the faith.

Father Balasuriya does not recognize the supernatural, unique and irrepeatable character of the revelation of Jesus Christ, by placing its presupposition on the same level as those of other forms of religion (cf. pp. [107–30]). In particular, he maintains that certain 'presuppositions' connected to myths were uncritically assumed to be revealed historical facts and, interpreted ideologically by the clerical 'power-holders' in the Church, eventually became the teaching of the Magisterium (cf. pp. [114–17]).

Father Balasuriya assumes, moreover, a discontinuity in the economy of revelation. In fact, he distinguishes between the faith due in Christianity to what Jesus teaches and to what the Churches have subsequently developed as interpretations of his teaching (p. [111]).[2] From this, it follows that the content expressed by various dogmas is considered to be on the same level as theological interpretations offered 'by the Churches', which are the fruit of their cultural and political interests (cf. pp. [114–16, 146]). This position involves, in fact, *the denial of the nature of Catholic dogma* and as a consequence, the relativizing of the *revealed truths* contained in them.

In the first place, the author relativizes *christological dogma*: Jesus is presented simply as 'a supreme teacher', 'one showing a path to deliverance from sin and union with God' (p. [112]), 'one of the greatest spiritual leaders of humanity' (p. [77]), a person who communicates to us his 'primordial spiritual experience' (p. [111]) but whose divine sonship is never explicitly recognized (cf. pp. [65, 119, 144]) and whose salvific function is only doubtfully acknowledged (cf. pp. [142–3]).

Ecclesiological errors

The ecclesiological errors of the text follow from this vision. In not recognizing that 'Jesus Christ wanted a Church – say the Catholic Church – to be the mediator of that salvation' (p. [143]). Father Balasuriya reduces salvation to a 'direct relationship between God and the human person' (p. [143]) and denies the necessity of baptism (cf. p. [134]).

A fundamental aspect of the thought of Father Balasuriya is the denial of the *dogma of original sin*, held by him to be simply a product of the theological thought of the West (cf. pp. [131–45]). This contradicts the nature of this dogma and its intrinsic connection to revealed truth.[3] The author, in fact, does not hold[4] that the meaning of dogmatic formulas remains always true and unchangeable, though capable of being expressed more clearly and better understood.[5]

On the basis of these positions, the author arrives at the point of denying, in particular, the *marian dogmas*. Mary's divine motherhood, her Immaculate Conception and virginity, as well as her bodily Assumption into heaven,[6] are not recognized as truths belonging to the Word of God (cf. pp. [37–8, 57, 119, 146ff.). Wanting to present a vision of Mary free from 'theological elaborations, which are derived from a particular interpretation of one sentence or other of the scriptures' ([cf. p. 77]), Father Balasuriya, in fact, deprives the dogmatic doctrine concerning the Blessed Virgin of every revealed character, thus denying the authority of tradition as a mediation of revealed truth.[7]

Finally, it must be noted that Father Balasuriya, denying and relativizing some statements of both the extraordinary Magisterium and the ordinary universal Magisterium, reveals that he does not recognize the existence of an infallibility of the Roman Pontiff and the college of Bishops *cum et sub Petro*. Reducing the primacy of the Successor of Peter to a question of power (cf. pp. [91, 115]), he denies the special character of this ministry.[8]

In publishing this *Notification*, the Congregation is obliged also to declare that Father Balasuriya has deviated from the integrity of the truth of the Catholic faith and, therefore, cannot be considered a Catholic theologian: moreover, he has incurred excommunication *latae sententiae* (can. 1304, par. 1).

The Sovereign Pontiff John Paul II, at the Audience granted to the undersigned Cardinal Prefect, approved this Notification, adopted in the ordinary session of this Congregation, and ordered it to be published.

Rome, from the offices of the Congregation for the Doctrine of the Faith, 2 January 1997, memorial of Saint Basil the great and Saint Gregory Nazianzen, Bishops and Doctors of the Church.

JOSEPH CARD. RATZINGER
Prefect
TARCISIO BERTONE
Archbishop Emeritus of Vercelli
Secretary

Notes

1 The text was published in the journal *Logos*, 20. 1–2, March/July 1990 (Colombo, Sri Lanka).
2 The same concept is found also in the Response of 14 March 1995, pp. 8–9.
3 Cf. Concilium Tridentinum, *Decretum de peccato originali*, DS 1511–1512; Paulus VI, *Sollemnis professio fidei*, AAS 60 (1968), 434, 445.
4 Cf. *Response*, p. 11: 'Are not the definitions of dogma made by Councils also particular expressions concerning an ineffable, inexpressible, ultimate divine, and that according to the needs of those who do so, their particular philosophical terms and according to the culture of a given time? To absolutize them could result in a narrowness which the Vatican Council II wanted to avoid.'
5 Cf. S. Congregatio pro Doctrina Fidei, *Mysterium Ecclesiae*, n. 51: AAS 65 (1973), 403–404.
6 Cf. Concilium Vaticanum II, Const. dogm. *Lumen Gentium*, n. 14; *Symbolum apostolicum*, DS 10; *Symbolum Toletanum*, DS 189; Concilium Constantinopolitanum II, DS 422. Concilium Lateranense IV, DS 801; Concilium Ephesinum, DS 252; Pius IX, *Ineffabilis Deus*, DS 2803; Pius XII, *Munificentissimus Deus*, DS 3903.
7 Cf. Concilium Vaticanum I, Const. dogm. *Dei Verbum*, nn 8–9.
8 Cf. Concilium Vaticanum I, Const. dogm. *Pastor Aeternus*, DS 3074; Concilium Vaticanum II, Const. dogm. *Lumen Gentium*, nn 18, 22, 25.

Note from the General Administration of the Missionary Oblates of Mary Immaculate on Fr Tissa Balasuriya OMI

Rome, 4 January 1997

1. The Congregation for the Doctrine of the Faith has promulgated a Note, dated January 2, 1997, in which, having examined the doctrinal position expressed by Fr Tissa Balasuriya OMI, in his book entitled *Mary and Human Liberation*, published in 1990, it declares that the author 'has deviated from the integrity of the truth of the Catholic faith and therefore, he cannot be considered a Catholic theologian.' It also declares that the author incurs the sanctions provided by the law.

2. Fr Tissa Balasuriya was born in Sri Lanka in 1924. He made his religious profession in the Congregation of the Missionary Oblates of Mary Immaculate in 1946 and, after the necessary ecclesiastical studies in Rome, he was ordained to the priesthood in 1952. He founded the Centre for Society and Religion in Colombo, an organization which aims to promote peace and social justice as well as the inculturation of the faith. He has authored a number of books and articles known mostly in the English-speaking world.

3. Because of questions raised by his book among a number of the faithful and theologians in his country and in Asia, the Episcopal Conference of Sri Lanka met with the author in January 1993. Having heard the opinion of a group of local theologians, the Conference issued a statement in June 1994 to the effect that they considered Fr Balasuriya's thesis harmful to the Marian devotion of the faithful, and that it cast doubts on the doctrine of original sin, the universal redemption of Christ, and the Immaculate Conception of the Virgin Mary.

4. Meantime, the Roman Congregation for the Doctrine of the Faith, although recognizing Fr Balasuriya's good intentions in trying to establish a dialogue between Christianity and the Oriental religions, contribute to the moral and social uplifting of Sri Lanka and present a new image of the Virgin Mary, sent him a series of *Observations* on his doctrinal opinions on July 22, 1994. These *Observations* concerned Christology, ecclesiology and Mariology, as well as the method used in his

book. The author replied with a lengthy document written on March 14, 1995, concluding that both the Episcopal Conference and the Roman Congregation had misinterpreted his work.

5. Not being satisfied with the Fr Balasuriya's reply and in order to dissipate any doubt concerning the accusations brought against him, the Congregation sent him a specially prepared Profession of Faith in November 1995, which he was required to sign before May 15, 1996. That deadline was later extended to the end of June but this did not achieve the expected results. In early December, Fr Balasuriya was offered anew the opportunity to demonstrate his unconditioned adherence to the faith of the Church. While again refusing to comply with this request, he had recourse directly to the Pope who, however, responded that he had personally followed the various phases of the procedure and had expressly approved the Notification prepared by the Congregation for the Doctrine of the Faith. The Holy Father, once again, urged Fr Balasuriya to 'rediscover the path of correct doctrine'.

6. Meanwhile, Fr Balasuriya threatened to summon all the Bishops of Sri Lanka and the editors of newspapers who had published the Bishops' statement of June 1994, before the State Mediation Board on a charge of defamation. He later desisted from this procedure.

7. During the more than three years of controversy and dialogue with the hierarchy, the Superior General of the Oblates of Mary Immaculate of which Fr Balasuriya is a member, has been in touch with him and with the Roman Dicastery. The Superior General asked three theologians of the Institute from three different continents for their views on the publication in question. All three expressed doubts and opinions similar to those of the Sri Lankan bishops and the Congregation for the Doctrine of the Faith. The Superior General has also served as mediator, seeking to provide an exact interpretation of Fr Balasuriya's theological thinking to the Congregation for the Doctrine of the Faith and trying to explain to the author the importance of conforming to the wishes of those whose duty it is to preserve the deposit of faith intact. He wrote numerous letters to Fr Balasuriya and met him personally and through members of his Council, inviting him to revise his statements and to give the full assent of faith and the religious respect due to the teachings of the Magisterium.

8. All of these suggestions and invitations did not bear fruit. It is to be hoped that the present measures taken by the Congregation for the Doctrine of the Faith will help Fr Balasuriya to understand the seriousness of his theological positions. It is also to be hoped that he will take the necessary steps towards reconciliation with the Church which it has always been his desire to serve.

❧❦❧❦❧❦❧❦

Information statement from Fr Tissa Balasuriya
6 January 1997

My book *Mary and Human Liberation* was published in 1990 as a double issue of the quarterly review *Logos*, published by the Centre for Society and Religion. 600 copies of it were printed. For three years it had a quiet readership. On 22nd December 1982, the Archbishop of Colombo, who was then also the President of the Catholic Bishops' Conference of Sri Lanka, invited me by letter to a special meeting on it on the 7th January 1993.

(A) Re Process

On 7th January 1993, between 10.15 and 11.45 am, at the headquarters of the Catholic Bishops' Conference of Sri Lanka (CBCSL). The Archbishop of Colombo, Nicholas Marcus Fernando, then President of the CBCSL, convoked the meeting, determined its participants and process. I was not given a prior agenda for it.

(1) At this meeting Auxiliary Bishop Malcolm Ranjith distributed and read a 5-page document on behalf of an Ad Hoc Theological Commission (AHTC) of the CBCSL set up for this issue. He stated 'The following observations were made by all concerned at that meeting' on 1st December 1992. The four members of that group were Bishop Vianney Fernando, Bishop Malcolm Ranjith, Fr Dalston Forbes OMI and Fr Emmanuel Fernando, Rector of the National Seminary.

(2) Subsequent correspondence with me and among them has shown that not all four members were agreed on the content of this report. It would seem that they had only one meeting at which Bishop Malcolm had read his own draft, which he developed into the document of 7.1.93. Fr Dalston Forbes did not agree with the document at the meeting of 7.1.93 as well as in subsequent correspondence. Fr Emmanuel Fernando said he saw the Report as such only when I sent him a copy of it two months later.

(3) The contents of this document are largely a string of misrep-

241

resentations, distortions and falsifications. Such distortions have been the source of charges against me for four years. But my objections to them have so far not been listened to by any Church authority dealing with this issue. Cf. Appendix I

(4) The presiding Archbishop of Colombo concluded the sessions abruptly at about 11.45 am without giving an adequate opportunity to discuss the issues raised by that report or to listen to my views on why I had written that book. He asked me to reply to the charges in writing without delay.

(5) Over the next few months, despite all my other work and foreign travels, I elaborated my responses to these accusations and sent them to all the Bishops in stages and as a collected response of 47 single-spaced pages on 7.1.94. I pointed out 6 falsifications, 5 distortions, and 3 manipulations of my text and several other misunderstandings and misrepresentations of my intentions and views. I have had no reply from the Bishops to this.

(6) Hence after 7.1.93 no official discussion or dialogue has taken place on the process or content of the charges of the AHTC.

(B)(1) On 20th April 1994 morning, I was suddenly called by telephone to come for a meeting of the Catholic Bishops' Conference in session at Kandy (120 kilometers from Colombo). I was asked to come alone, not even with the Provincial Superior of the Oblates. The meeting with me, begun at about 5.30 pm, lasted only about 55 minutes. At his meeting the presiding Archbishop informed me that the Bishops had decided to make a public statement on my book, and that they would write to me in a few days to give me prior intimation of it. Again I requested an objective investigation into the content of my book and into the working of the Ad Hoc Theological Commission of the Catholic Bishops' Conference. Once again I was dismissed without any serious discussion on content or any evaluation of my researched and careful responses to the AHTC charges of 7.1.93, and its mode of operation.

(2) These were the only two meetings with me held by the Church authoritative bodies on my book during the past four years viz. (a) on 7th January 1993 and (b) 20th April 1994. I have never had the opportunity for a dialogue or discussion of the theological issues involved in my book *Mary and Human Liberation* and/or the accusations against me due to it with the official Church authorities.

(C) (1) On the 5th June 1994 the CBCSL published in the SL Catholic press their statement on my book. It is a more nuanced statement, that gives credit to my objective in writing the book to relate Marian theology to the milieu that is multi-religious and socially unjust. It refers to 'four glaring errors' and admonishes the Catholics to refrain from reading it. They did not point out how I could correct my 'errors'.

(2) The same Church media refused to publish my reply to these charges asking for exact references from my book for such charges. Neither did I discuss them through the public news media.

(3) This statement too had unproved charges, and a grave falsification of my position called the '2nd glaring error'.

(4) During 1994 I worked on my responses to these charges of the CBCSL and sent them on 27th March 1995 to the Bishops' Conference in a 53-page single-spaced typed document, with an 8-page summary placing their texts and mine side by side with brief comments, and a two-page summary of all these. I responded carefully to each charge. But I received no response to this either. (Cf. my 'Doing Marian theology in Sri Lanka', *Logos*, volume 33, nos 3 and 4 (CSR, Colombo, 1994).)

(5) There was no inquiry into these issues thereafter. The theological community of Sri Lanka was not consulted by the Bishops on this.

(6) The Archbishop of Colombo wrote to me on 14th May 1996:

> At our conversation of 14th February 1996 your proposal was that the issues related to your book *Mary and Human Liberation* should be referred to a mediation body within the Church. My reply was that I would present your proposal at the next meeting of the CBCSL (Catholic Bishops' Conference of Sri Lanka) as correctly stated in your present letter. I did present the proposal but then it was observed that the matter was now with the Congregation of the Doctrine of the Faith. *I have now received a personal letter from the same Congregation in which it is stated that competence in this particular case of your book pertains exclusively to that particular dicastery* ([italics] added).

Thus the Vatican Congregation for the Doctrine of the Faith has authoritatively impeded the Catholic Bishops Conference of Sri Lanka from arriving at a settlement of this issue by a process of inquiry and/or mediation within Sri Lanka.

(D) (1) On 22nd July 1994 the Vatican Congregation for the Doctrine of the Faith (CDF) sent me (in Italian) their 11-page 'Observations' on my book, without anyone taking personal responsibility for them. It was only at my request that an English translation was sent to me. Misrepresentations of my statements on account of language problems cannot be ruled out.

(2) After long study and reflection I replied on 14th March 1995 in a 55-page single-spaced typed document discussing each issue. I sent also a summary of 22 pages placing side by side each charge and the relevant text of my book with short comments. Further I summarized

all this in two pages as containing 58 misunderstandings, misrepresentations, distortions and falsifications of my text.

(3) All I received from the CDF in response to this serious study of seven months was just one word viz. 'unsatisfactory'.

(4) In response to my request for a fair inquiry into my 58 counts of 'unproved generalizations, misunderstandings, distortions and falsifications by them of my work', the CDF wrote to me on 2nd May 1996

> *In order to overcome your objections concerning the correct interpretation of your thought, this Dicastery formulated a Profession of Faith concerning the truths held by the Church and taught by her Magisterium. From this Profession of Faith it would be possible to verify if you accept these truths, which were expressed with lack of clarity in your book.*

(i) Thus the CDF recognized my objection that their interpretations of my thought were incorrect. But they did not discuss, clarify or correct them.

(ii) Their proposed POF was to be a substitute for a fair inquiry into their view of the shortcomings of my book and/or their incorrect interpretation of it.

(iii) It was to be a remedy for the 'lack of clarity' with which I have expressed the truths of the Catholic faith. 'Lack of clarity' in exposing truths is not an affirmation of 'grave errors' or denial of truths.

(5) These are the only documents and discussions (if they can be so called) between the Church authorities and me on the content of my book since 22/12/1992.

(6) The Ad Hoc Theological Committee of the CBCSL, the CBCSL itself and the unknown officials of the CDF never responded to my replies to their charges. The correspondence clearly proves this. I have documented all this, writing out myself minutes of the meetings of 7/1/93 and 20/4/94 and sending them to the CBCSL for approval. Further the meeting of 20/4/94 was tape-recorded by the secretary of the CBCSL.

(E) Re 'Profession of Faith'

(1) The CDF did not present me with corrections of my 'errors' in specific terms, but took refuge in their specially constructed PoF. I was asked to sign the specially drafted 'Profession of Faith' (PoF). Failure to do so would result in my excommunication under Canon 1364. This was said to have been approved by His Holiness the Pope on 12th May 1995.

(2) This decision, communicated to me only on 20/XI/95, seemed an unreasonable and unnecessary device for resolving the problem, a device which is far removed from the spirit of intellectual investigation and fraternal correction. It is a punitive act assuming that the judgments

of the CDF on my book are correct.

(3) I asked that this PoF be authenticated by the CDF as Catholic doctrine binding on all Catholic theologians. But this has not been done.

(4) One of the reasons for this is its unfaithfulness (by omission) to Vatican II teaching (*Lumen Gentium* 16) on the possibility of salvation outside the Church. Due to this omission I was unable to sign it in conscience. On the other hand it was precisely for holding such a position as in this PoF of the CDF that Leonard Feeney SJ of Boston was excommunicated in 1953. The solemn Profession of Faith of Pope Paul VI which I have signed includes numbers 14, 15 and 16 of the Vatican *Lumen Gentium* which is a more comprehensive expression of the Church's teaching on this issue.

(5) Under urgent pressure by the CDF (by Fax) to sign this POF within four days before 15th May 1996 or be excommunicated, I signed on 14th May 1996 the more complete 1988 Profession of Faith of Pope Paul VI which contains all these items and more (*et amplius*).

(6) Once again there has been no dialogue or objective inquiry concerning this.

(7) I am asking for an elucidation of how I should correct my 'grave errors'. My signing a profession of faith does not remove the 'errors' in the book as such and undo the supposed damage to the faithful. The problem is the supposed errors in my book, not the personal assent of faith by me. Neither does it correct the CDF's incorrect interpretations of my views.

(8) On the night of 7th December 1996, the Apostolic Nuncio in Colombo merely read to me the 'Notification' of the CDF and said I had to sign the special PoF then and there or face automatic excommunication (*latae sententiae*) with effect from the following day, 8th December 1996, the feast of the Immaculate Conception. There was no discussion whatsoever on that occasion.

(F) Profession of Faith of Paul VI

(1) As the CDF Notification of 2nd January 1997 states:

> *In May 1996 Fr Balasuriya responded by sending a different text, the Solemn Profession of Faith of Paul VI which had been signed by him with the addition of the following clause: 'I, Father Tissa Balasuriya OMI make and sign this Profession of Faith of Pope Paul VI in the context of theological development and Church practice since Vatican II and the freedom and responsibility of Christians and theological searchers, under Canon Law.' Prescinding from the fact that the author had responded with a different text from the one requested, the addition of such a clause rendered the declaration defective, since it diminished the universal and permanent value of the definitions of the Magisterium*

(2) May I ask what are the defects or deviations from the Catholic faith in the very comprehensive Profession of Faith of Pope Paul VI, which I signed?

(3) May I remind the CDF that I have made a profession of faith, along with Pope Paul VI, in all the doctrines which I am now accused of denying or erroneously interpreting by the CDF notification? This includes Christology, Mariology, ecclesiology, original sin and redemption. The CDF letter of 2nd May 1996 wrote of their PoF 'in order to overcome your objections concerning the correct interpretation of your thought' and 'it would be possible to verify if you accept these truths, which were expressed with a lack of clarity in your book'.

(3) Is not the solemn Profession of Faith of Paul VI a more authentic and integral expression of the Catholic faith than the special text drafted by the CDF for me personally, but not signed by anyone, not even by them despite repeated requests by me for it? Pope Paul VI expressly declared that, 'without being properly speaking a dogmatic definition', his profession of faith 'repeats in substance the creed of Nicaea, with some developments called for by the spiritual condition of our times'. Why should the CDF take the position of *'prescinding* from the fact that the author has responded with a different text from the one requested'?

(4) It is true in his PoF Paul VI does not say that the Church could never confer priestly ordination on women. But can this be imposed on Catholics under pain of excommunication?

(5) In declaring that 'Fr Balasuriya has deviated from the integrity of the truth of the Catholic faith, and therefore, cannot be considered a Catholic theologian', after I signed the Profession of Faith of Pope Paul VI, is not the CDF declaring in effect that Paul VI too 'deviated from the integrity of the truth of the Catholic faith, and therefore cannot be considered a Catholic theologian'?

(6) What is wrong with the *addition of that clause prior to my signature of the Profession of Faith of Paul VI? How does it render 'the declaration defective, since it diminished the universal and permanent value of the definitions of the Magisterium'?* What is wrong with 'context of theological development and Church practice since Vatican II, and the freedom and responsibility of theological searchers under Canon Law'?

(7) If there is anything wrong with the development of theology and Church practice since Vatican II should not the CDF correct those errors? My profession of faith would then be in the context of such corrections too. The 1985 Synod of Bishops, convened by Pope John Paul II, declared 'Vatican II as the greatest grace of the 20th century'.

(G) Non-Functioning of Church Structures for Justice and Conciliation.

(1) In this case all the structures for dialogue, mediation and justice within the Church have been atrophied. My numerous appeals and those of the Conference of Major Religious Superiors and numerous others for a fair deal on this issue have not been entertained within the Sri Lankan Church by

(i)   The National Justice and Peace Commission,
(ii)   The National Pastoral Convention and its follow up Committee
(iii) The CBCSL Commission for Theology and Canon Law. It has had no members other than its Bishop Chairman during the past four years.
(iv)   The CBCSL itself,
(v)   The Apostolic Nuncio in Colombo.

(2) At the Vatican level, I forwarded a petition on 13th June 1996 to the Signatura Apostolica concerning the injustice done to me by the AHTC and the public statement of the CBCSL. The Signatura replied to me on 21st June 1996 that, as they were the court of final appeal, I should address my petition to the relevant Vatican Dicastery. After inquiry I addressed my petition to the Congregation for the Evangelization of the Peoples on 17th July 1996. I received no acknowledgement from them. The 'Notification' published by the CDF read to me by the Apostolic Nuncio stated that the Congregation of the Evangelization of Peoples had referred my petition to the CDF. I have had no acknowledgement from the CDF either – except through this 'notification'.

(3) Thus at the Vatican CDF level too my legitimate petition for a judicial trial on the processes and an objective scholarly inquiry into the theological issues has not been listened to.

(4) All my persistent pleas during four years have fallen on deaf ears. This is a far cry from intense dialogue and a refusal to correct my 'error'.

(H) Re Theological Issues

(1) Other than for the exchange of few letters, the theological issues were never discussed with me by the

(a) Ad Hoc Theological Commission which, as such, never met me,
(b) The CBCSL, which met me only on 20/4/94 and that for 55 minutes.
(c) and the CDF which never responded to my replies to their charges. There has been no face-to-face contact with the unknown officials of the CDF – not to mention meeting of minds and hearts in a Christ-like and Mary-like manner.

(2) There were no repeated requests to correct my 'errors' as the CDF stated through the Vatican Press on 12th December 1996 and as mentioned in the letter of the Vatican Secretary of State Angelo Cardinal Sodano of 27th December. It is not true that I have 'reiterated refusal to recognize and correct the grave errors which have been condemned'.

(3) This position is very much at variance with the spirit of dialogue mentioned by Pope Paul VI in *Ecclesiam Suam* (1964) and in many presentations of Pope John Paul II to various groups, as well as in his *Tertio Millennio Adveniente* (1996).

(4) My book *Mary and Human Liberation* was written in the Asian and especially Sri Lankan multi-religious, socially unjust and conflictual context. It endeavours to bring out the enduring relevance of the loving mother of Jesus and our common mother as His Holiness Pope John Paul II, Pope Paul VI and Cardinal Ratzinger have written, concerning her relation to the changing contemporary world, especially for the recognition of the dignity of women.

(I) Negation of Due Canonical Process
In this entire four-year period there has been a sad neglect of due canonical process, not to mention natural justice. Canon law is invoked for imposing excommunication under Canon 1364: para 1. But many other canons that deal with the process of imposing penalties have not been observed.

Some examples of these are:

'*Canon 18: Laws which prescribe a penalty, or restrict the free exercise of rights, or contain an exception to the law, are to be interpreted strictly*' (i.e. in favour of the accused on the general principle that 'odiosa sunt restringenda': what is odious is to be restricted).

'*Canon 50: Before issuing a singular decree, the person in authority is to seek the necessary information and proof and, as far as possible, is to consult those whose rights are harmed.*' The CDF has not done this.

'*Canon 211: All Christ's faithful have the obligation and the right to strive so that the divine message of a salvation may more and more reach all people of all times and places.*' This means that the message and mission be thought in terms of the contemporary world correcting past centennial mistakes as the Pope mentions in his Third Millennium exhortation. Along with other Asian theologians I too am trying to respond to this call of the Spirit in our times.

'*Canon 221 #1   Christ's faithful may lawfully vindicate and defend the rights they enjoy in the Church, before the competent ecclesiastical forum in accordance with the law.*' The history of this case is largely one of the consistent transgression of this canon due to the non-functioning of the structures for dialogue, justice and conciliation.

'Canon 221 #2   If any members of Christ's faithful are summoned to trial by the competent authority, they have the right to be judged according to the provision of the law, to be applied with equity.' In this case there has been no trial as such. Neither is there equity as many theologians with views similar or identical to mine have not been dealt with in a similar fashion.

'Canon 221 #3   Christ's faithful have the right that no canonical penalties be imposed upon them except in accordance with the law.' In this case several very relevant laws have been breached, especially in not holding a judicial trial.

'Canon 1321 #1   No one can be punished for the commission of an external violation of a law or precept unless it is gravely imputable by reason of malice or of culpability.' I cannot be accused of malice when I have consistently during four years asked for dialogue and a fair trial from all the levels of Church authority in Sri Lanka and the Vatican. I have always expressed my readiness to correct my views if I am proven wrong at the level of sound contemporary theological scholarship. Since I am charged under Canon 1364 #1, my supposed heretical positions have to be proved. The CDF has not done so. It has only substituted its PoF for gauging my orthodoxy.

'Canon 1342 #1   Whenever there are just reasons against the use of a judicial procedure a penalty can be imposed or declared by means of an extra-judicial decree; in every case penal remedies and penances may be applied by decree.

#2   Perpetual penalties cannot be imposed or declared by means of a decree; nor can penalties which the law or precept establishing them forbids to be applied by decree.' Commentators say

> The legislator's preference for judicial procedure is affirmed implicitly in paragraph one, which requires due cause if judicial procedure is to be waived.
>
> On the contrary the most serious penalties, those of a perpetual or irrevocable character, can be declared or imposed only through formal judicial procedure #2. There is a proportion between the seriousness of the penalty, e.g. dismissal from the clerical state, and the seriousness of the procedure declaring or inflicting it. When the consequences of a penalty are so weighty, every effort should be made to provide maximum legal protection for the accused, e.g., services of advocate, access to all relevant documentation for self-defence purposes, possible appeal of adverse decision to higher court.
>
> (*The Code of Canon Law, A Text and Commentary* commissioned by the Canon Law Society of America, ed. James A. Coriden *et al.* (New York: Paulist Press, 1985), pp. 911–12)

It is clear that this grave act of excommunication on a matter of doctrine should be executed only after at least a fair and objective theological investigation, if not judicial trial. In this case the accuser and judge is the same body, the Vatican Congregation for the Doctrine of the Faith whose membership is not known to us and are not open even to dialogue. The CDF mentions complaints it has received from others concerning my book. I have never had information about them for examination of such witnesses and response.

'Canon 1733: When a person believes that he or she has been injured by a decree, it is greatly to be desired that contention between that person and the author of the decree be avoided, and that care be taken to reach an equitable solution by mutual consultation, possibly using the assistance of serious-minded persons to mediate and study the matter. In this way, the controversy may by some suitable method be avoided and or brought to an end.'

The CDF did not leave room for a mediated solution even by the Bishops Conference of Sri Lanka. The CBCSL public statement was a more nuanced and pastoral one than the approach of the CDF.

The November 1971 Synod of Bishops on 'Justice in the World' says:

> The Church recognizes everyone's right to suitable freedom of expression and thought. This includes the right of everyone to be heard in a spirit of dialogue which preserves legitimate diversity within the Church.
>
> The form of judicial procedure should give the accused the right to know his accusers and also the right to a proper defence. (Section III)

The CDF action is deficient in both the letter and spirit of this norm.

(J) Briefly

(1) I maintain that the charges made against me are incorrect in relation to what I have written. *I have not said what they say I have said.*

(2) There has been no meaningful dialogue or objective inquiry into these issues. Canon Law is invoked for my punishment, but it has not been observed in the due process of the investigations especially numbers 50, 221, 1321, and 1733.

(3) What I have written is within the bounds of Catholic orthodoxy. I am prepared, as I have repeatedly stated, to publicly correct any errors which are proved to me at an objective and fair evaluation of my views at the level of accepted contemporary theological scholarship.

(4) Many other writers, especially in the West, have expressed similar or identical views. None of them, as far as we know, has been treated so severely and with the threat of excommunication (*latae sententiae*, without trial). This seems to us to be the most severe treatment of a Catholic theologian since Vatican II. Why am I subjected to such unique and selective discrimination, against all norms of canonical equity? Is there a different criterion for Asian theologians?

(5) The CDF 'Notification' of 2nd January 1997 is incomplete and should be subject to discussion as it is a unilateral declaration by the

CDF operating as accuser, witness, judge and executor all in one. This is contrary to both the letter and spirit of Canon Law. I intend to reply to it in due course after careful study of it.

(6) The specially drafted 'PoF' is not a good means for gauging my faith, nor is it a suitable substitute for an impartial, theological investigation into the issues. The sad history of intolerance in the Church during several centuries of this millennium teaches us that faith can and must tolerate a diversity of theological expressions. His Holiness the Pope has often referred in recent months, including in his New Year message of 1st January 1997, to the need of correcting the causes of past inter-religious conflicts. I am trying to contribute to that cause, especially in the background of centuries of misguided violence against others in Asia and elsewhere by Christians, often with Church approval and blessings. The Holy Father himself has called for such repentance in the preparation for the third millennium as in his 1994 Apostolic Letter *Tertio millennio adveniente*, 'On Preparation for the Jubilee of the Year 2000'. The Pope acknowledged the centennial blunders of the Catholic Church:

> Another painful chapter of history to which the sons and daughters of the Church must return with a spirit of repentance is that of the acquiescence given, especially in certain centuries, to *intolerance and even the use of violence* in the service of truth. (No. 85)

The Church needs to seek and correct the deeper theological motivations for such violence by the disciples of the loving and lovable Jesus and of his mother Mary.

(7) The task of theological searchers is to endeavour to present the content of the faith in an expression that is intelligible and meaningful to the people of our time, place and culture. This has been and is an accepted ongoing process in the Church. It has contributed towards the development and elucidation of doctrine.

(8) I hold my faith in God, in Jesus and in the Church as a serious life commitment. I cannot honestly buy my non-excommunication by blindly signing unconditionally a specially crafted 'Profession of Faith' with some elements of which I am not convinced. Further this PoF, as it stands, is harmful to the Church. I trust the CDF does not want me to do a Galileo saying 'Eppur si muove'.

(9) My faith in Jesus is a hope against hope that love and justice would ultimately prevail in the Church, the community he founded.

(10) In any case, conscious of my fleeting life at the age of 72 and with a clear conscience, I entrust myself to the judgment of God, who is love, and to the verdict of human history.

Praying that all of us involved in this issue may discern it listening to the Spirit of God who is love and truth, and that we may all grow in wisdom and virtue through this exceptional ecclesial experience.

TISSA BALASURIYA OMI

Appendix 1 An example from the AHTC document gives an indication of the extent and gravity of the distortion of my thought. This document states:

> After an analysis of chapters 4 and 5 of the book all of us felt (sic) that the basic theological flaw in the book is that Fr. Balasuriya seems (sic) to deny the very divinity of Jesus. This is at the basis of the whole book. He denies in toto the following classical theological presentation of the nature of Jesus.

The classical argument:–

Major premise:–
   All mankind is under original sin
   Redemption is to be freed from the power of original sin
   This can be done only by a divine/human saviour
   Jesus Christ is the Saviour
   Through his death and Resurrection He saves us ontologically from original sin
   Therefore Jesus Christ is the divine/human Saviour and God's Son.

Father Balasuriya's argumentation:
Major premise:
   There is no original sin
   No redemption is necessary
   No saviour is necessary
   Jesus Christ is not the saviour
   He is not God.

It will be remarked how subjective this assessment, on such an important issue, is: 'All of us felt' and 'Fr Balasuriya seems'. This is hardly a rational or theological argument on which to ask for ecclesiastical sanctions as this Document does.

In contrast to this, what I have written on original sin is:

> We have no difficulty with original sin in the sense of a human proneness to evil, that we all experience; nor with the concept of the collective sinfulness of a society or an environment that has a corrupting influence on persons. What we question is the hypothesis of original sin as propounded in traditional theology according to which human beings are born in a situation of helpless alienation from God due to the originating original sin of the first parents. ([Cf. p. 132])

The statement of the Oblates of Sri Lanka on the excommunication of Fr Tissa Balasuriya OMI

21 January 1997

The Provincial Superior of the Oblates of Sri Lanka together with his Council and the Oblate Theology Circle met on Thursday 16th January 1997, to assess the sad situation that has arisen by the excommunication inflicted on our brother Oblate Fr Tissa Balasuriya, omi.

Fr Tissa is a distinguished member of our Province. He worked as Rector of Aquinas College and he is the Founder-Director of the Centre for Society & Religion which has done so much for national development, inter-religious dialogue, ecumenism and justice and peace in our country. His ministry has been in line with the vision of Vatican Council II and the missionary priorities of the Oblate Congregation worldwide. His ministry has been approved and supported by his Oblate Superiors.

The initial cause of his condemnation was the so-called theological errors of his book, *Mary and Human Liberation*. It is important to note that Fr Balasuriya's intention in writing his book was 'not to dilute Marian devotion but to make it more meaningful and truly fulfilling for all' (Preface, p. [19]). The process to evaluate these so-called errors began in December 1992 by the Bishops' Conference and has gone on since then through various steps.

A public statement listing these alleged errors was published in the *Catholic Messenger* and *Gnanartha Pradeepa* on the 5th June, 1994. Unfortunately Fr Balasuriya's reply did not find a place in the same media. The matter was then referred to the Congregation for the Doctrine of the Faith (CDF), Rome, which sent him observations concerning these alleged errors in July 1994. His detailed response to these observations was dismissed by the CDF with a curt phrase 'unsatisfactory'.

The CDF wished him to sign a Profession of Faith which touched many of the themes outlined in his book to assure them of his orthodoxy. Fr Balasuriya did not sign this Profession of Faith since it contained certain ambiguities especially with regard to the people of other religions and the ordination of women to the priestly ministry.

In place of this Profession of Faith, Fr Balasuriya signed the much richer Profession of Faith of Pope Paul VI, Credo of the People of God, written after Vatican II, with the addition of the following note, 'I, Father Tissa Balasuriya OMI make and sign this Profession of Faith of Pope Paul VI in the context of theological development and Church practice since Vatican II and the freedom and responsibility of Christians and theological searchers under Canon law'. In the Notification of Fr Balasuriya's excommunication, the CDF held that this addition rendered the Profession of Faith of Pope Paul VI defective. We feel that this note does not touch the substantial value of the Profession of Faith and expresses common methodological presuppositions of modern theologians.

The CDF insisting that Fr Balasuriya should sign their version of the Profession of Faith formulated especially for him with no conditions or qualifications. He refused to do so because it would do violence to his conscience. To cut a long story short, this led to his final excommunication.

There has been some misunderstanding in this country as to the meaning of excommunication. It is a rare sanction and in terms of the Canon Law means only the following:

An excommunicated person is forbidden:
1. to have any ministerial part in the celebration of the Sacrifice of the Eucharist or in other ceremonies of public worship:
2. to celebrate the sacraments or sacramentals and to receive the sacraments;
3. to exercise any ecclesiastical offices, ministries, functions or acts of governance. (Can. 1331, *1)

Nothing more is to be arbitrarily added to these.

The inflicted excommunication does not mean that Fr Balasuriya is derobed or defrocked. He continues to be an Oblate of Mary Immaculate, priest and religious and a Catholic Christian.

It is a matter of deep sadness to note that the whole process against Fr Balasuriya has been heavily flawed from the beginning by the failure to dialogue with him. At no stage (either in Sri Lanka or in Rome) was he given an opportunity to dialogue about his book or his alleged errors. Nor was there any inquiry at which he could answer the accusations against him. Whatever took place was by correspondence. Nor was there any dialogue between Fr Balasuriya and a Board of competent theologians. All attempts to establish a Conciliation Board in Sri Lanka to solve the question were fruitless.

He is now accused in the 'Notification' of not explicitly recognising the divinity of Christ, denying Marian dogmas and the teaching power of the Popes and Bishops. However, in the Professions of Faith Fr Balasuriya swore all these points are explicitly mentioned, with the exception of the one concerning the ordination of women, of which no explicit mention is made in the Notification. He cannot therefore be accused of having posited some action which calls for the sanction of excommunication. We therefore entertain serious doubts about his incurring the penalty of automatic excommunication.

In any case, the excommunication seems to us a penalty out of tune with the spirit of the Gospel which should animate us in this day and age after Vatican II. It acquires added incongruity when applied to a senior priest and religious who has contributed so much to Church and Society for the past 51 years and who passionately desires to remain within the Church.

We, therefore, insistently urge that the CDF should repeal the penalty of excommunication. Other means should be devised to deal with these alleged theological errors of this book and to place them before the International Theological community and the Church.

JOHN CAMILLUS FERNANDO OMI
Provincial Superior
Sri Lanka
ANSELM SILVA OMI
President
Oblate Theology Circle
21st [January] 1997

A response to Joseph Cardinal Ratzinger from Fr Tissa Balasuriya
1 February 1997

Dear Cardinal Ratzinger,

May I make the following observations with reference to the 'Notification' of the Congregation for the Doctrine of the Faith published by you through the world's mass media on 5th January 1997 and your press conference of 24th January reported also in the mass media.

1. It pains me deeply that you are reported to have said on 24th January 1997 that:

(a) 'The heresy, condemnation and the excommunication were inflicted after the priest refused to sign a statement, renouncing all his various positions, particularly his rejection of the dogma of original sin' (Reuter, 24/1/97).

(b) 'Father Balasuriya has been excommunicated ... for his doctrine of original sin, according to which original sin has been invented by the clergy in order to be able to exercise power over the souls of the faithful' (ANSA, Città del Vaticano, 24/1/97).

(c) 'Fr Balasuriya's theses have nothing to do with the theme of inculturation of the Christian faith among the Asian peoples, rather they are deduced from European theses which can be taken back to the Marxist interpretation according to which religion and priests construct for themselves a position of power over the souls of the faithful' (ANSA).

2. On Divinity of Christ and Original Sin

(a) You say that I have rejected the truths of the first level of the Catholic faith such as the divinity of Christ and the doctrine of original sin.

I do not accept the charge in the CDF 'Notification' of automatic excommunication that I have 'deviated from the truth of the Catholic faith'. The CDF has not proved this. Further, I formally professed the Catholic Faith integrally when I signed on 14th May 1996, before witnesses, the solemn Profession of Faith of Pope Paul VI. It was immediately delivered to the CDF through the Oblate Superior General in Rome. You quote this same document of Paul VI in your PoF specially drafted for me and in your Notification of my excommunication.

(b) What is there defective in the doctrine of Pope Paul VI on the Catholic truths of first level such as the divinity of Christ and on original sin?

(c) If there is anything defective invalidating my signature of the Profession of Faith of Paul VI, why did the CDF not inform me soon after 15th May 1996 and not merely in the 'Notification' of my excommunication on 7th December 1996?

(d) My position is that in the unsigned 11 pages the CDF sent me (in Italian) the CDF distorted my view of original sin and divinity of Christ as written in my book. The CDF did not deal at all with my detailed analysis in response to their charges.

(e) Do not many other writers, especially from Europe, hold views on original sin similar to mine? What then of canonical equity?

3. 'Nothing to do with Inculturation' in Asia

Many of the issues in the CDF 'Observations' had to do with the relation between Christian theology and other religions. Here are a few references from the 27/7/94 CDF Observations or charges against me.

'1. Methodological deficiencies': ... 'All Church teaching can be modified in order to construct a theology that is capable of serving the inter-religious dialogue and woman's liberation.'

2.1 View of revelation, criterion of love for evaluating Christian theology. 2.1 'relativism' equalizing religions, 'sacred books of other religions', comparison of religions.

'3.1 Christological problems' ... 3.2 'From the point of view of the Christian faith it is quite surprising to see Jesus aligned with Buddha, Mohammed and seers of other religions, as if the question of Christ's identity were not already radically clarified by the gospels and the great Ecumenical Councils. According to the author, in Asia it would be necessary to revise all the elements of Christian faith which impinge on the sentiments of Asian countries and oriental religions, particularly the concept of salvation.'

'4. The Doctrine of Original Sin' ... and discrimination against other religions, ... understanding of redemption, ... erroneous way of mission 'ad gentes'.

The action of the CDF against me and its special PoF have done much damage to the image of the Church here among those not of the

Catholic faith – an image we have tried to reconstruct by acknowledging and redressing, in so far as lies in us, the massive blunders Christians have committed against others in the past, as the Holy Father invites us to do in his *Tertio Millennio Adveniente*, no 35.

Are you not *now* changing the ground of your critique of my book?

4. Not concerning Women's Ordination

In addition to other references the final words of the CDF 'Observations' are:

'6.2 ... Finally, the author, in an effort to enhance the figure of Mary, presents her as the first priest of the New Testament in so far as she participated in a particular way at the sacrifice of the cross. On the basis of this Marian reality it cannot be understood why the Church does not permit the ordination of women.'

If women's ordination was not a critical issue why did the CDF introduce the clause concerning it in the Profession of Faith drafted for me? Women's ordination is one of the main points of difference between the PoF of Paul VI and the CDF drafted PoF which I did not sign. Women's ordination is not in the PoF of Paul VI.

5. Marxist Interpretation

(a) This is the first time that the issue of Marxist influence has been raised concerning my work during the past 50 months and more of this affair, here in Sri Lanka or in Rome. How do you come to this conclusion *now*?

(b) Your CDF 'Observations' of June 1994 begins thus:

Good intentions can certainly be found in this work of Fr Tissa Balasuriya: the desire to favour the dialogue between Christianity and oriental religions; the desire to contribute to the moral and social advancement of his people; the desire to link Mariology to Christology; the desire to [offer a] view [of] the figure of the Blessed Virgin that illuminates her values of mature and responsible womanhood; the desire to emphasize the centrality of the doctrine of love; the desire to criticize aberrations in certain expressions of Marian piety.

(c) The Catholic Bishops Conference of Sri Lanka in their public statement of 5th June 1994 on my book states:

In it [this book] the author has made an attempt to give a fresh interpretation to Jesus and Mary. It is obvious that he has cherished the hope of making these sublime figures more acceptable to our milieu – a milieu that is multi-religious in character, and scarred by social injustices.

(d) Was the Jesus gospel of social justice 'deduced from European theses which can be taken back to the Marxist interpretation according to which religion and priests construct for themselves a position of power over the souls of the faithful'? Was the Asian Jesus influenced by Karl Marx when he condemned the falsified religiosity of the high priests, the hypocritical Pharisees and other religious exploiters of the day? Was it Marxist influence that made Jesus chase the money changers from the temple of Jerusalem? Was the *Magnificat* of Mary with its radical message of social, political and cultural transformation influenced by the 19th century European Karl Marx?

(e) Are not many of humanity's radical social and religious leaders from Asia, and that long before Marx, even before Christ as in the case of Buddha? They indulged in a ruthless critique of religious doctrines, religious practices and religious leaders. Did not European thinkers and mystics too have a radical critique of religion before Marx? Permit me to say that I have from my youth been influenced by Mahatma Gandhi and the social liberation dimension of religion and spirituality. I have personally known and been with some of the great Indian spiritual and radical social leaders like Jaya Prakash Narayan and Vinobha Bhave, and the Ashramic tradition of Sri Aurobindo and Rabindranath Tagore. Are we in Asia today incapable of thinking out things on our own? Please do not thus add insult to injury.

(f) How is the rethinking of the classical teaching of original sin connected with Marx?

6. Unclarity in Interpretation and Profession of Faith

(a) The Cardinal said 'of *Mary and Human Liberation*' that it was a 'very difficult task' to interpret a book exactly down to the final word and the final phraseology; the author could always say that one had not respected the context. But in order to avoid interminable discussion which would not be useful to anyone, the CDF opted for a 'more positive way forward by inviting him to sign a profession of faith'. (*Tablet* 1st February 1997)

(b) By this observation you clearly admit that the *CDF has not established error in my book*. After I pointed out the grave deficiencies in the CDF Observations, the CDF opted for a unilateral way out of dialogue or investigation of my work as well as their charges and my responses to them.

(c) How can you speak of 'interminable discussion', when there was no discussion at all between us? The first CDF decision of 22nd June 1994 was without consulting me, and subsequently in the first CDF communication to me of 27th July 1994 the CDF condemned my book and me, and wanted me to withdraw my views (as understood or distorted by the CDF) or be subject to ecclesiastical penalties.

(d) This document of 27th July 1994 was the only communication the CDF sent me on the content of my thinking. Thereafter in May 1995 the CDF curtly dismissed my 55-page single-spaced, seven-month study and detailed response to its 'Observations' with only one word: 'unsatisfactory'. After that the issue between us was only about my signing the ad hoc PoF or being punished under canon 1364 i.e. excommunicated. Is this not far from what you say *now* that:

> we are very sensitive to the situation of this great Asian continent. We are very attentive not to quench the flame of the appropriation and creation of an Asian identity for the Catholic faith. (*Tablet* 1st February 1997)

(e) If the CDF found my book was difficult to interpret why did it expressly prevent the Sri Lankan Bishops' Conference from dealing with it, even when the Archbishop of Colombo was open to a solution by mediation within our country? They know the context better.

7. A Strange Type of Evidence

After claiming that my note before my signature of the Profession of Faith of Paul VI 'renders my signature invalid', the Cardinal *now* proceeds to argue that:

> By non acceptance of the profession of faith, Fr Balasuriya created the evidence that he did not share the faith of the Church. But the Cardinal added, 'he can always deny that evidence by signing the profession of faith'.

This 'evidence' which the CDF thinks is against me is based on the presumption that my not signing their special PoF is proof of my rejection of the Catholic 'truths of the first level'. This is preposterous. The fact of the matter is as follows:

(a) The Cardinal admits that some views in the book are at most unclear and need greater clarification before I could be held responsible of rejecting Catholic doctrines of the first level. This view was expressed in a letter by the CDF on 2nd May 1996 also. The fact that the CDF decided to overlook or ignore the earlier charges against me indicates that those charges are not valid.

(b) If, as I now see, the mere signing of that profession of faith would remove the blemish attributed to me, it is either that what I have stated in the book does not offend the truths at the first level, or the blemishes I am alleged to have committed are of such a minimal gravity that they could be corrected with a signature to a profession of faith. The CDF seems to have decided on a new barometer of my faith (their PoF) with the same ease with which they made the earlier charges and decided to ignore them when they were responded to.

(c) Could not my 72 years as a Catholic, 51 and $\frac{1}{2}$ years in the Oblate Congregation and nearly 45 years as a Catholic priest be considered a clear, cogent and convincing evidence of my professing the Catholic faith and of my commitment to the Church. Even in the midst of the manifold and diverse trials of these four years I am persevering against immense odds to maintain my communion with and in the Church.

(d) Therefore I am now utterly at a loss to discover that I am said to have done (by omission) something which is so grave as to incur automatic excommunication, and, even more, how I could now ritually correct myself and regain the faith by such a signature to what I see as against my conscience.

(e) May I repeat what I have said earlier that I could not in conscience sign this specific profession of faith:
  (i) as it is punitive, and presumes my error, guilt and malice, which are required for excommunication.
  (ii) It is not a PoF that the Church proposes regularly to all Catholics or theologians.
  (iii) The CDF and the Cardinal, though requested several times by me, did not authenticate the proposed PoF by signing it as doctrine binding on all Catholics.
  (iv) it is not in keeping with Catholic truth as proposed by Vatican II concerning the salvation of those who are not Catholics.

8. Permit me to sum up the situation as I see it as one in which I am subject

to unfair charges, with witnesses unknown to me,
to judgment without trial
and punishment without proof.

This is against both Canon Law and natural justice.

9. As you have been informed I have appealed to the Supreme Court of the Vatican, the Signatura Apostolica, on 13th January 1997, for judicial redress against the CDF declaration of my automatic excommunication, in so far as it may have had any validity. Such appeal, according to canons 1353 and 1638, automatically suspends the excommunication. Since you are aware of this can you please inform the world through the mass media of this changed situation, and that my position in the Catholic Church is the same as prior to your Notification of 5/1/97.

10. Since you say that there are unclarities concerning the views in my book, and the CDF finds it very difficult to sort them out, may I request you to appoint a reconstituted *international theological commission*, with recognized Asian theologians, also to evaluate them. As I have stated from the beginning of this issue: if there are proven theological errors in my book in terms of accepted contemporary theological scholarship, I will correct them publicly.

Dear Cardinal Ratzinger, we have never met, seen or even heard each other (except perhaps as students in Rome). We are both of an advanced age when the intimations of mortality are daily felt and sensed by us. Though you are in the Centre of the Church and exercise power and I am in the periphery and subjected to your authority, let us settle this issue justly and with the required dialogue, so that it may be for the good of the Church which both of us have served during this half century and more.

Yours fraternally in Jesus Christ and Mary Immaculate.

TISSA BALASURIYA OMI